Social Work and Disability

Social Work and Disability

PETER SIMCOCK & RHODA CASTLE

polity

First published in 2016 by Polity Press

Polity Press
65 Bridge Street
Cambridge CB2 1UR, UK

Polity Press
350 Main Street
Malden, MA 02148, USA

ISBN-13: 978-0-7456-7019-5
ISBN-13: 978-0-7456-7020-1 (pb)

Library of Congress Cataloging-in-Publication Data

Names: Simcock, Peter, author. | Castle, Rhoda, author.
Title: Social work and disability / Peter Simcock, Rhoda Castle.
Description: Malden, MA : Polity Press, 2016. | Series: Polity social work in
    theory and practise | Includes bibliographical references and index.
Identifiers: LCCN 2015031160| ISBN 9780745670195 (hardback) | ISBN
    9780745670201 (paperback)
Subjects: LCSH: Social work with people with disabilities. | Social
    service--Practice. | BISAC: POLITICAL SCIENCE / Public Policy / Social
    Services & Welfare.
Classification: LCC HV1568 .S536 2016 | DDC 362.4/04532--dc23 LC record
available at http://lccn.loc.gov/2015031160

Typeset in 9.5 on 12 pt Utopia by
Servis Filmsetting Ltd, Stockport, Cheshire
Printed and bound in the UK by Clays Ltd, St Ives PLC

The publisher has used its best endeavours to ensure that the URLs for external websites referred to in this book are correct and active at the time of going to press. However, the publisher has no responsibility for the websites and can make no guarantee that a site will remain live or that the content is or will remain appropriate.

Every effort has been made to trace all copyright holders, but if any have been inadvertently overlooked the publisher will be pleased to include any necessary credits in any subsequent reprint or edition.

For further information on Polity, visit our website:
politybooks.com

920720525

Contents

Introduction

Social work with disabled people is an area of practice that has seen significant change. This change is the result of not only legislative reform and new policy initiatives but also the work of the disability movement in challenging our understanding of 'disability' and what it is that disables people. Undoubtedly, it is a complex yet rewarding specialism. However, while social work is part of many disabled people's lives, it has received limited attention in practice and has been marginalized in academic and professional literature. Social work for disabled adults has been described as an underfunded 'Cinderella service', and practitioners have reported having limited experience of working with disabled young people. Disability activists, disabled people's organizations, academics and commentators have all questioned the role of social workers in the lives of disabled people; this has been the case particularly in adult social care services as a result of increased personalization and self-directed care. Disabled people can now commission, coordinate and manage their own care and support directly.

Not all disabled people need social work intervention. Furthermore, as highlighted by many people with physical and sensory impairments, social work services and social work itself have been disabling barriers in their lives. However, this book explores how social work practice can, and indeed does, contribute to the promotion of disabled people's rights and the securing of positive outcomes. We suggest that such positive practice requires the following: a focus on human rights; critical reflection on the disability movement's critique of social work; a full understanding of the barriers that disable people with impairments; and working in partnership, as equal allies, with disabled people and their organizations.

Social workers spend considerable time supporting people with physical and sensory impairments, both older people and those of working age, yet the amount of attention given to these issues in the professional literature seems to lack balance. There are also significant numbers of disabled children, many of whom have physical impairments. As such, while other social work texts consider learning disability, in this book we focus on practice with people with physical and sensory impairments. We do not mean to suggest that social work intervention is needed solely because of such impairment; however, this focus could still be considered problematic. Most disability studies scholars would agree that disability is about more than the nature of a person's impairments. If it is the barriers that disabled people face in the social and physical environment that are crucial in shaping their experience, why should demarcation between different types of impairment be relevant? While we are sympathetic to this argument, we still consider that there is room for consideration of disability associated with physical and sensory impairment. The nature of the barriers and restrictions that disabled people face results from the interaction between the environment and the individual. There is wide variation between the restrictions that people with different atypical physical attributes will face, and variation again between their experience and that of people with learning disabilities.

Although we have chosen to concentrate on what we consider to be a neglected area in the professional literature, a rigid dividing line between physical and intellectual impairment is untenable. People with learning disabilities may also have physical impairments, and some 'syndromes' and degenerative conditions have both physical and intellectual manifestations. This is particularly marked in the case of disabled children, many of whom have a learning disability; in fact this is the largest impairment-related group within social care services for disabled children. Children with complex health problems whose parents require support with day-to-day care may also have learning disabilities. Therefore, despite the primary focus of the book, we have attempted to take a holistic approach to the experience of disabled people. This is in keeping with the need for professionals to avoid compartmentalizing people's lives in ways that are unhelpful and adds to the stress experienced by individuals and families. One of the potential strengths of social work is the capacity to take a holistic view of the barriers, difficulties and strengths of people's situations.

The book is divided into three parts. Part I, 'Perspectives: Understanding Disability', covers chapters 1 to 4. Drawing on lived experience, theory and models, law and policy, this section examines how disability is, and continues to be, defined, explained and understood. We highlight the implications of these definitions and understandings for social work practice through a series of case profiles. Chapter 1 is co-written with a disabled woman who has experience of social work intervention as both a child and an adult. It offers personal reflections on a range of issues, which are then further explored throughout the book. Starting with a brief overview of the historical context of understandings of disability, including early sociological approaches, chapter 2 explores theoretical perspectives, with a particular focus on theory arising from the experiences of disabled people. In chapter 3 we consider the knowledge that can be gained from taking a life course perspective on disability and analyse the implications of this knowledge for social workers. The final chapter in this part, chapter 4, offers a critical analysis of the interface between law, policy and social work in relation to practice with disabled people. Starting with a brief overview of the historical development of law and policy in this area, we go on to consider contemporary legal frameworks, such as the Care Act 2014, the Social Services and Well-Being (Wales) Act 2014 and the Children and Families Act 2014, and highlight the importance of the UN Convention on the Rights of Persons with Disabilities.

Diversity, inequality and oppression are the focus of Part II, 'Diversity, Inequality and Disability', which consists of chapters 5 and 6. In chapter 5 we explore the research on inequalities and oppression experienced by disabled people, considering issues such as discrimination, employment, victimhood of crime, access to education, debt and poverty, and access to health and other public services. The place of social work in addressing and challenging discrimination and oppression in this context is outlined. Challenging assumptions of homogeneity among disabled people and acknowledging the need for social workers to consider the impact of characteristics such as race, gender and sexual orientation, chapter 6 considers the experience of disability across a range of diverse communities. It then turns to examine disability as a dimension of human diversity itself and highlights the implications of this knowledge for social work practice.

Part III, 'Disability and Social Work Practice', consists of chapters 7 to 11 and addresses social work functions, roles, processes and practice with disabled people. Each chapter here highlights strategies for best practice. Chapter 7 considers the importance of strong communication skills. In chapter 8 we focus on social work practice with disabled children, exploring core functions such as assessment and intervention and also practice with looked after disabled children, while in chapter 9 we look at the social work role with disabled adults in an increasingly personalized system of adult social care. Arguing that social work has a central role in safeguarding both children and adults, chapter 10 explores this function in the context of disability settings, with a particular spotlight on the concepts of risk and vulnerability. Chapter 11 concludes this section by examining collaborative practice in this field, before a final conclusion is offered at the end of the book.

The chapters contain case profiles, many of which have been drawn from our own practice experiences, to illustrate key points and practice implications. Additionally, the 'voices' of disabled people, social workers and carers are included throughout to encourage the reader to reflect on lived experiences. Links are made to relevant domains of the Professional Capabilities Framework (PCF) and sections of Professional Codes of Practice. We end each chapter with a summary of the key messages, activities for reflection and independent study, and suggested further reading.

The book is intended for use by qualifying students on social work degree programmes, students on post-qualifying courses seeking to develop specialist knowledge, and current social work practitioners involved with disabled people. Though the focus of the book is on social work, it may also be of interest to those on health and social care courses, third-sector practitioners, advocates, advice workers, and service users and carers.

PART I

PERSPECTIVES: UNDERSTANDING DISABILITY

1 Lived Experience of Impairment, Disability and Social Work

Co-written with Helen Burrell

Introduction

Now in my fifties, I have had physical impairments since the age of twelve, following a fall during cross-country running at school. Slipping on the wet grass, I did the 'splits' and dislocated my hip; however, this diagnosis didn't come until some months later, as the ongoing pain in my hip was dismissed as growing pains. Since I was in pain and constantly falling over, my mother pushed the matter with the medical staff, and I got to see a consultant who diagnosed the dislocation. Surgery followed, and I was on crutches for six weeks. As I turned thirteen, I remember experiencing further pain in my hip. This was initially dismissed, and I was told I was simply seeking attention. After further falls and what can only be described as agonizing pain, my mother took me to casualty. An X-ray identified that the blood supply to the hip had been affected and the bones had disintegrated; the screws implanted during previous surgery were also poking out where they shouldn't have been! I remember spending nine weeks in hospital, on an adult ward – a thirteen-year-old girl surrounded by older women having hip replacements.

I have had further surgery throughout my life, and ultimately, after a series of unsuccessful hip replacement operations, the hip joint was removed. I recall a conversation with the Benefits Agency, which advised me that I *must* have a hip joint as 'hip replacement' was the only option on the benefit application form on their system. I assured them I didn't. I now mobilize with either elbow crutches or a wheelchair. As I have developed additional conditions over time, my consultant is insistent that I use the wheelchair far more than I have done previously; I have mixed feelings about this. I also have mixed feelings about and experiences of social work and social workers.

First encounters with social work

Having spent long periods of time in hospital as a child, I missed a lot of my schooling. My mother was concerned that I wasn't having any teaching, but my old school would not take me back; because of my crutches I was described as 'a liability' and 'a risk' to myself and others. My mother was advised to make contact with social services with a view to my attending a special school. She visited a special school and was very concerned: 'Helen will be bored to tears here.' She wanted me to attend mainstream school and contacted the local authority, highlighting my need for appropriate schooling.

I remember a social worker visiting my home around this time. I recall her greeting me, but then being sent to bed while she and my mother discussed my situation.

I believe she was completing some sort of assessment. I heard my mother take her to the kitchen, saying, 'This is where Helen has to wash, in the sink.' The bathroom upstairs at home was no longer accessible. Fortunately we had a downstairs toilet, but unfortunately, as I couldn't bend my knees when I sat on the toilet, I couldn't shut the door; imagine the impact on my dignity, a teenage girl with such limited privacy. I recall my mother putting up net curtains in the kitchen so I wouldn't be seen as I washed. The visiting social worker advised that, as I couldn't get up the stairs, this was acceptable. My mother explained her concerns about my lack of schooling and also my mobility, telling the social worker that I couldn't walk far on the crutches. Following this visit, a wheelchair was arranged for me, and the social worker also facilitated arrangements for a home tutor, who visited three times a week. Though I hardly spoke to her, the social worker had made things happen that made life somewhat easier.

I recall my home tutor teaching me outside in the garden, as she was pregnant at the time and experienced bouts of morning sickness; she felt less nauseous outside in the fresh air. After a period of time, a place at a mainstream school was identified for me. It was a small school, just for girls, and the headmistress was very supportive. Once I was there I don't recall any further involvement with social work as a child; my next encounters with social workers would be in my adult life.

Encountering barriers

My place at school was sorted, but getting me there proved quite a challenge. The school I attended was a long walk away, and my mother spent the spring and early summer months pushing me there in the wheelchair; with the bad weather coming, she believed this would no longer be possible and contacted social services to request support. The solution that was made available to me was a place on the bus that transported children to the special school, the school that my mother did not want me to attend. Its hours were shorter than those at my mainstream school, and the bus times reflected this; I was dropped off at my school at 10.00 a.m., thus missing early morning lessons, and collected for the home run at 2.30 p.m., missing another hour of schooling. I had already missed two years of my education because of time spent in hospital and now I was missing over a day a week. Fortunately, a chemistry and biology teacher saw my interest and potential in her subject areas and spent additional time with me over lunch breaks, helping me to catch up.

My curiosity in the sciences continued, and I developed an interest in pursuing a nursing career. This interest was quashed by the school careers advisor: 'People like you don't go into nursing.' I didn't challenge this advice and resigned myself to the fact that I wouldn't be a nurse because I was disabled. Some time later, the local NHS organized an information event showcasing the range of career options available and offering opportunities to shadow different professionals. My curiosity and interest motivated me to attend, and I ended up spending time with the radiographer. My interest in nursing was replaced: I had discovered my vocation. After further study and training, I achieved my goal and became a qualified radiographer. It was a career I loved and one I continued in for some years. It gave me professional identity, purpose and financial independence. However, it wasn't to last to a 'normal' retirement age. I had ongoing health problems and further physical impairments and ended up taking early retirement on health grounds. Looking back, it all seemed to be something of a *fait accompli*; I recall no appeal, no fight with the health authority – just a tacit agreement that I would take my money and retire.

While this was the end of my radiography career, it was certainly not the end of my working life. I have designed and delivered 'disability awareness' training, provided consultancy work, led expert patient programmes, and coordinated service-user involvement in public services and higher education institutions. I have also taught on a range of health and social care programmes at two universities. Securing employment has not always been easy, however, and I have often found myself on temporary contracts or short-term projects; while enjoyable, such work reduced my financial security and often complicated my welfare benefit entitlement. Learning to drive and having an adapted vehicle has facilitated my engagement in all kinds of activities, enabling me to travel independently with much greater ease. However, even a planned shopping trip to the supermarket becomes problematic when the 'disabled' parking bays are all taken (and not always by disabled parking permit holders!). What may appear to be nothing more than difficulty finding a parking space is actually a wasted journey, a period of stress, and a necessary rescheduling of the weekly shop.

Models of disability, law and policy

Following changes in the law relating to chronically ill and disabled people, I recall receiving a leaflet through the post that outlined health and care pathways. The diagrams showed a range of services and support through which people would 'travel'; the end of the pathway was 'being cured'. In tiny letters at the bottom of the leaflet were the words 'Not all illnesses can be cured', followed by a full stop. As I re-read the pathways, I thought, 'Well, doesn't that just sum it all up!' Disabled people are put into the pathway machine and they come out cured or not cured. The 'cured' person carries on into education, training and employment; the 'not cured' person is given a full stop. The medical staff had been unable to fix me. I had not been cured and I had been given a full stop.

I started to volunteer at a DIAL (Disability Information and Advice Line) service and underwent a six-week training course to support my involvement. During the course I met a wheelchair user from the Greater Manchester Coalition of Disabled People (a woman with whom I am still great friends). She spoke about these 'models of disability' – the medical model and the social model. Hearing her speak, I suddenly started to put the pieces together. Up until that point, I saw my difficulties as entirely my fault: I must have done something wrong to end up this way. The hip replacements didn't work and I couldn't walk; doctors had tried to fix me but had not succeeded. This, I was told, reflected a medical model of disability. Hearing about the social model was a 'Eureka moment'. I realized that the problems I had encountered (missing education, not being able to secure employment, being made redundant from the health authority with no appeal or fight, problems with housing adaptations) were not *my* fault; they were a result of society's inability to accommodate me as a physically impaired wheelchair user. I felt as if I had fallen asleep in one world and woken up in another. The medical model glasses through which I viewed the world had been replaced by social model glasses. One life for me had stopped and this new life was opening up; just as if I was emigrating, I needed to do my research about this new world I had come into, this social model of disabled Helen. It was a new language, it was new values, it was a new world. I finally realized that my illness and impairments played only a small role in my daily challenges. It was the barriers imposed by society that truly disabled me, and, in the 1980s, the most challenging of all of these were other people's attitudes.

It was suggested that I go on a disability awareness training course led by the Disability Coalition, and I revelled at the chance to learn more about this new world. Eight people were there, all training to become trainers for the coalition. The excitement of the new social model world, however, became complex and confusing. As the training programme developed and I heard the views and perspectives of others, for the first time ever in my life I was ashamed to tell people what job I had done. I realized that a lot of the people who were involved with the training didn't see healthcare workers in the same light as I did. We had one or two lively discussions about healthcare and health professionals' attitudes – but I had been a healthcare professional! It was then I realized that the social model carried with it a great deal of responsibility. I also realized that people with acquired impairments, especially people like me who acquired increasing impairment over a period of time through childhood and into adulthood, often had different experiences from those with impairments from birth or early childhood. I sometimes found it quite intimidating being around people with very strong views on the social model, and at the end of the training I didn't sign up to be a trainer for the coalition. I didn't feel comfortable. Life – my life – wasn't black and white; there were and are many shades of grey.

Since that health and care pathways leaflet came through my door, there have been numerous legal and policy changes. For someone who doesn't take a lot of notice of policy and law, I have to say I really started to notice changes after the Disability Discrimination Act came into force. People may think of parking and accessible toilets, but for me it was transport. I remember travelling on a train in the guard's van. You couldn't travel on a train in a wheelchair, so I was in the unheated guard's van. I remember sitting near the window, waving out so I wasn't forgotten and taken to the wrong place! Now I can sit in a train in a proper wheelchair space and travel comfortably.

Later in life I began delivering training on the Disability Discrimination Act. I had great hopes for the Act and thought it would help bring down barriers. I also thought it would help me find a job and receive realistic welfare benefits; however, it hasn't done any of that. It is the cheap and the superficial that has been addressed, not the majority of barriers. As a wheelchair user, I still can't get into half the shops in my town. I'm so disappointed, because I really had big hopes.

Life as a disabled adult

I was in my mid- to late twenties by the time I had undergone the unsuccessful hip replacements and my hip joint was removed. At this point I recall being visited by a social worker. He queried why, following the surgery, I wasn't moving back 'home' to live with my parents, so that they could help me. I hadn't lived at 'home' for some years at that time. Why would I want to sell my house now? I hadn't considered this. The social worker felt it would be so much easier because my parents 'could look after me'. I felt that I was being seen as the 'perpetual child' in being asked to consider such a move; throughout my life I have met other disabled adults who have been encouraged to stay at home with parents or return to live with them. I feared that I'd never get the chance to grow up (what I term 'Peter Pan syndrome') and that I'd have limited experience of good and bad things. Everyone thought that what I had gone through was bad enough – but we all have to go through bad things and difficult experiences. They make us who we are; they have made me who I am. They haven't taken away from my life, they have added to my confidence. I'm far more self-assured about what I believe and what I stand for.

I remained living in my own home and the social worker facilitated access to what is now called a Disabled Facilities Grant (DFG). The outside toilet and coalhouse were converted into an accessible toilet and shower room. I was also issued with a raised toilet seat and a perching stool and advised to purchase two 'helping hands' to enable me to put my stockings on. No more sitting on the toilet with the door open, no more washing in the sink with just a net curtain between the outside world and me! But the equipment was all so clinical looking: white rails that didn't go with the décor, halls cluttered with medical equipment and supplies. My home was important to me, as was its style. As a woman, it was important to me. But I'd discovered that DFG funding didn't cover personal choices relating to décor when it came to equipment, which was to meet my professionally identified needs.

While I now associate my dissatisfaction with the equipment with gender issues, it was really only after I started going to the Greater Manchester Coalition for Disabled People (GMCDP) and met other disabled people that I became aware of unsettling issues around being a woman with a disability. Even deciding on a term for myself was confusing. Was I a disabled woman, a woman with a disability or, as before my disabling event, still a woman? I began to research the women's movement and to feel that, because of my impairments, I wasn't a woman anymore. Would my impairment prevent me carrying out my 'womanly' roles and functions (wife, mother and partner)? I began to feel that it meant that I should not have children; doing so might run the risk of their being removed by social services.

When I sought help from the local hospital for treatment for my endometriosis, I went in my wheelchair. The consultant told me that getting rid of that 'monthly mess' (my period) via a hysterectomy was the much better option and would give me a much improved quality of life. I was just thirty-five years old at the time, but the 'expert', the consultant, made me think this was the best idea. It was only afterwards that I discovered that a friend, with no physical impairment, also met with the same consultant for the same health problem. She was offered a raft of hormone treatments and, when she asked about having a hysterectomy, she was told that this was the very last resort for someone of her age; she was forty-two.

I remember talking to a disabled friend about these experiences, and she suggested I should read the work of Jenny Morris (cited in this book). Her work opened my eyes to so many issues and highlighted how certain models of disability had robbed me, and so many disabled women, of our status as women.

Positive social work practice: my perspective

For me, best practice has always been centred on positive relationships. Social workers who took the time to build positive and sustainable working relationships were those I valued the most; inevitably, they were also the ones who were able to secure positive outcomes with and for me. Social workers need to build relationships that are founded on genuine care and compassion, trust, professionalism, and excellent communication skills.

Genuine care and compassion   I value social workers who create an atmosphere of care and empathy, not sympathy and superficial kindness. Social workers must recognize that I have knowledge, skills and expertise in my own situation and work in partnership with me on equal terms. In my experience, such approaches have not only secured positive outcomes but also built my confidence. I need to know the social worker will act as a strong advocate for me, or support me to advocate for myself, in order to promote and protect my human rights.

Trust   During contact with social workers, particularly through assessment processes, I have needed to share private thoughts, very personal information, my fears, and my concerns. In order for a social worker to enable me to share this information, I need to know that they will protect my right to privacy and maintain confidentiality appropriately.

Professionalism   I do not equate professionalism with unnecessary formality but, rather, with appropriate confidence in role, suitable appearance, and honesty. I always welcome positive eye contact, a pleasant demeanour, a smile. I want up-to-date information and social workers who are knowledgeable; it doesn't matter to me if they have to check information on the computer or ring the office, provided what they tell me is the truth. Recognition that I am a source of knowledge and expertise on my own life must not lead to assumptions about what I know about social care systems: sharing and exchanging knowledge is key to an equal social worker–service user relationship.

Communication skills   Social workers do not need good communication skills; they need outstanding ones! I recall one less than positive experience during a social work assessment in which I felt 'talked at'. There was very little inclusion in the interaction, which involved questions of a personal and emotive nature. I needed time to think, reflect and consider my responses; however, while I was considering how to respond, the social worker was already writing something down, smiling, as she said, 'I fill hundreds of these things in. I'll read it back to you at the end.' There was an immediate sense that 'this is how it was going to be done'. I felt I had limited options to alter things once the assessment form was filled in and signed off; time was short and she needed to get back to the office. This approach led to some unhelpful and awkward exchanges. For example, following a question about my personal care needs, the social worker said, 'I can see that you are on your own at the moment, but do you have a man friend who can help out?' I responded, with some frustration, 'I might well have a "man friend", but I am not going to ask him to help me get washed and dressed!' 'Oh', she replied, 'I didn't mean like that. I meant going out socializing.' I reminded her that we had been talking about personal care, but she was already moving on with 'her' form. Assumptions have also been made that, because my impairment is physical (and visible), I have no particular communication needs; not once in all my years of having contact with social services and social workers has anyone asked about my dyslexia and the resulting difficulties it causes me with the written word.

Concluding thoughts

I am woman with physical impairments. These impairments result in some restrictions and sometimes cause me pain and discomfort. I am also a disabled woman; physical barriers, attitudinal barriers, social and economic barriers have all disabled me in the past and continue to do so. I am also a Christian, a niece, a carer, a qualified radiographer, a friend, a theatregoer, a home-owner. I value social workers that see me as this person, not just as a list of medical conditions and limitations. I value social workers who recognize that my need for their involvement is not always related to my physical impairment. And I value social workers who protect and promote my rights – not just my rights as a user of social work services but my fundamental human rights.

Activities

- Make a note of your initial thoughts and feelings after reading this personal account. Revisit your notes as you read other chapters in the book and reflect on how they relate to Helen's experiences.
- What issues does the chapter raise that should be of concern to social work?
- How do Helen's views on positive social work practice relate to the domains of the Professional Capabilities Framework (PCF)?

Suggested further reading

Beresford, P., Croft, S., and Adshead, L. (2008) 'We don't see her as a social worker': a service user case study of the importance of the social worker relationship and humanity, *British Journal of Social Work*, 38: 1388–407.

Evans, C. (2008) In practice from the viewpoint of disabled people', in Swain, J., and French, S., eds, *Disability on Equal Terms*. London: Sage.

2 Theories and Models of Disability

Issues considered in this chapter:

- The way that disability has been conceptualized
- The social model of disability and its critique of existing disability policy
- Critiques and further developments of the social model of disability
- The search for a theory of disability
- The implications of theories and models for social work practice

Introduction

This chapter begins by exploring the way that understandings of disability have developed in their historical context and how these have influenced responses to disability. Social work practice with disabled people does not take place in isolation from the beliefs held in contemporary Western societies about disability, and these beliefs have inevitably been influenced by our history and culture. Having considered this, along with early sociological approaches to disability, the chapter will continue by describing the major reconceptualization of disability brought about by disabled activists and academics. The result was the *social model of disability*, which has been integral to the disability movement in Britain (Campbell and Oliver 1996). It is also of fundamental importance for social work, as it has been influential in the reform of a range of policies, including social care. However, the social model itself has been subject to critique. This has resulted in some spirited debates between the originators of the model and those who have argued that it needs to be developed (Thomas 1999) or even jettisoned (Shakespeare 2006).

The relevance of these theoretical debates for social work lies in their links with professional practice. The way that disability is defined and explained, and indeed the language and terminology adopted, can have a significant bearing on policy, the experience of disabled people, their interactions with professionals, and their relative status in wider society. This is further explored in chapters 4 and 5. Arguing that the social model of disability should inform social work practice, Oliver et al. (2012: 20) point to the dangers of current claims that theory should arise from practice: '... to rely on practice to inform theory when practitioners may have already internalised an inappropriate model is to perpetuate the problem, for it would merely result in the reinforcement of the individual model of disability.'

This chapter will focus particularly on theory arising from the experience of disabled people. As Ife (2012: 216) observes: 'Because of [social work's] grounding in the world of day-to-day practice, it cannot afford theoretical formulations that are not similarly grounded in lived reality.' Also, reflection in social work involves examination of the (often unstated) assumptions that have influenced practice (Knott and Scragg 2007) (PCF 6.4). In order to make sense of the situations in which they practise, social workers sometimes draw explicitly on theory, but also often on 'common-sense' understandings, ubiquitous in our culture.

Case profile: Marion

Marion is fifty-five, lives alone and has severe arthritis. This has affected her mobility, and she uses a wheelchair outdoors. Her children have grown up and left home, and two years ago her marriage ended. This followed a period when friends and neighbours suspected that she was the victim of domestic violence. Marion has managed to earn her living as a clerical worker for the council. However, her arthritis has recently become worse and has affected her hands, which has made it very difficult for her to do her job. She has become exhausted and depressed and is at present on long-term sick leave. She feels socially isolated and misses the company of colleagues. Because of the arthritis in her hands she is struggling to cope at home, and she was recently seen at Accident and Emergency after scalding herself when trying to lift the kettle.

If you were the social worker asked to assess Marion, what would you identify as the main problems in her situation, and what do you consider has caused them? What do you think would be helpful in improving her situation? It would be very easy to assume that her difficulties all arise from her arthritis. If it was not for this she would be able to work and do everything for herself at home. Marion is indeed affected by severe arthritis and may be depressed because of the loss of physical function that it involves. As the social worker allocated to her, you might ask whether she is receiving all the medical treatment she needs, together with any necessary physiotherapy. This might improve her condition and enable her to carry out the ordinary tasks involved in everyday living. You might also assess whether she needs care workers to support her.

Neither of these responses is necessarily wrong. Marion may indeed benefit from further medical treatment and assistance in the home. However, both are based on the assumption that her problems arise from her medical condition and her inability to carry out the tasks of everyday living for herself. In other words, this is a problem concerning Marion as an individual. She is a disabled person, and her disability is the result of her arthritis. However, there are several indications in her story which suggest that her problems are also caused by extrinsic factors, or factors outside herself. Could her employer have made adjustments to her role and provided equipment? If so, her period of sick leave might have been avoided. If she has been the victim of domestic violence, how has this affected her sense of self-worth? Has this, along with her current difficulties in seeing friends and colleagues, played a role in her depression? How accessible is her home, and is there any specialist equipment that would make it easier for her to carry out domestic tasks? Does she have access to suitable transport to enable her to travel into town and participate more in community life?

This discussion has only begun to consider the issues that might be impacting on Marion's situation. There are other issues that could be raised. However, it is sufficient to demonstrate that the same situation can be seen through more than one lens. These lenses are the assumptions, or implicit theories, that are held about disability.

The assumptions that people hold about the nature of disability are likely to have been influenced by the society around them. The views of family and friends, and sometimes personal experience, may play a part in this. The way that disabled people are represented in newspapers, literature, films and television programmes also exerts an influence. Disabled people have been portrayed as 'pitiable and pathetic' (Barnes 1992), unable to take control of their own lives and deserving of sympathy. The birth of a disabled child has been represented as a 'tragedy' for parents, involving many disappointments (Kandel and Merrick 2003), which relates to another of the stereotypes identified by Barnes (1992): 'the disabled person as burden'. Oliver (1990) maintains that disabled people have been over-represented among the 'villains' of fiction or as 'superheroes' who achieve great things through exceptional determination, personality or talents. Examples would be the evil Dr No, in Ian Fleming's novel of the same name, and Christie Brown in the film *My Left Foot*, who becomes a successful artist by 'transcend[ing] pity through grit, will, and self-determination' (Hayes and Black 2003: 115). As Barnes and Mercer (2010) point out, disabled people tend not to be portrayed as 'ordinary members of society engaged in everyday activities'.

These examples portray disability as something to be avoided if at all possible and, if not, as something to be heroically 'overcome'. However, the way that disability is defined and how the boundary is drawn between those whose need is legitimized in terms of eligibility for welfare services and benefits is clearly important in terms of policy and practice.

What the examples above have in common is the underlying assumption that disability is an attribute of the individual. Although recognition as a disabled person denotes a particular *social* position, in practice it is dependent on individual 'deficits' that are assessed by medical examination. Official responses to disability have included social work practice. It is pertinent that the *social model* of disability was associated with a radical critique of the community care system implemented by social workers and, eventually, with the introduction of new forms of policy and practice. However, the social model itself has been subject to challenge, and this indicates that understanding of disability continues to be 'work in progress'.

The historical context

Historical comparisons need to be made with care, as what constitutes 'ability' and 'disability' can vary between cultures (Edwards 1997). For example, Depoy and Gilson (2008) suggest that, due to widespread poverty during the Middle Ages, only the most extreme deviations from the typical were regarded as exceptional. Conversely, in the late nineteenth century, the introduction of compulsory schooling is thought to have led to the categorization of those children who could not benefit from the standard approach to education. Children who might not have attracted official attention previously became classified as atypical, sometimes with the label of 'feeble mindedness'. For example, when exploring the historical background to 'special' education, the Warnock Committee reported:

> Mental disability was for many children no substantial handicap in coping with the simple demands of everyday life in a largely uneducated and relatively uncomplicated world … Their needs first became apparent after 1870 when large numbers of children of below average or poor intellectual ability entered public elementary schools. Many of them made scarcely any progress. (Department of Education and Science 1978: 12)

In addition, historical responses to disability have been linked to explanations for atypical bodies (Depoy and Gilson 2008). In ancient Greece, for example, those injured in war were treated more favourably than others with atypical bodies, while babies with the most severe and visible 'deformities' were left to die (Mallett and Runswick-Cole 2014). During the Middle Ages, atypical bodies were often associated with the supernatural. Many people put to death for witchcraft were likely to have been suffering from neurological or emotional disorders (Winzer 1997). Conversely, the presence of those with atypical bodies was also thought to be an opportunity from God to demonstrate charity – hence the beginning of faith-based care.

The trend from the seventeenth century onwards was towards institutionalization for the protection of the non-disabled population. By the nineteenth century this trend towards segregation had intensified, with an increase in institutionalization and the promotion of 'freak shows', which allowed the middle classes to view those with atypical bodies (Braddock and Parish 2001). However, this existed alongside responses motivated by Victorian notions of Christian charity.

Modern disability scholars have maintained that the rapid progress of industrial capitalism exacerbated the exclusion of disabled people. The growth of large residential institutions in Victorian Britain has been associated with the need to deal with those who either could not or would not conform to the new disciplines of wage labour and therefore were regarded as potentially disruptive. Whereas disabled people could make a contribution to production in an economy based on cooperative and communal approaches to agriculture and small-scale production, in a system based on individualized wage labour they were excluded (Finkelstein 1980). Also associated with institutionalization was the rise in status of the medical profession, with its developing capacity to classify 'deviant' groups. This offered opportunities to distinguish 'scientifically' between those whose incapacity was no fault of their own (for example, those who today would be regarded as 'disabled' or 'mentally ill') and those whose failure to support themselves was due to idleness and irresponsibility.

This medical approach, which interpreted diversity in terms of pathology, was linked to the concepts of 'able-bodiedness' and 'able-mindedness', which were criteria for inclusion in employment in Victorian Britain (Oliver 1990). Davis (1997) argues that the concept of *normalcy*, which gained currency in the mid-nineteenth century in England, has created the 'problem' of disability and has led to the pathologizing of atypical bodies. In explaining how disability became associated with 'abnormality' and exclusion, Davis describes the rise of statistics. The notion of 'normality' arose originally from the desire to eliminate error from observations in the physical sciences. However, the Belgian statistician Quetelet (1796–1847) identified that the same 'law of error' could be applied to human attributes. It was a short step from this to the formulation of the concept of the 'average man'. The norm came to be seen as kind of ideal in itself and to be associated with progress and the perfectibility of the human population. For example, Quetelet is quoted as follows:

> One of the principal acts of civilization is to compress more and more the limits within which the different elements relative to man oscillate. The more that enlightenment is propagated, the more will deviations from the mean diminish ... The perfectibility of the human species is derived as a necessary consequence of all our investigations. Defects and monstrosities disappear more and more from the body. (Cited in Davis 1997: 12)

This is the context for the analogies that were drawn between the disease of individuals and that of the nation. Although this is a false analogy (Davis 1997), it found favour at a time when industrialization appeared to require uniform, fit and interchangeable workers.

Galton, the leading eugenicist, was in fact the originator of the statistical term 'normal distribution'. In 'normal distribution', when measurements taken from a population are plotted on a graph, the majority fall within a symmetrical 'bell curve' that encloses the average measurement. Those whose measurements fall outside the bell curve are the extremities outside the 'normal' range. In terms of Darwin's theory of natural selection, disabled people were evolutionary 'defectives', a belief which underpinned attempts to control their reproduction and promote their segregation in institutions. They were also grouped together with a range of other 'defectives' displaying 'undesirable' characteristics, including criminality, alcoholism and destitution. In this way, disability was conflated with 'depravity' (Davis 1997). This led to calls for the sterilization of people with a wide range of atypical attributes. To the eugenicists, heredity was thought to account for all variation in human beings, to the exclusion of any environmental influence. Therefore, 'marks of physical difference became synonymous with the identity of the person' (ibid.: 15).

The influence of eugenics and individualism can be seen in early modes of social work practice. For example, Mary Dendy (1855–1933), a member of the Charity Organization Society, described her motivation for setting up permanent institutional care for children who were 'mentally deficient'.

> I rather suddenly realized that nearly 2 per cent of our elementary school children would never be fit to undertake the direction of their own lives. I also realized that three-fourths of our charitable work must be absolutely wasted if we could not, by some means, take possession of these feeble lives, and make certain that they should not have the opportunity to reproduce themselves. (Dendy 1903)

The Charity Organization Society lobbied the government for the introduction of a legal framework for such segregation, resulting in the 1913 Mental Deficiency Act. While learning disability is not the focus of this book, physical and mental impairment was conflated in some nineteenth- and early twentieth-century policy and legislation, with epilepsy in particular often being dealt with in conjunction with 'mental deficiency' – for example in the report of the Departmental Committee on Defective and Epileptic Children in 1898. As described in chapter 4, ideologies supporting segregation continued to exert an influence well into the latter half of the twentieth century.

Social theory and disability

Abberley (1993) has identified that it is 'abnormality' which disabled people share with oppressed groups such as women, black people, older people, and LGBT people. He further remarks that these 'abnormal' groups may in fact constitute the majority of the population. This seems to indicate that the processes through which such groups come to be defined as 'abnormal' requires explanation in social rather than individual terms.

Disabled activists and academics have critiqued the way in which disability has been understood as an individual 'personal tragedy' (Oliver 1990). They have argued that many of the consequences for disabled people result not from their impairments but from the oppressive social relationship that is 'disability'. This distinction between disability and impairment is crucial to the social model of disability, developed by disabled activists, and has been described as follows: 'Disability is something imposed on top of our impairments, by the way we are unnecessarily isolated and excluded from full participation in society. Disabled people are therefore an oppressed group in society' (UPIAS 1976: 14). The main premise of the 'social model' is that the restrictions experienced by people with impairments result from physical and social environments which take account only of the requirements of non-disabled people (Barnes 1991; Oliver 1996b).

However, the social model is not the only attempt to explain disability in terms of social processes and structures (Priestley 1998a). The social model, as described by Finkelstein (1980) and Oliver (1990), considers disability 'as a product of the material conditions of life at a particular socio-historical juncture' (Thomas 2007: 53), in particular the restructuring of working life that occurred with the industrial revolution. As such it has been described as *materialist*, while other *idealist* theories focus on the way that responses to impairment have been shaped by human values and beliefs. The following paragraphs explore these varying approaches in more detail.

It is possible to consider the theorization of disability as a chronological process which runs alongside, and is often integral to, disability politics and the experience of disabled people. It was life in residential care that informed the work of Paul Hunt (1966b), whose critique of the controlling ethos of much staff practice is described in chapter 4. Sociological study of disability before the development of the social model utilized a range of theoretical frameworks, but, as Thomas (2007) has maintained, the approach of the medical sociologists who carried out most of the theoretical and empirical work on disability and 'chronic illness' was, with few exceptions, informed by a *deviance paradigm* which did not distinguish between disability and impairment and sought to explain the deviance of disabled people rather than to challenge it.

For example, sociologists have explored the *role* of disabled people in society, taking a functionalist approach. This was influenced by work on the 'sick role' within society by Parsons (1951), who argued that the effective operation of the social system was dependent of individuals carrying out their social roles. Arguing that sickness was disruptive to the social system, and therefore deviant, Parsons defined a sick role that permitted those accepted as 'sick' to be relieved of 'normal' responsibilities. However, this was on condition that medical diagnosis was sought and professional advice followed, so that there would be a prompt return to health and productivity. As this fitted best with short-term acute illness, a more permanent 'impaired role' was later identified (Siegler and Osmond 1974). This was associated with the denial of full membership of society. Similarly, a 'rehabilitation role' (Safilios-Rothschild 1970) set out the social expectations of those undergoing rehabilitation. For example, they must maximize their remaining abilities, assume as 'normal' a function as possible, cooperate with professionals, and adapt to their new identity. This approach has had a continuing influence on policy and practice (PCF 5.1).

Levitas (1996) and Prideaux (2005) both linked 'welfare to work' policies introduced by New Labour (and subsequently intensified under the Conservative–Liberal Democrat coalition government) to functionalist sociology. This stresses social cohesion through integrating people into required roles. The moral aspect of such an integrationist discourse (Levitas 1996) includes attacks on irresponsibility and welfare dependency, both of which are perceived as 'deviant'. The social exclusion of disabled people may once have been 'functional' in warning the general population of the consequences of failing to comply with 'normal' responsibilities. However, when the maintenance of economic competitiveness required a reduction in welfare dependency, government aimed to further restrict access to the 'sick' and 'impaired' roles.

Sociologists have also addressed the way individual identity is formed through social interaction. Those taking this *symbolic interactionalist* approach maintained that the 'sick role' was 'deviant' in a society grounded in individual responsibility. Disability, therefore, was also regarded as a form of social deviance. However, negative attitudes towards disabled bodies in an aesthetic sense also play a part in the creation of such deviance. The best-known exponent of symbolic interactionalism was Goffman (1964), whose identification of *stigma* had particular relevance for disability. He maintained that certain attributes (including impairments, disfigurements and physical or psychological 'abnormality') are interpreted as signifying a spoiled identity. Therefore people with atypical bodies have to find ways of managing interaction. Concealing the impairment is an option for some but not for others. Disability can be understood as a 'stigma' which arises from the perceived attitudes of others. However, interactionist explanations do not attempt to explain *why* disablist ideologies and attitudes that lead to the labelling of disabled people are so prevalent (Abberley 1993).

Policy implications arising from this *idealist* conception of disability include proposals for changing negative attitudes towards disabled people and also the principle of 'normalization', later known as 'social role valorization' (Wolfensberger 1995). This advocates 'the use of culturally valued means in order to enable, establish and/ or maintain valued social roles for people' (Wolfensberger and Thomas 1983: 23). Abberley (1993) comments that 'social role valorization' assumes that 'abnormality' is located in the disabled individual, whereas disabled people are oppressed through society's failure to meet their human needs, particularly that for inclusion in social relations. He also argues that many disabled people do not aspire to the 'normal' modes of social life promoted by social role valorization.

A particular research study grounded in the same deviance paradigm became a catalyst for an emancipatory approach to research and theorizing about disability. Following a dispute between residents and management at the 'Cheshire Home' Le Court over the residents' demands for more control over their own lives, researchers from the Tavistock Institute were invited by the residents to investigate their living

conditions. While Paul Hunt and other residents anticipated that the institutionalized regime at Le Court would be critiqued, the researchers themselves were anxious
to avoid 'taking sides' in disputes between residents and management. They decided
to investigate the way that the organization could be made to work better through
the lens of 'social defence' theory (Menzies Lyth 1960). The resulting publication,
A Life Apart, focused on the staff's anxieties in carrying out work with the residents.
The researchers (Miller and Gwynne 1972: 80) defined the situation of the residents
as 'social death' and as regards the purpose of the organization: 'The task that society assigns – behaviourally though never verbally – to these institutions is to cater
for the socially dead during the interval between social death and physical death.'
Carrying out this task creates stress and anxiety for staff. Of particular interest to the
researchers was the way that staff, and the culture and practices of the organization
more generally, interpreted the task in ways that would defend workers against pain
and anxiety. They found that institutional practices worked to create social distance
between residents and staff and to obscure the individuality of residents. Two models
of care were identified: 'warehousing' and 'horticultural'. The meaning of the former
is self-evident. The latter refers to the development of the unfulfilled capacities of
residents. Both, in the view of Miller and Gwynne (1972), were social defence mechanisms which enabled staff to cope with the 'real' task that society had implicitly set
them.

Hunt (1981) strongly challenged this concentration on the problems for staff and
the failure of the research to challenge the institutionalized regime to which residents
were subjected. He considered that the only 'side' the researchers were on was their
own and referred to them as 'parasite people'. He also criticized their unquestioning
acceptance of the medical approach to disability, in which

> the root cause of the whole problem is in our defective bodies and not in the social
> death sentence unnecessarily passed on us … The half concealed assumption that
> our severe impairments actually *cause* our social problems is essential for Miller
> and Gwynne's attempt to justify their concentrating on the task of reconciling us to
> the inevitability of our social death, and for legitimizing their research into how the
> sentence may most humanely be carried out. (Hunt 1981: 41–2)

Hunt maintained that Miller and Gwynne, despite their concern to be 'unbiased',
'restrict themselves to a narrow, blinkered approach to the issue, i.e. to try to make
the institutions work a little better' (ibid.: 40). *A Life Apart* is often cited by disability
studies authors as fundamentally exploitative of disabled people, the conclusions
being contrary to their interests. Calls for disabled people to have control over
research agendas and for research to be grounded in the social model of disability
have been informed by the experience of disabled research participants, including
those at Le Court (PCF 5.11).

Historical materialism and the 'social model'

It was disabled activists struggling for civil rights and independent living who made
a vital contribution to the development of the 'social model' (Campbell and Oliver
1996; Oliver 1996a). This has involved a recognition that disabled people are a
minority group subject to structural discrimination and oppression. Such accounts

recognize that the experience of disability is specific to particular points in history and to particular socio-economic systems. They also draw clear distinctions between impairment and disability.

Although there are now variants of the social model, the 'classic' social model as expounded by Oliver (1990) is materialist. Gleeson (1997: 193) asserts that a materialist account of disability needs to acknowledge that 'all social relations are products of the practices which humans pursue in meeting their basic needs for food, shelter, affective ties, movement and the like.' While impairment is physiological, the extent to which this is transformed into 'disability' will depend upon the way society organizes its basic material activities such as work, transport, leisure and reproduction. This tends to be supported by anthropological accounts such as those of Hanks and Hanks (1980), which indicate the variety of ways in which impairment is experienced and the relationship between such variation and socio-economic structures. They found that the individualized 'tragedy' model of disability was far from universal but tended to be prevalent in modern industrialized societies. Materialist scholars such as Finkelstein (1980), Oliver (1990) and Abberley (1987) regard attitudes and discourses as 'the product of the social practices which society undertakes in order to meet its basic material needs' (Gleeson 1997: 194).

Oliver (1990) argues that segregation from the rest of society and exclusion from the productive process are features of industrial capitalism. Therefore, if disablement is to be eliminated, radical transformation rather than reform will be necessary. In changing the material structures which marginalize and oppress disabled people, Gleeson (1997) emphasized the need to transform more than the built environment. For example, the physical design of workplaces may seem to be the cause of the marginalization of disabled people. However, socio-structural forces such as the commodity labour market and the principle of competition help to shape the design of workplaces which enable the participation of some and exclude that of others whose contribution is devalued.

This collectivist/materialist approach has been crucial in shaping the political agenda of the disability movement and has also played an important part in transforming the self-identity of disabled people, who were formerly encouraged to attribute their restricted opportunities to individual deficit. For example:

> For years now this social model of disability has enabled me to confront, survive and even surmount countless situations of exclusion and discrimination. It has been my mainstay, as it has been for the wider disabled people's movement. It has enabled a vision of ourselves free from the constraints of disability (oppression) and provided a direction for our commitment to social change. It has played a central role in promoting disabled people's individual self-worth, collective identity and political organization ... Gradually, very gradually, its sphere is extending beyond our movement to influence policy and practice in the mainstream. The contribution of the social model of disability, now and in the future, to achieving equal rights for disabled people is incalculable. (Crow 1996: 55–6)

As Crow has observed, the social model has influenced social policy, including social care. With its origins in a critique of existing residential care services, the social model has also been the basis of critiques of community care through the philosophy of *independent living* (Morris 1993b, 2003). The tenets of independent living are that disabled people should have the same rights to choice and control over their own lives as non-disabled people; that independence does not mean being able to do everything for oneself; and that disabled people should be in control of any assistance they require. These are, however, seen as means to an end: '[T]he "right to independent living" argument rests on the contention that disabled people have additional requirements, which must be met if they are to experience a level playing field in terms of their access to human and civil rights' (Morris 2003: 5).

Morris continues by identifying the barriers to independent living within a community care system in which disabled people had few substantive rights. For example, under the NHS and Community Care Act 1990 there was no right to live at home rather than in residential care. Many local authorities operated a cost ceiling on care at home and therefore had a financial incentive to place people with high support needs in residential care. This contravenes the right to a private and family life under the Human Rights Act 1998 (ibid.: 15). Negative professional attitudes towards capacity and risk also impeded choice and control for disabled people. This could lead to assumptions that individuals were unable to take decisions for themselves (the Mental Capacity Act 2005 later sought to strengthen the safeguards against such assumptions). Eligibility criteria and the need to ration scarce resources led to a focus on risk to 'life and limb' rather than risk of social exclusion. Access to lower-level preventative support had diminished, posing a risk to people's health.

The social model and the philosophy of independent living have informed the introduction of direct payments, through which disabled people can exercise more choice and control over their social care services (PCF 4.2). On account of campaigning by disability activists, awareness of discrimination and barriers in society increased; this eventually led to the introduction of anti-discrimination legislation, developments which are discussed further in chapters 4 and 9.

A more recently developed model, the affirmative model of disability (Swain and French 2000), challenges the tragedy approach to disability by asserting that, for many disabled people, disability is viewed in positive terms. The idea that many disabled people do not aspire to non-disabled norms is a challenge in itself (Abberley 1993). The affirmative model does not claim to replace the social model, as French and Swain (2012) identify implications for professional practice emerging from both (PCF 5.1).

Jenny Corbett has developed similar ideas in terms of positive identity and 'coming out'. Acknowledging that there are pressures to deny difference and to assimilate, she asserts that assimilation 'carries a high price in terms of human suffering and frustration' (Corbett 1997: 166). Using as an example the social skills training that aims to change the behaviour of people with learning disabilities that varies from the norm, she writes:

> Hiding our identities and presenting social masks is presented as an element of social decorum and an essential ingredient of social assimilation. Thus, we are encouraged to feel fear of exposure and to practice the art of concealment ... The journey into self-respect seems to me to be a critical element of coming out. (Ibid.: 167)

There are some parallels between the 'proud label' referred to by Corbett and the Deaf identity celebrated by members of the Deaf community, considered further later in the chapter. Other emerging positive identities include that of autistic activists who celebrate their difference as 'neurodiversity' rather than impairment (Singer 1999).

However, there have been a number of challenges to the 'social model' in recent years, some of which have come from within the disability movement. While these arise from the experience of disabled activists, they also reflect more generally feminist and post-structuralist critiques of historical materialism. The social model has concentrated on the social and environmental barriers faced by disabled people, and these provide an important focus for intervention. However, its relative neglect of individual agency and 'the experiential aspects of disablism' (Thomas 1999) gives it limitations as a sole framework for social work practice. If it has marginalized both particular groups and the impact of chronic illness and impairment, as critics maintain (Crow 1996; Morris 1996), social workers will require an approach that is capable of synthesizing these concerns with the structural analysis of the 'social model' (PCF 5.1).

Critiques of the social model

Many criticisms of the social model are concerned with the binary distinction it draws between impairment and disability and its reluctance to include impairment. There are two broad strands to this argument, the first of which is the claim that impairments are themselves socially constructed and therefore cannot be dismissed as irrelevant to any social or political approach. The second concerns the view that the removal of environmental barriers may not be sufficient to ensure the full participation of all disabled people (Abberley 1996). In support of this contention, feminists have argued for the incorporation of the experiential aspects of impairment into the social model and have pointed to the way that impairment has been dismissed by advocates of the social model as a personal or private matter, while disability has been favoured as part of the public sphere.

For Hughes and Paterson (1997: 325), the body has social as well as biological meaning; they refer to the social model as 'conced[ing] the body to medicine'. This viewpoint reflects trends in the sociology of the body, which has identified that interest in the body no longer focuses on its contribution to 'national efficiency' but, rather, on its significance in the construction of personal and political identity (Shilling 1993). As Shilling points out, whereas the body once symbolized the assigned social position of an individual, it is now regarded as the manifestation of personality and self-identity. The maintenance and 'improvement' of the body therefore becomes an important personal project. Disability has not figured prominently in such discussions. However, these arguments have significant implications for disabled people, whose capacity for bodily control and self-presentation may be more restricted than that of non-disabled people. It is the body which mediates between self-identity and the identity that is socially assigned (ibid.). For example, Goffman's work on 'stigma' and the presentation of self, mentioned earlier, stresses connections between bodily appearance and the identities which are assigned during processes of social interaction.

The work of social constructionists illuminates the ways in which the body and received ideas about acceptable bodily forms and idioms are shaped by society. This is taken further by Foucault (1979), who regards the body as wholly constituted by the 'discourses' through which power is exercised. Indeed, the medicalization of disability could be regarded as generating a particular discourse (a system of language, meanings and classifications) which has determined the way that disability is perceived and experienced. This approach is termed *post-structuralist* and is drawn upon by some authors within disability studies and Deaf studies. For example, some feminists have maintained that there is no essentially 'normal' body from which the 'deviations' associated with impairment can be identified. Shildrick and Price (1996) argue that the 'boundaries' of 'sameness' and 'difference' are being continually redrawn through discursive practices and performativity. In connection with the experience of deaf women, Corker (1999) identifies the discourse of 'phonocentrism' through which deafness is constructed as an impairment. This is despite the fact that many Deaf people do not regard themselves as impaired or disabled and instead identify as a cultural and linguistic minority. This has posed a challenge to the social model as, rather than prioritizing inclusion, Deaf activists have argued for the facilities to maintain and reproduce their culture.

This demonstrates a clash between two paradigms: one (the social model) conceptualizes the embodied difference that is called deafness as an impairment, and therefore as a precursor to disablism, while the other conceptualizes it in terms of linguistic diversity and cultural oppression. Of course, a third way of conceptualizing deafness is provided by the medical model, which would regard it as a deficit which is responsible for any social disadvantages experienced by deaf people. This demonstrates the importance of discourse in the way that embodied difference is *perceived*. However, a strong post-structuralist position would assert that the body can only be *experienced* through discourse, and differences do not exist prior to discourse. For example, Mallett and Runswick-Cole (2014) provide the example of the unpleasant experience of dealing with faecal incontinence, which they argue exists only within cultural expectations. Shakespeare (2006) takes a different view, describing his own theoretical position as *critical realist*. He argues that differences can be 'real' irrespective of our knowledge and understanding of them. However, he would agree that they can be interpreted very differently, and that different socio-historical contexts can have an impact on whether they are actually considered to be impairments.

Priestley (1998a) and Thomas (1999) acknowledge that post-structuralism has added to understanding by stressing the socially constructed nature of knowledge, but they refer to its limitations in accounting for the rise of particular discourses. It also leaves little space for the experiential aspects of impairment and disability (Hughes and Paterson 1997), considered next.

There is a strand within the sociology of the body that has attempted to integrate the experience of living within the body and the issue of social inequalities. Inevitably the account provided here is limited and selective, drawing on work that does not directly involve disability. One approach which addresses the 'lived' experience of the body while maintaining a focus on the 'social' is Elias's work on the civilizing process. Taking a historical approach, Elias (1978) traced the growing importance of the 'socialization' of the body, which included the hiding of natural functions and the growing importance of socially approved codes of behaviour. One result of this was that emotions and drives came to be expressed *within* rather than *between* individuals. The relevance of this has been extended by work on the 'emotional body' and 'emotion work' in terms of the effects of greater demands for bodily control on bodily well-being. This approach also seems to have potential in explaining the experience of disabled people.

Freund (1982, 1990) stresses the close integration which exists between body and mind and that, in order to maintain bodily well-being, people should have sufficient control over this integration. The constant necessity to interrupt the connection between emotion and its response can undermine well-being. Emotions arise through interaction with others and are the mechanism that connects the body to social relationships. To maintain well-being and avoid illness, people should be able to remain 'in touch' with their emotions and mobilize bodily resources to deal with these. However, the ability to do this is socially differentiated. One source of emotional stress is the inability to maintain self-identity in the face of being redefined by someone who is more powerful. The capacity to resist such processes is limited for people in subordinate positions, who may not be able to maintain their original self-perception in the face of such redefinition from 'above' and may be 'trapped' as a result.

A related concept is that of 'emotion work' (Hochschild 1983), which provides some important insights into the way that people are expected to manage their emotions in social encounters. In employment situations, it is often not enough to perform tasks efficiently; people must also display the required type of social interaction. The 'acting' that this requires can lead to inconsistency between emotion and bodily demeanour.

The question of 'emotional bodies' and 'emotion work' is closely related to social inequalities, as the demands for 'emotion work' can be more onerous for people in less powerful positions. For example, research about the experiences of disabled social workers has found that feelings of vulnerability led many disabled workers to hide their anger and frustration about the attitudes of colleagues and the failure of organizations to provide necessary equipment and support (Castle 2007) (PCF 3.2). As one research participant observed, there were dangers in 'creating an atmosphere'. Some participants also felt responsible for making non-disabled colleagues feel comfortable about working with a disabled person – for example, by making jokes and 'giving them permission to laugh'. If this is the case for disabled people at work, there may be parallels in the interactions that take place between social workers and disabled service users, something considered further later in this chapter.

Debate about the body and impairment is beginning to re-emerge within the disability movement, and Abberley (1996) has linked these concerns to the centrality of access to paid work in the social model approach to disability. He points out that the classical Marxist theories on which the social model draws ascribe a crucial importance to work as a means to social integration. Work is regarded both as a need and as a potential source of identity. However, even in the 'Utopia' envisaged by Marxism, some people with impairments would continue to be disadvantaged, by biology if not by society, and the integration of all impaired people into work is unlikely ever to be possible.

The centrality of work to the materialist social model may result from the history of disability activism, in which disabled white men of working age played a key part. This has led to critiques of the failure of the social model to incorporate racism, sexism and other forms of multiple oppression (Watson 2004). Oliver (2004: 9) has asserted that '[t]he fact that the social model has not so far adequately incorporated these dimensions does not mean that it is unable to do so.' However, it is apparent that this is still work in progress, and that there is scope to further address issues in the private sphere.

There are experiential accounts that support Abberley's contention that impairment continues to impose restrictions even when environmental barriers have been removed (Morris 1993b; Crow 1996). Many disabled people have impairments which cause pain and fatigue or which otherwise make paid work problematic. This can also limit their participation in disability politics. Thomas (1999) coined the phrase 'impairment effects' to describe such restrictions and advocated a 'social relational' definition of disability (Thomas 2004). This is intended as a corrective to interpretations of the social model which imply that *all* restrictions result from social and environmental barriers.

Case profile: Eileen

Eileen is eighty-nine years old and has lived alone since her husband's death. Until recently she led an active social life, based mainly on her friendships at the lunch club and her interest in crafts. Two years ago she was admitted to hospital after breaking her hip. She responded well to physiotherapy and regained sufficient mobility to return home, where she has since been assisted by an agency care worker. Eventually she was able to go out as far as the corner shop on her own using a walking aid but was reliant on help from friends and relatives to go further. However, since she has found it more difficult to go out, her circle of friends has contracted. Following her hospitalization she has taken some time to regain her strength. She has also developed osteoarthritis in her hands, and this has made it difficult for her to carry out basic tasks, including making a hot drink. She tires easily if she tries to do too much. She is also afraid of falling, and this has discouraged her from going out alone; she is worried about 'being a nuisance' to others if she needs help while out and about. Her daughter has been living with her since she came out of hospital and has taken annual leave so she can be around during the day. She is worried about how her mother will cope when she returns to work. Eileen feels anxious and depressed about the future and fears that she might have to go into residential care.

Consider the factors that are restricting Eileen's life. Which of these arise from impairment? Is disability also restricting her? How would you respond to this situation as a social worker? It is apparent that Eileen's impairments have an impact on her ability to participate in the activities she used to enjoy. In particular, her fear of falling has made her reluctant to risk going to the lunch club, which would have kept her in touch with friends. There are activities that have become difficult as a result of impairment. However, as the advocates of Independent Living have stated, independence is not about doing everything for oneself. A social worker would be able to assess Eileen's need for assistance in the home and perhaps for support outside the home. This might overcome some practical difficulties, as might aids provided by an occupational therapist. However, the brief description above indicates that disability is also an issue. Why should Eileen be worried about having to ask for help while she is out? This suggests that she wishes to avoid being a 'burden' to others and also that people might think less of her as a result. The paragraphs below explore these issues, in particular that of internalized oppression.

Thomas (2004) argues that disability is more than a restriction of activity, and that it is not only impairment that can be associated with pain and 'psycho-emotional effects'. Identity and psychological well-being can be affected by disabling processes which undermine self-worth (Thomas 1999). Thomas refers to these as restrictions on 'being' rather than the more active 'doing' normally associated with the social model. For her, the issue is not only impairment but the marginalization of much experience as 'personal' and thus outside the remit of the social model, thus denying that experience in the private sphere can be the subject of politics. Reeve (2004b: 10) has emphasized that the psycho-emotional effects of interaction with others can lead to internalized oppression (discussed further in chapter 5): 'I consider internalised oppression to be one of the most important manifestations of psycho-emotional disablism because of its unconscious and insidious effects on the psycho-emotional well-being of disabled people and because it has a direct impact in restricting who someone can "be".'

Others have written of the marginalization of the physical and psychological pain of impairment within the social model, to the extent of 'deny[ing] the experience of our own bodies' (Morris 1991: 10). Crow (1996) argues that the social model should fully integrate the experience of impairment with that of disability. Referring to pain, fatigue and chronic illness, she points out that 'the suppression of concerns related to impairment does not mean that they cease to exist or suddenly become more bearable' (ibid.: 59). In addition, this silence tends to marginalize people whose impairments (rather than disabling barriers) make it difficult to participate in disability politics. This may lead to a partial understanding of disability:

> What we risk is a world which includes an 'elite' of people with impairments, but which for many more of us contains no real promise of civil rights, equality or belonging. How can we expect anyone to take seriously a 'radical' movement which replicates some of the worst exclusionary aspects of the society it purports to challenge? (Ibid.: 60)

Arguing that, as a social construction, the 'personal tragedy' interpretation of impairment is not inevitable, Crow advocates a greater focus on the subjective experience of impairment. She argues that, although they are conceptually distinct, impairment and disability interact. For example, the negotiation of environmental barriers may increase pain and fatigue. Conversely, external barriers may become irrelevant at certain points in a progressive illness. Also, people may find that access to the medical treatment or pain relief which would facilitate their social participation is restricted. Poverty, inequality, discrimination and cultural variation in approaches to pain can all exacerbate impairment. Some of the points raised by Crow are similar to those of Shakespeare, who argues that the distinction between impairment and disability is untenable. He continues by asserting that pain can be generated by a combination of physiological, psychological and socio-cultural factors, so that 'the individual experience can never be separated from the social context' (2006: 34). He is in agreement with Crow (1996) and Abberley (1987) that impairments can be caused or exacerbated by social factors. Lastly, he maintains that 'what counts as an impairment is a social judgement' (Shakespeare 2006: 35).

An interesting approach to the judgements through which people are assigned to categories arises from the application of *explanatory legitimacy theory* (Depoy and Gilson 2008). Assignment of individuals to particular disability [*sic*] categories is argued to be dependent on the *explanation* for their atypical behaviour or appearance. Depoy and Gilson assert that current explanatory frameworks involve either medical judgements or judgements based on 'disability as a construction', including social and political models of disability. However, they maintain that, in practice, 'constructed' explanations are applied only to those with bona fide diagnoses, and that this obscures the primacy of medical/diagnostic explanations (ibid.: 12). This may therefore include some people while excluding others for whom an acceptable medical explanation cannot be identified.

For example, Molloy and Vasil (2002) have referred to the social construction of Asperger's syndrome as an example of 'pathologizing difference'. Asperger's syndrome (AS) is an autism spectrum condition without an associated learning disability. As Baron-Cohen (2002) argues, people with AS have an IQ within the normal range, possess many strengths, and could just as appropriately be considered different rather than impaired. However, AS was added to the American diagnostic guide DSM-4 in 1994 and has been subsumed under 'autism spectrum disorder' in DSM-5. Asperger's syndrome is now commonly recognized as a disability. However, there are conditions for which official medical recognition took some time, with 'sufferers' experiencing the consequences of this lack of perceived legitimacy. A relevant example would be 'chronic fatigue syndrome' (or myalgic encephalomyelitis), which is now recognized, although its cause remains uncertain.

In order to overcome this problem, Depoy and Gilson (2008: 12) offer a third explanatory framework – *disjuncture theory* – which involves 'the ill fit of the body (broadly defined) with the environment'. They assert that what is regarded as typical has determined the design of the built environment and also social environments and professional practices, which disadvantages people with atypical bodies. This has much in common with Shakespeare's conceptualization of disability: 'The experience of a disabled person results from the relationship between factors intrinsic to the individual, and extrinsic factors arising from the wider context in which she finds herself' (2006: 55). Depoy and Gilson (2008) also argue that the current diversity paradigm, which tends to categorize minority groups on the basis of shared 'bodies and backgrounds', needs to be broadened to include 'the uniqueness of all people'. Their approach to diversity shares with post-structuralism a critique of the way in which both the medical and the social model have 'othered' disabled people. It is this 'othering', post-structuralists have argued, that has left people with impairments open to oppression. The question that is addressed later in the chapter is whether the deconstruction of the distinctions between 'impaired' and 'not impaired', 'disabled' and 'non-disabled', has the potential to increase social justice and the participation of those currently identified as disabled in social life.

Implications for social work

The theoretical and conceptual debates in this chapter have significant implications for social work. These are now discussed, beginning with disjuncture theory. This has much in common with the approach to disability formulated by Shakespeare (2006) as regards implications for social work. Both suggest that the focus of intervention should be at the intersection of the body and the physical, social and political environment. Depoy and Gilson (2008) consider that their reformulation of the current diversity paradigm provides additional opportunities for social work to broaden its social justice remit so as to include the full range of diversity.

A commitment to human rights and social justice means that social workers need to be prepared to engage in challenging oppression (PCF 4.1). Group work and community work were formerly important components of social work education but have now slipped to the margins. However, social workers may need to draw on a wider menu of methods and skills than is currently the case in order to work with disabled people to tackle social barriers (PCF 5.8). Since the introduction of care management in the 1990s, the role of social work has contracted, although the Care Act 2014 supports a return to a more preventative approach (see chapter 4). There is much to be gained from a return to some of the activities that took place earlier, in particular collective advocacy. Social workers should be prepared to engage with the collective issues identified by organizations of disabled people (PCF 7.7). This may include promoting such issues and 'rais[ing] questions about traditional assumptions and conventional approaches' within the agencies that employ social workers (Mullaly 2007: 323). It may also include supporting campaigning organizations or promoting their agendas through trade unions or professional associations. In addition, social workers may signpost service users to organizations in which they can link with others experiencing shared difficulties.

However, both Thomas (1999) and Shakespeare (2006) suggest that work with individuals remains important. Thomas, for instance, refers to the psycho-emotional effects of both disability and impairment, as well as to the limitations imposed by impairments. These cannot be ignored, and social workers may need to draw both on the relationship-based skills that have been traditional in social work and on assessment and support planning skills, including advocacy with service users, the promotion of self-advocacy and independent living. There has been debate about the use of counselling skills with disabled people, as they have traditionally been associated with 'help[ing] people come to terms with their impairment' (Oliver et al. 2012: 164), notably the restrictions caused by disablism. However, Oliver and his colleagues conclude that counselling can be useful in empowering disabled people, raising their consciousness and tackling barriers arising from low self-esteem.

In their relationships with service users, social workers are in a position of relative power (PCF 3.3). It is recognized that social work itself may make demands for emotion work, but not always that this may also be an issue for service users. Ken Davis (2004) has identified the disempowering nature of the professional–'client' relationship, and Finkelstein (2004: 208) has described the demeanour he felt was expected of him when visited by a professional:

> I was obliged to feed information into one of the longest forms I have yet encountered. I, of course, complied by adopting the usual 'fool' role expected from a subservient patient and answered all the questions without even joking that all the information was available in the referring GP's file.

In the case of this particular encounter, Finkelstein found that he was not able to maintain the 'fool role' for very long before he 'exploded'. However, social workers need to be aware that service users may feel impelled to act the role they have learned is expected of them despite any impulse to the contrary. There is clearly a need both for more recognition of the abilities and knowledge of disabled people and for greater equality and respect in their face-to-face interaction with professionals (PCF 7.3, 5.12).

Shakespeare (2006: 55–6) has identified some of the 'intrinsic factors' which affect the experience of disability, including 'the nature and severity of her [sic] impairment, her own attitudes to it, her personal qualities and abilities, and her personality'. As regards 'extrinsic factors', he includes 'the attitudes and reactions of others' and 'the extent to which the environment is enabling or disabling' (ibid.: 56). Again, these issues appear amenable to modes of practice which may already be familiar to social workers, including strengths-based approaches with individuals and their families (PCF 5.8), and in this context it may be empowering to foster service users' understanding of the social model, which has been regarded as vital by disabled writers (Crow 1996). Multi-professional approaches to support planning may also contribute to tackling barriers within the home and immediate environment. However, this needs to be in the context of the principles of independent living and designed to enhance the degree of choice and control the service user has over her own life (PCF 2.4, 2.5).

Towards a theory of disability?

Oliver (2004) has responded to critiques of the social model of disability by asserting that it should not be expected to perform as a social theory of disability. It was merely intended to be a model. Finkelstein (2001: 3) maintains that 'models do not *explain* anything.' He argues that the social model was intended as a device to aid understanding, being 'a multidimensional replica of reality that can trigger insights which we might not otherwise develop'. The social model is a description of how impairment, environmental barriers and disability are related, a simplified version of a complex reality, but this does not of itself explain why this relationship works in the way that it does. However, Oliver (1990) has linked the model to a theoretical framework which operates at a more general level. The 'classic' social model draws on Marxist theory as a means of explaining the relationship between impairment and disability. In this respect, the social model links a theoretical framework (historical materialism) with a particular phenomenon in the contemporary world (disability). However, it is possible to explain the relationship between the three components of the social model (impairment, barriers and disability) in a number of different ways, of which historical materialism is only one.

Critics have suggested that an adequate social theory of disability would be more inclusive than the social model, and also that it would allow for differences between disabled people. Corker (1999) has argued that the structural analysis of the social model should be complemented by the approaches based on discourse and language, and that this would result in a focus on the relationship between impairment and oppression. It is contended that this would allow differences on the basis of gender, ethnicity and sexuality to emerge. However, Watson (2004: 113) has questioned whether discursive approaches of this kind are consistent with normative standards of social justice, as, in post-modernism, 'there are no universal truths, no concept of universal justice.' If the intention is to decouple embodied difference from normative judgements about impairment, Watson has identified limitations in terms of its potential to guide moral decisions and the just distribution of material goods: 'The disadvantage related to disability is to a great extent a matter of economic injustice, and before this injustice can be corrected we have to be able to identify those individuals and social groups that have been disadvantaged by social arrangements' (2014: 647). This suggests that, although post-structuralism contributes a great deal to understanding the way that normative judgements are made about embodied differences, it appears to pull in a different direction from the social model when it comes to their practical implications. However, there is potential for widening the inclusiveness of the social model through dialogue with feminists, who have argued for the greater recognition of the experience of impairment (Morris 1991; Crow 1996), the issues arising in the private sphere, and the psycho-emotional effects of both impairment and disability (Thomas 1999). This could extend the concerns addressed by the social model to those which are important to women, older disabled people, and those experiencing debilitating and painful impairments (PCF 3.1). Oliver himself (2004) asserts that the social model has the capacity to include issues of multiple oppression and could be developed so as to be more inclusive of the experiences of all disabled people. Thomas (2007) has also argued for closer links with medical sociology but warns against the deviance paradigm that has been predominant in this discipline. There is within medical sociology a stream of work in which illness and disability are understood as products of capitalism (Doyle 1979) and which identified social determinants of health inequality (Marmot and Wilkinson 1999). Medical sociologists have also carried out qualitative research investigating the experience of 'chronic illness'. From within disability studies, Watson (2004) argues for more qualitative research which would illuminate the diversity of disabled people's lives and the contextual nature of both disability and impairment. In this way, 'a more comprehensive and inclusive social theory of disability can emerge' (ibid.: 115).

This indicates that the social model as currently constituted provides a partial explanation of the experience of disability. Watson (2004: 17) argues that the model should emphasize 'interpersonal relations' as well as the material, as 'people's experiences of disablement … occur at the interpersonal [level].' This is consistent with the work of Reeve (2004), who has identified a relationship between day-to-day interaction and internalized oppression.

For social workers, the social model provides an invaluable insight into the experience of disability. Understanding of the model should focus professional attention on the barriers to social participation faced by disabled people and broaden the range of social work practice beyond the individual. More recent theorizing throws light on the continuing importance of impairment and the interpersonal, as well as the restrictions and psycho-emotional effects of experience in the private sphere. It has also questioned the way that atypical bodies have been conceptualized in terms of deficit. This has implications for a more empowering practice which acknowledges the impact of oppression but also draws on the affirmative model and the positive identities which celebrate embodied difference.

Key messages

- The social model makes a clear distinction between impairment and disability, which arises from environmental barriers and social oppression.
- Social workers should focus on the barriers that prevent disabled people from achieving their human and civil rights. They should engage with the political issues that affect disabled people in partnership with disabled people's organizations. This will mean regaining skills in group and community work.
- The social model of disability has been criticized for its neglect both of other social divisions and of impairment and the private sphere. Restrictions can arise from 'impairment effects' as well as from disability. Whether an atypical characteristic is regarded as impairment can involve value judgements.
- There is still a place for social work intervention with individual disabled people. Social oppression can threaten self-worth and lead to internalized oppression. In their work with individuals, social workers should engage in forms of practice that promote the independence and positive identity of disabled people. In this context, independence involves having control over one's life.

Activities

- To what extent is the 'rehabilitation role' relevant today? Consider either any experience you may have had working with adults or university-based learning about intermediate care or reablement.
- Consider Miller and Gwynne's research *A Life Apart* (1972). Evaluate their approach, including their findings and ethical issues arising. Are there any positives? How might findings have differed if disabled residents had determined the aims and theoretical orientation of the research?
- Does disjuncture theory provide a feasible basis for social work practice? What challenges might social workers face in trying to implement it?

Suggested further reading

Barnes, C., and Mercer, G. (2010) *Exploring Disability*. 2nd edn, Cambridge: Polity.
Oliver, M. (2009) *Understanding Disability: From Theory to Practice*. 2nd edn, Basingstoke: Palgrave Macmillan.
Shakespeare, T. (2014) *Disability Rights and Wrongs Revisited*. 2nd edn, Abingdon: Routledge.

3 Disability from a Life Course Perspective

Issues considered in this chapter:

- The knowledge and understanding of disability gained by adopting a life course perspective
- Perceptions of disability and their relationship to pre-birth and end of life decisions
- The experience of disability throughout the life course
- Implications for social work practice

Introduction

The experience of disability is not static but one that is intertwined with the ageing process throughout the life course; disability may be experienced very differently in childhood, youth, adulthood and old age. Adopting a life course approach to disability therefore offers insight into the relationship between disability, human growth and development, policy and practice. Indeed, much can be learned about experiences of disability by exploring them through a life course lens. Priestley (2003b) argues that such an approach not only highlights how people at different life stages can experience disability differently but also develops our understanding of the social construction of disability, how disabling barriers emerge, and also how disability and impairment impact on life transitions. Social workers often engage with people at times of transition, and the importance of sound knowledge of life course issues is reflected in both the Health and Care Professions Council (HCPC) Standards of Proficiency (SoP 13.4) and the PCF (Domain 5).

This chapter explores the experience of disability throughout the life course and considers the implications of the knowledge gained from this perspective for social work practice. While knowledge of human growth and development is important for practice, the social work profession's commitment to recognizing and valuing diversity (HCPC SoP 5; PCF Domain 3) is also essential in this context. Boushel et al. (2010) observe the risk of disability, when explored in the context of the normative concepts of growth and development, being associated with difference and deviance rather than diversity. This risk is evident when one acknowledges the pervasive notions of a 'normal' life course that social policy (see chapter 4) and social institutions have constructed. The disability movement has had an active role in redefining not only disability but also the notion of a 'normal' life course (Priestley 2003a).

Pre-birth choices

Exploration of disability from a life course perspective begins with pre-birth choices. Considering such choices compels one to reflect on the criteria used to determine which lives are valued by society (Priestley 2003a) and highlights the impact of social policy and disabling barriers on the life course and life chances of those with embodied difference before they are even born (Priestley 2000). The announcement in November 2013 of an NHS trial of a new blood test in pregnancy to detect Down's syndrome in a developing foetus reflects the increasing number of options made available to parents; such options, emerging from medical and genetic research, include pre-natal screening and selective abortion. It is the common use of such practices that has revived debates about which lives have value and which human features are desirable (Priestley 2003a). While such eugenic debates have historically been linked with population-level policy (for example, the Nazi regime under Hitler), Shakespeare (2008: 27) argues that the range of pre-birth choices facing individual parents has resulted in 'privatized eugenics'. However, whether at a population or an individual level, such debates and decisions are frequently informed by perceptions of impairment as inherently undesirable. For example, Priestley (2000, 2003a) notes the practice of requiring parents to discuss termination when offering pre-natal screening for impairments and the use in some countries of 'wrongful life' lawsuits, where parents sue medical professionals who fail to identify foetal impairment before birth. In this latter instance, the clear implication is that the life of the impaired child should never have been. Actions taken to reduce the numbers of children born with impairments, in turn, strengthen such negative perceptions.

Disability activists have been highly critical of 'privatized eugenic' practices on the basis that they express negative views about the value of disabled people's lives. This challenge, or 'expressivist objection' (Shakespeare 2008: 29), strongly rejects the notion of 'wrongful' lives and perceives embodied difference as a reflection of human diversity (Priestley 2003a). Applying the social model of disability to the debate, commentators have argued that 'it is not disabled lives that are wrongful but disabling societies' (ibid.: 39). Disability activists have also drawn attention to the human rights issues raised in this context. The UN Convention on the Rights of Persons with Disabilities includes explicit reference not only to the 'Right to life' (Article 10) (a right also contained in the Human Rights Act 1998) but also to 'Respect for difference and acceptance of persons with disabilities *as part of human diversity and humanity*' (Article 3). However, failure to recognize embodied difference as human diversity is evident in law and policy. For example, during contemporary debate about amendments to the Human Fertilization and Embryology Act 1990, deafness was labelled as a 'serious medical condition' and 'abnormality'; this categorization was in the context of a suggested amendment concerning preference being given to embryos without such conditions. Unsurprisingly, the Deaf community queried why their lives are considered less worthy than those of hearing people (Young and Hunt 2011).

Despite this challenge, Shakespeare (2008) argues that disability activists are wrong to suggest that all human impairment is merely human difference. While he is critical of those who suggest all impairment is undesirable, he suggests that the emotive language of eugenics overshadows the complexity of both the debate and people's lives. He also questions the extent to which disabled people themselves support the challenge mounted by disability activists, observing that many are involved with organizations that support medical research into the prevention of their conditions and impairments. Social workers are therefore placed in a highly complex situation when working with parents seeking advice, guidance and support in the face of pre-birth decisions: challenging a termination decision could be seen as criticism, and indeed judgement, of individual parents, while failure to challenge could be seen as contributing to dominant negative perceptions of impairment and, therefore, a failure in anti-oppressive practice. In addressing such practice dilemmas, social workers should focus their attention on ensuring parents are *fully* informed, thereby enabling them to exercise choice. This involves challenging perceptions of impairment as inherently undesirable or inexorably tragic (ibid.). For example, in the practice experience of one of the authors, facilitating meetings between hearing parents and Deaf adults proved a very positive and non-threatening way of challenging negative assumptions about hearing loss.

Disability and childhood

Given the negative value often placed on the unborn disabled child, it follows that the emotional response of parents to the birth of a disabled child has been interpreted in terms of loss (Ellis 1989). Parents have been described as 'mourning' the child they expected to have, and the diagnosis of an impairment is interpreted as a 'family crisis' (Fortier and Wanless 1984). Read and Clements (2001: 82) state that 'there are very many reasons why [parents] may feel desperate when they discover that they are the parents of a child they were not expecting.'

Avery (1999), who has analysed parental stories of living with childhood disability, comments on the preponderance of guilt and shame in these narratives. She refers to 'a deep parental investment in our culture's conflated ideologies in the areas of 'good' parenting and 'perfect' children' (ibid.: 119). Many parents pinned their hopes on a 'cure', and the wheelchair became a symbol of the end of these hopes.

This focus on parental loss is informed by a deficit model of impairment. It has been challenged by disability activists and academics, who stress the normalizing ideologies which underpin this (Priestley 2003a). Shakespeare and Watson (1998) point out that the difference of disabled children is devalued by society as a whole. This is reinforced by traditional approaches to child development, which measure individuals against developmental norms and monitor those who are 'failing' to meet milestones or develop the behaviours and competences of independent adulthood. There are parallels between this and early sociological approaches to childhood, with their emphasis on socialization (Parsons 1951). Both regard childhood primarily as preparation for independent adulthood.

Given their pervasiveness, it is not surprising that normalizing ideologies influence the initial response of some parents. While acknowledging the impact of this on parents, Read and Clements (2001: 82) identify the danger of an overemphasis on parental distress: 'If the prevailing attitude is that parents need to be helped to cope with something that is unequivocally tragic, disabled children may feel devalued and undermined.' An interesting response has come from Jim Sinclair, a man with an autistic spectrum condition, who urges parents 'don't mourn for us'. He acknowledges that parents may need to mourn for the loss of the child they expected to have, but adds that:

> it shouldn't be our burden. We need and deserve families who can see us and value us for ourselves, not families whose vision of us is obscured by the ghosts of children who never lived. Grieve if you must, for your own lost dreams. But don't mourn for us. We are alive. We are real. And we're here waiting for you. (Sinclair 2012: 3)

Although parents may be encouraged to value diversity and to recognize the abilities of their disabled child, social workers need to be mindful of the challenges families are likely to encounter. Research evidence suggests that they will face additional barriers to social inclusion (Clarke 2006), will have to provide extra care over and above that of the parents of non-disabled children (Roberts and Lawton 2001), and may experience difficulties in accessing the support they and their child need (Care Quality Commission 2012). This indicates that the social model of disability has much to offer in explaining the restrictions experienced by disabled children and their families, and that many of these are the result of social, environmental and attitudinal barriers. Social workers may find that the distinction that Thomas (1999) draws between 'impairment effects' and 'disability effects' (see chapter 2) provides a useful tool for analysing the restrictions experienced by families.

The social model of disability is an important source of challenge to perceptions of the disabled child as a 'burden'. Another challenge arises from the new sociology of childhood. It is this field of study which has identified that it is independent adulthood that is most valued in Western societies, and this has led to the exclusion of children from the rights of citizenship (Priestley 2003a). If childhood is socially constructed in this way, children can be regarded as a minority group with little opportunity to participate in the decisions that affect their lives (Mayall 1993). This contrasts with notions of childhood as merely a preparatory stage for adulthood. Recent sociological approaches have been concerned with the relationship between children and other social groups, with their experiences and understandings of childhood, with their capacity for agency and ability to exert influence. It is this approach which is most consistent with recent policies involving children's rights and, consequently, the imperative to listen to disabled children directly rather than just through intermediaries.

When asked about their lives directly, disabled children have described constant surveillance by adults. Although much of this arises from attempts to meet the support needs of disabled children, for example in school, it has led to a relative lack of privacy and has affected relationships with other children (Watson et al. 1999). These relationships were limited by the wider social and physical environment and often dominated by the assumption that the disabled child needed the care of the non-disabled friend. Children found that adults categorized them primarily as disabled, with everything explained in terms of their impairments, and tried to resist this. Their difference from other children was reinforced through procedures and use of physical space within schools. In addition, these children had experiences of being bullied.

The separation of disabled children from their peers can be reinforced by policies and processes in education. The most obvious of these is the allocation of some disabled children to special schools or units, which may separate them from other children in their home neighbourhood. Linda Derbyshire (2013: 31) has written about what happened to her friend David:

> He was sent, on his own, to the local special needs school. I remember at the time talking to my mum and saying that it wasn't fair that he couldn't go to the same school as his best friend Nick as they were both very close, and inseparable. And I knew how miserable I would have felt if I had moved away from my friends. Soon after the move we would go round and ask David to play out with us, but he wouldn't come any more, and eventually we moved on through secondary school and lost touch.

However, it is increasingly recognized that there can also be segregation *within* mainstream schools through processes of labelling whereby abilities are given less attention than inability to achieve developmental milestones (Davis and Watson 2001). Pippa Murray (2006: 34–41) has written about her son's experience:

> Having begged, pleaded and fought for a place in the school his non-disabled sister attended, I naively thought his presence there would be all that was required. I knew that staff would be on a steep learning curve, and that it might take some time for things to work out, but I could not have anticipated the reality he encountered: of exclusion wearing the face of inclusion; of his being there without any real sense of belonging.

This is consistent with the experience of the children in the study by Watson et al. (1999), who identified the way that they were categorized and separated from non-disabled peers, primarily on the basis of their impairments. However, their own identification with disability was much more fluid, suggesting that context was important. At times, they might regard themselves as the same as others with the same impairment, and at other times they might identify with a wider group of disabled children. Alternatively there were situations in which they did not feel that they were disabled. Watson and his colleagues conclude that disabled children are active in negotiating identities and relationships rather than being the passive recipients of labelling by others, and that there is fluidity in the way they perceived disabled identity.

Of particular relevance for disabled children is cultural preoccupation with bodily perfection, discussed later in this chapter's section on youth. This has led to a concern with the 'cure' or 'correction' of 'imperfections'. The assumptions underpinning this are apparent in classic children's fiction; for example, both Johanna Spyri's *Heidi*, written in 1880, and Frances Hodgson Burnett's *The Secret Garden*, published in 1911, include a disabled child who is restored to health and functional 'normality' by the end of the story. In *Heidi*, it is the loss of the wheelchair (the symbol of disability) that motivates the disabled child to begin to walk again. Cooper (2013) has explored the impact of medical constructions of normalcy on the disabled child, noting that child-care manuals demonstrate a shift from concern about sickness in the nineteenth century to concern about normalcy in the twentieth. While acknowledging that medicine may have offered 'physical emancipation' for some disabled people, Cooper asserts that the impact of the medical construction of normalcy has been oppressive for disabled children. For example, in referring to a recent television documentary, she comments: 'The children's lives are constructed as narratives of success or failure to mimic the "norm" of able-bodiedness' (ibid.: 139).

Much corrective surgery and therapy takes place during childhood, and social workers may be working with parents who have been advised that their child should undergo medical intervention. For example, parents may have been told that, without this, their child's mobility is likely to decrease significantly. In these circumstances, a social worker may be able to support the family in obtaining accurate information about the procedure and its likely outcome, as the efficacy of some treatment has been questioned (Middleton 1999). The accounts of adults who were disabled from childhood indicate that, in some cases, children have exceeded initial medical prognoses:

> At two years old my Dr 'M', as I called him, tested my reflexes by holding me down and running his thumb up my bare foot. My mother was told I would not do anything, not walk – but at two, I walked naked down the hospital corridor to show them! (Skitteral 2013: 23)

> With only dramatic and terrifying information from the doctors about my 'severe' impairment and that my life was a ticking time bomb, my parents were supposed to be confident and help themselves in their new role as parents of a disabled (and said to be dying) little girl. (Haraldsdóttir 2013: 13)

Priestley (2003a) is critical of the normalizing imperatives which underpin corrective surgery, and Shakespeare and Watson (2001) state that the disability community has been critical of the imperative towards 'cure' and the maximization of function. Some children have been subjected to repeated orthopaedic surgery in the past, irrespective of their wishes (Borsay 2005). However, while admitting that some treatments 'cause more harm than good', Shakespeare and Watson (2001: 13) go on to argue that 'it would be to commit an equivalent error if we discounted all possibility or benefit of impairment-avoidance and reduction.' As they note, not all impairments are stable, some are highly unpleasant to live with, and many have at least *some* medical implications.

Parents and children have to balance any likely benefits arising from prolonged medical treatment with the disruption that this causes to disabled children's lives (French and Swain 2012) and with the pain and discomfort involved. However, John Davis (2004) comments that decisions about medical treatment are often taken by parents and professionals on the assumption that children lack competence. Article 12 of the United Nations Convention on the Rights of the Child specifies that children have the right to be involved in decisions which affect them, although there is a caveat that he or she should be 'capable of forming his or her own views'. Alderson (1993) argues that, if treatment is explained in an accessible way and sufficient time is allowed for disabled children to consider, they may be well able to make decisions and express their views. Davis (2004) points out that medical decisions are made on the basis of the future quality of life of the child, but the issues taken into account may not accord with what is valued by that child. It is therefore important for social workers to support and encourage communication with children when there are perceived barriers to obtaining their views. For example, communication with children with learning difficulties or communication impairments is likely to make consultation more time consuming.

Particular issues arise for families considering cochlear implants for a deaf child, as this technology has been regarded by Deaf activists as 'an attack on the culture of the Deaf' (Sparrow 2005: 136). Deaf parents may choose to bring up a child without implants as a part of the Deaf community. In these cases, they may be able to support the language development of their child using their first language, British Sign Language, and may already be part of the Deaf community. However, the issues may be more problematic for hearing parents, and, as Sparrow (2005) points out, 90 per cent of deaf children are born to hearing parents. Such parents would have to become proficient in British Sign Language and establish links with the Deaf community if their child is to be brought into contact with this world. However, there are ethical issues involved in parents choosing a cultural identity for a very young child who may not yet have developed language. Irrespective of whether D/deafness is regarded as a culture or a disability, it is associated with considerable social disadvantage in a predominantly hearing society. Certainly many of these disadvantages are socially created, and they would be much reduced through rigorous enforcement of equalities legislation. However, in an imperfect society, being unable to learn the language of the majority may restrict opportunity. Decisions about cochlear implants will need to take a wide range of issues into account, including the wishes of the child (where this can be ascertained), the age and current language development of the child at the onset of deafness, and the resources and support available to the family. Although families will consult medical personnel about this issue, there is a role for social workers in assisting families to consider the social and emotional aspects. Social workers with knowledge and understanding of sign language and Deaf culture, the barriers that may be faced by D/deaf people, and strategies for dealing with these will be helpful.

There is a danger of disabled children becoming socially isolated as a result of policies and practices in education and, in some cases, through prolonged medical treatment. It is also well documented that access to leisure activities can be problematic (Beresford and Clark 2009). However, the priorities of disabled children are not 'special'. As children told the Audit Commission (2003: 2), they value 'being respected and listened to, being able to play and have friends, feeling safe and comfortable'. These are ambitions common to all children, but they are not always attainable for disabled children on account of a range of social, attitudinal, environmental, and sometimes impairment-related barriers. By assisting families in tackling these barriers and meeting impairment-related needs, social workers may also help disabled children to become 'children first'.

Disability, youth and transitions to adulthood

Youth can be an exciting, yet difficult and challenging time for all young people, as they manage puberty and emerging sexuality, develop new social networks and relationships, and finish compulsory education. It is also a time of transition and significant change, as young people move towards adulthood; indeed, Priestley argues that the life course category of 'youth' has been structurally constructed as a '*transitional* generational category between childhood and adulthood' (2003a: 106; emphasis added). This transition involves increased responsibility and decision-making and may include a desire to move away from the parental home and increased independence. Disabled young people encounter these same issues, and there is clear evidence that they hold similar ambitions and aspirations for adulthood as their non-disabled peers (Hanisch 2011; Hendey and Pascall 2002). However, young disabled people have not always been included in public consultations on younger persons' issues (PMSU 2005), and research suggests that they face a number of disabling barriers in relation to the move into adulthood; this includes barriers related to housing and leaving the parental home, access to further and higher education, and financial difficulties (Hendey and Pascall 2002; PMSU 2005). There is also some evidence, albeit not all UK-based research, that younger disabled people have lower levels of life satisfaction than their non-disabled peers (Göransson 2008; Roebroeck et al. 2009; PMSU 2005). Consider the disabling barriers and their impact on life satisfaction in the following case scenario.

Case profile: Giselle

Giselle is seventeen years old and lives with her mother, Sue. The council home they share is in a small village. Giselle is keen to move out of this home and live independently in some new mainstream council housing in a larger town, where she feels she will have more opportunities and be closer to her boyfriend, Ed. Giselle has congenital muscular dystrophy, and Sue is worried that she won't be able to continue to support her as much as she does now if they do not live together. The current home also has some adaptations to meet Giselle's needs. Although the property has two bedrooms, mother and daughter are currently sleeping in the same bedroom, as the other is used to store hoisting equipment for Giselle's transfers. Sue is not supportive of Giselle's intention to move, as she is very concerned about her ability to cope alone; she also feels that Ed is putting undue pressure on her to move and that this is the real reason Giselle is pursuing it. She comments to the social worker that Giselle has many other friends, so does not see any particular need for her to be near Ed. Giselle comments that her relationship with Ed is the first serious relationship she has had; while she is happy in the relationship, she does feel Ed may be trying to move things on too quickly and wants to establish her own independent life before considering his suggestion that they live together. The housing officer has commented that they are both clearly adequately housed.

The development of one's own identity is of particular significance at this stage of life. Erikson (1968) considered this period as central to his theory of human growth and development, arguing that identity formation proper begins at this point. He goes on to suggest that failure to develop a strong identity will adversely impact on the experience of adulthood, particularly in relation to forming positive intimate relationships. Establishing a positive self-identity involves not only reflection on who one has come to be but also interaction with others. A sense of group belonging, which could be based on shared interests, language, music and/or clothes, is particularly important in this process (Göransson 2008). Most of us will remember that, as young people, we had a desire to identify with others 'who are like us' in order to affirm a positive sense of identity. For disabled young people, negative perceptions of impairment in society and the lack of positive images of disabled people in the media may impact on the formation of positive identity and self-esteem (Harpur 2011). Two life course issues appear to be of importance here: youthful bodies and embodied difference; and emerging sexuality.

The body, and indeed bodily perfection, is undoubtedly linked to idealized notions of youth and youthfulness. Priestley (2003a) refers to the mass marketing of bodily perfection as a marker of youthfulness; one needs only to review television advertisements and popular magazines to observe this imagery. However, as access to positive images contributes to the formation of a strong identity, presentation of perceived bodily perfection in this way may have a particularly adverse impact on those, such as Giselle, with visible embodied difference. Indeed, Priestley (ibid.: 95) argues that 'the myth of bodily perfection is an important factor in the construction of impaired people as inferior' and notes the significant disadvantage to disabled young people this creates. Consider how many times you have observed those with visible physical differences being portrayed as attractive or sexually desirable.

Emerging sexuality, sexual feelings and sexual expression are all important features of youth, and young disabled people do develop intimate sexual relationships. However, in research with disabled young people, issues related to sexuality and relationships have been raised as areas of concern (Clarke et al. 2011). Opportunities for these disabled young people to express their sexuality are often limited or even denied, owing to regulation by parents and carers, the portrayal of disabled people as less attractive or asexual and the consequent impact on self-esteem, and limited access to places for social interaction (Priestley 2003a). In Giselle's case, the importance of her relationship is not presently being recognized by either her mother or the housing officer; Giselle and, indeed, her mother have limited options to engage in an active sexual life while they share a bedroom. The fact that the housing officer does not view this arrangement as unsatisfactory suggests that he may, albeit tacitly, see Giselle as asexual. Sue equates Giselle's relationship with Ed with other friendships rather than seeing it as a potential sexual relationship. While issues related to sexuality have been seen by transition services as the responsibility of schools (Clarke et al. 2011), Priestley (2003a) highlights evidence that young disabled people are often excluded from or encounter poorer levels of sex education, impacting on their sexual knowledge and therefore development. However, for many younger disabled people, the barrier is not a lack of knowledge about sexual acts but, rather, accessing places where their peers gather in order to meet potential sexual partners. As such, the challenges range more widely than sexuality and relate to the development of other increasingly important relationships at this life stage, such as social networks and friendships.

In a study by Hendey and Pascall (2002), many of the seventy-two young disabled people interviewed reported the difficulties they had in meeting people and maintaining relationships. Clarke et al. (2011) describe high levels of unmet need in relation to social life and social activity among younger disabled people, noting limited income, inaccessible transport and the negative attitudes of social centre staff as key barriers. These may certainly be barriers for Giselle, especially as she currently lives in a rural area. The social worker involved should place importance on these factors in any assessment, as Giselle has identified relationships and limited opportunities as key issues impacting on her current life satisfaction. It is indeed unsurprising that limited social opportunities, having few or no friends, and challenges in maintaining relationships have been raised as key concerns by both disabled young people and their parents (PMSU 2005; Göransson 2008; Clarke et al. 2011). Indeed, in the Prime Minister's Strategy Unit's (2005: 123) consultation with disabled young people, they 'emphasized that maintaining friendships and a leisure life were issues of *primary* importance to them.' However, within the same consultation, they go on to note that such issues were not considered as important by those involved in support planning for them.

The disability movement has been active in challenging the perception of disabled people as asexual and in campaigning for services and a society that enable full engagement in social and leisure activity. Social workers can also contribute to this work and engage in activity to support young disabled people. Some issues linked to sexuality and relationships, such as those raised by Giselle, may be related to 'being a teenager' rather than to impairment or disability. In her study with younger deafblind people, Göransson (2008) observes that many valued the support of workers who were able to distinguish between problems that are typical for youth and those that are connected to impairment or disability. This was particularly important when supporting young people in developing positive self-identity and self-esteem. Ensuring that issues around sexuality and relationships (and any associated safeguarding concerns) are discussed in assessments and support planning is also essential. There is evidence that facilitating peer group meetings among young disabled people provides a supportive environment in which to have such discussions, drawing on their own personal experiences and expertise; such peer interaction has been linked to strengthened self-esteem and is of particular importance to young disabled people from black, Asian and minority ethnic (BAME) communities who may experience high levels of isolation (PMSU 2005; Göransson 2008).

Social workers, as part of their responsibility to promote social inclusion, should also contribute to the provision of opportunities for young disabled people to develop an active social life (HCPC SoP 6.1). This may involve working alongside disabled people's organizations in campaigning for more accessible mainstream leisure and social activity and also supporting young disabled people to benefit from direct payments (first extended to sixteen- and seventeen-year-olds under the Carers and Disabled Children Act 2000) and personal budgets (see chapter 9). For younger disabled people moving to adult social care services, increasing eligibility thresholds may pose a threat to support for social activity, which is often deemed low level or low risk. However, adopting a human rights approach can support social workers in advocating for ongoing publicly funded support. Local authorities have been successfully challenged when failing to meet such needs. The right to respect for family and private life, enshrined in Article 8 of the Human Rights Act 1998, includes sexual life and the formation of relationships. In *Price* v. *UK* (2001) the court acknowledged that Article 8 places a positive obligation on the state to take all practicable action to ensure disabled people have access to social activities. Reference to the United Nations Convention on the Rights of Persons with Disabilities, with its inclusion of a right to be included in the community, rights to participate in cultural life, recreation, leisure and sport, right to reproductive and family planning education, right to sexual healthcare, and the obligation on states to eliminate discrimination in matters relating to marriage and relationships, also proves useful in the context of issues related to sexuality and relationships.

As young people grapple with issues of identity, sexuality and relationships, they also commence the transition into adulthood. Based on identifiable themes within this transition, three key markers of adult status are noted: employment, independent housing and the establishment of one's own family (Priestley 2003a). In her study with thirty young disabled people, Dean (2003) observes that, for many, a key indicator of adulthood was leaving the parental home, a move which was linked to a desire for increased independence. However, there is evidence that young disabled people face several barriers in all three areas noted above (Hanisch 2011; Hendey and Pascall 2002). The challenges in making the transition to 'full adult status' have contributed to the construction of disability as a 'liminal yet enduring adolescence' (Priestley 2003a: 113), something experienced by Helen (see chapter 1).

Focusing on leaving the parental home in particular, Dean (2003) highlights three key barriers for young disabled people: lack of information; poor or limited local services; and the attitudes of parents and professional staff. The young disabled people and parents interviewed in the study often had limited information about the housing system, housing allocation processes, and housing and care options available to them. Some young people reported not knowing who to ask for information, while those who had sought advice from professionals remained uninformed. Many were unaware that support could be organized separately from the allocation of housing, which may explain why the most frequently reported housing option among young disabled people responding to the survey by Clarke et al. (2011) was supported housing. Limited information may be a factor in Sue's views on Giselle's desire to move out of the parental home; Sue refers to the challenges such a move will pose to her ability to provide care for Giselle and fears about her coping alone. She appears to have no awareness that support could be provided to her daughter separately from the allocation of housing. A lack of local accessible and affordable housing provision also presented a barrier to young disabled people wishing to move, especially for those with severe impairments. Although the White Paper *Caring for our Future: Reforming Care and Support* (HM Government 2012) commits to a £200 million investment in specialist housing for older and disabled people, this may be undermined by the challenges posed to disabled people by removal of the 'spare room subsidy' (or 'bedroom tax'), as widely reported in the media. While opposition to a move from parents also creates a barrier for young disabled people, social workers' failure to listen to their aspirations and to draw on these to inform support options and support planning strengthened rather than removed this barrier. Giselle's social worker, while acknowledging Sue's concerns, should listen carefully to Giselle's explicitly stated aspirations and not allow her mother's concerns to dictate the support plan for her.

For some disabled young people, transition may mean transition from children's to adult social care (and, in some cases, health) services, and not just from being a child to becoming an adult. This aspect is of particular significance for social workers, especially as poor transition experiences can undermine the benefits of early intervention work (PMSU 2005). Government policy has endeavoured to improve such services for young disabled people. *Aiming High for Disabled Children* (HM Treasury and DfES 2007) established the Transition Support Programme (now ended), and the good practice guides *A Transition Guide for All Services* (DCSF et al. 2007) and *Transition: Moving on Well* (DCSF and DoH 2008) offered practitioners good practice examples and strategies. More recently, the Care Act 2014 has sought to improve transition by giving young people (and the carers of children) the legal right to request an assessment from adult social care services before they reach the age of eighteen.

The full impact of the Care Act 2014 provisions is not yet known. However, despite previous government policy, there is much research evidence suggesting that young disabled people encounter barriers which impact negatively on their move into adult services. Provision of transition support services has been identified as 'patchy', and young disabled people have reported high levels of unmet need (Clarke et al. 2011). Where transition services have been in place, these have concentrated on young people with severe learning disabilities and have not necessarily addressed the needs of those with physical impairments, such as Giselle. The fact that such young people have been poorly supported is noted in the *Transition: Moving on Well* (DCSF and DoH 2008) good practice guide, which focuses specifically on those with neuro-disability.

Barriers to positive transition experiences include a lack of effective multi-agency working, failure to consider the concerns and priorities of younger disabled people themselves, and the use of differing eligibility criteria between services. Such barriers result in what many reports call a 'cliff edge' experience, where services fall away suddenly as the young person reaches adulthood. Examples of excellence in practice and the characteristics of good transition services can be found in the two good practice guides cited above. However, key aspects of good practice for social workers to consider are:

- conceptualizing transition as a process, not an event. Transition does not end when a young disabled person enters adulthood and begins using adult social care services, but continues throughout the life course.
- enabling young people to control the process, focusing on what is important to them. This involves forming positive working relationships with younger disabled people, exploring their individual aspirations and needs, and ensuring these influence transition planning.
- working collaboratively across agencies (see chapter 11). As moving from the parental home has been identified as a key priority for young disabled people, work closely with housing providers and support young people to complete housing applications. Collaboration between children's and adult's social care services is also essential; the Care Act 2014 includes a statutory duty of cooperation to support successful transition.
- providing accessible and quality information on transition, the transition process and local services, making use of social media, websites and DVDs. Liaison with and referral to user-led disability organizations and advocacy services are both key here. Having a transition worker based in adults' services to provide such information and work directly with young people is another approach to facilitate this. However, in some local authorities, children with disability teams and adult disability teams have merged to form a disability service.
- applying the principles of personalization to transition. This includes developing peer and user-led supportive networks (HCPC SoP 9.5), referral to advocacy services and, when young people are ready, maximizing the potential of personal budgets. The Children and Families Act 2014 seeks to support this by creating 'birth-to-25 years' education, health and care (EHC) plans, which offer families personal budgets.

Disability and adulthood

In Western societies, adult status is synonymous with the notions of independence and autonomy. Blatterer (2007) argues that social policies and institutions have had a particular role in constructing an idealized adulthood (see chapter 4), which is central to notions of the 'normal' life course. Priestley (2003a: 114) suggests that it is the achievement of 'competence, independence and autonomy' that enables access to an adult status so defined. Young disabled adults in the study by Hendey and Pascall (2002) identified paid work, independent housing, citizenship and social relationships as key ambitions, but went on to highlight the barriers they faced in achieving these, particularly in combination. For example, those who had established an independent household often had difficulties securing paid employment.

There is a significant contrast between the construction of adulthood centred on notions of functional independence and autonomy and the association made between the need for assistance with daily living and 'dependence'. As such, and in the context of considerable barriers in relation to householding, paid employment and social relationships, Priestley (2003a) argues that it becomes clear why disabled people have been excluded from adult status and had their claims to 'adult' rights denied. This poses a key challenge to the social work profession, which claims to be committed to upholding the rights and autonomy of service users (HCPC SoP 2.7; PCF 4).

The disability movement has challenged definitions of 'independence' that have focused narrowly on 'functional independence' – being able to carry out functions without assistance. They have drawn attention to the reality of 'interdependence' in human life, noting that adult competence is achieved in relationship with others and through existing social networks (Priestley 2003a). Fraser (2013) argues that all adults are in some ways dependent on others, and that recognition of this fact is essential if support staff and services are to be compassionate. Consider your own current situation and identify any others upon whom you are dependent; this may be for practical, emotional or financial support. Does such 'dependence' undermine your 'independent' adult status? In her examination of the legal and policy framework for community care, Morris (2004) identifies numerous barriers to independent living (see chapters 2 and 9). Within her critique she draws on Simon Brisenden's definition of independence, highlighting that self-determination and 'adult status' are clearly possible even where one needs assistance: 'Independence is not linked to the physical or intellectual capacity to care for oneself without assistance; independence is created by having assistance when and how one requires it' (Brisenden, 'Charter for Personal Care', 1989; cited in Morris 2004: 427–8). Such an approach to independence may be realized through the use of direct payments and personal budgets, though these services have been subject to critique by academics, commentators and members of the disability movement (see chapters 4 and 9). However, the key point is that the use of or need for care or support services should not exclude disabled people from enjoying 'adult' rights and exercising adult responsibilities.

Two central markers of adulthood are work and parenting. While earlier social policy linked 'disability' with 'inability to work', thus further contributing to the exclusion of disabled people from adult status, contemporary policy has focused on moving disabled adults from the welfare benefits system and into paid employment (see chapter 4). In a recent consultation with disabled people undertaken by the Labour shadow work and pensions team (Labour Shadow Department for Work and Pensions 2013), a significant majority reported a real desire to work and suggested that support should be available for those who are seeking employment, including those able to work only on a part-time basis. However, research and the experiences of disabled people indicate that accessing paid employment remains difficult, both nationally and internationally (Hendey and Pascall 2002; Clarke et al. 2011; Harpur 2011; Office for Disability Issues 2014). While use of direct payments and personal budgets to appoint personal assistants has afforded some disabled adults the opportunity for paid employment (Prideaux et al. 2009), others have reported that their need for personal assistance proved a barrier to engagement in paid employment, particularly in relation to charges levied by local authorities for personal support (Hendey and Pascall 2002). Furthermore, in the second national personal budgets survey, 80 per cent of service users reported that use of personal budgets made no difference to them in acquiring and maintaining paid employment (Hatton and Waters 2013), and the evaluation of the 'Right to Control Trailblazers' pilots, in which disabled adults received personal budgets integrating a number of funding streams (see chapter 9), produces no evidence that such an approach had a positive impact on employment outcomes (Tu et al. 2013). However, Prideaux et al. (2009) suggest that increased use of direct payments and personal budgets by disabled adults should result in a reconceptualization of 'work'. Highlighting the skills required in employing one's own personal assistant, such as recruitment, interviewing, budgeting and supervision, they argue that such cash for care schemes make disabled adults into active small businesses creating employment opportunities rather than merely being passive welfare recipients. This should result in qualification for the tax incentives available to other employers.

Addressing the structural barriers to paid employment experienced by disabled people may appear overwhelming for individual social work practitioners. However, social work does not operate at an individual level only; in the context of work with disabled people, Gillman (2008) notes what can be undertaken at the organizational and policy levels and suggests that social workers form alliances with disability organizations to challenge and promote change within their own organizations. She also encourages social workers to enhance their political awareness and to become involved in promoting policy reform. Such work may involve raising awareness and maximizing the impact of the UN Convention on the Rights of Persons with Disabilities (Harpur 2011). Indeed, while a right to work and protection against unemployment has previously existed under the 1948 Universal Declaration of Human Rights, Article 27 of the UN Convention on the Rights of Persons with Disabilities explicitly includes state obligations in relation to securing disabled people's right to work.

Parenting has also been emphasized as a marker of adult status (Priestley 2003a), and, although it is difficult to quantify, there are approximately 1.7 million disabled parents in Britain (Morris and Wates 2006). Priestley (2000) notes that the competence of disabled people as parents has been consistently challenged, and that many disabled parents have experienced 'stricter assessments' of their abilities to parent and 'higher levels of surveillance' (Priestley 2003a: 132). Disabled people undoubtedly experience numerous barriers to becoming parents and parenting.

These barriers are explored further in chapter 9, but include those related to limited finances and funding, uncoordinated service provision, and the attitudes of health and social care professionals. In relation to attitudinal barriers, Reeve (2008), in her doctoral research, identifies how failure to recognize disabled people as potential parents can result in practice that is oppressive. In her thesis, she relates the story of one disabled mother (Lucy) who, when informing the social worker of her pregnancy, was offered support in accessing a termination. The social worker failed to recognize Lucy's potential as a mother. There is a clear lesson for social work here; adopting a social model of disability in such interactions would lead social workers to explore with pregnant disabled women the services, peer-led social networks and advocacy that would serve to remove barriers and support their future parenting.

Disability and old age

When considering disability and old age, it is important to recognize two groups of people: those ageing *into* disability and those ageing *with* disability. Research has identified important differences between these two populations, though the former has received more attention than the latter, both in the literature and in social work education (Jeppsson Grassman et al. 2012). Verbrugge and Yang (2002) argue that social care services have often overlooked those ageing with disability; this is reflected in the way services are organized, with 'disability services' usually being focused on those aged between eighteen and sixty-five, while support for those over sixty-five is provided by mainstream older people's services.

Case profile: Muriel

Muriel is a 94-year-old woman who has lived alone since the death of her husband eight years ago. She has age-related hearing impairment and wears two hearing aids. Her vision is affected by cataracts and age-related macular degeneration. In addition, Muriel has angina and osteoarthritis in her knees, hips and hands. For the last four months she has had help with her personal care needs from her granddaughter Gemma at the weekends and from care workers organized by adult social care during the week. At a recent review meeting with the social worker, Muriel reported feelings of boredom, isolation and loneliness; she states that her 'poor vision, hearing and mobility' stop her from visiting family, enjoying books and radio, and writing letters, all of which she enjoyed.

Social care services for Muriel would almost certainly be arranged by the team for older people. When reading her case profile, do you view her as an older person experiencing some of the normal challenges of old age or as a disabled adult with a range of sensory and physical impairments? The majority of disabled people are aged sixty-five or over, and yet older people are rarely considered as 'disabled people' in the same way as those younger. Social workers, carers, family and older people themselves have all been found to associate impairment as an inevitable feature of ageing (Pavey et al. 2009), and older people often do not perceive themselves as 'disabled' (Verbrugge and Yang 2002; Darling and Heckert 2010).

While the majority of disabled people are over sixty-five years of age, the perception that old age inevitably leads to ill health and impairment is unsubstantiated by gerontological research. Indeed, the majority of older people are neither ill nor impaired. However, contemporary Western culture views ageing and the onset of impairment as unequivocally linked; this reflects the social construction of old age as problematic, characterized by a dominant discourse of 'inevitable and irreversible decline' (Andrew 2012: 47). One needs only to peruse a selection of birthday cards for older people to be faced with numerous images and references to this supposed association. Although natural biological ageing processes may increase the risk of illness and impairment, and certain impairments (such as Muriel's age-related hearing loss) are common in older age, they are neither inevitable nor experienced by all older adults. However, impairment has come to be considered by many as a 'normal' part of ageing. This may explain both why older people are not considered as 'disabled people' in the same way as children or younger adults and why older people's voices have been somewhat neglected in disability activism and politics (Priestley 2003a).

The normalizing of impairment in old age may itself result in the experience of disability and therefore has significant implications for social work practice with older disabled people. The impact of the impairment, particularly sensory impairment, may be overlooked or misinterpreted, resulting in a failure to address needs and a disinclination to refer on to specialist services (Brennan et al. 2005; Sense 2006). Assessment of Muriel's sensory impairment as an inevitable part of ageing engenders a 'nothing can be done about it' attitude. This then acts as a barrier to her accessing services such as those from technical officers for the deaf, rehabilitation officers for visually impaired people, or one-to-one communicator guides, despite local authorities having responsibilities to provide or arrange such services. The increasing use of self-assessment (see chapter 9) may result in 'under-assessment' of needs when older people themselves perceive impairment as inevitable in old age. Consequently, care and support packages will be inadequate or incomplete.

Limited or lack of involvement in disability politics, disability organizations or disability activism means that older disabled people are often less aware of the social model of disability. Indeed, some argue that the social model has had a minimal impact on older people (Phillips et al. 2010). Muriel clearly attributes her difficulties to her impairments rather than considering the role of inaccessible literature, media and transport in creating disability. Darling and Heckert (2010) suggest that older people ageing into disability are more likely to adopt a medical model to explain their experiences; as non-disabled people in earlier life, they have been socialized to accept this dominant normative view. This may lead not only to the continuing pursuit of a cure but also to feelings of exclusion and low self-esteem, particularly where there is comparison to a non-disabled peer group of which they were previously a part. Consider the impact this would have on Muriel's well-being, particularly as she has already experienced a significant bereavement and is increasingly isolated.

Disabled older people's needs may also be assessed and defined in ways reflecting medical models of both old age and disability in order to facilitate access to social care services, particularly as eligibility criteria have often focused on the notion of *risk* and not *need* (DoH 2010c). As a result, subsequent services address care rather than help or personal assistance and can be experienced as controlling and concerned solely with physical safety. Research at the University of York suggests that many older people want support packages that consider occupation/activity and mobility rather than just safety (Patmore et al. 1998). Muriel's support package clearly addresses her personal care needs, but it has failed to meet her needs relating to activity and mobility, resulting in increased boredom and isolation.

In addition to those ageing *into* disability, such as Muriel, a second population of older disabled people exists: those ageing *with* disability. This includes those born with impairments and those acquiring impairments in childhood or earlier adulthood. This population has grown as a result of increased life expectancy and advances in medicine and rehabilitation (Putnam 2002; Roebroeck et al. 2009). While a number of studies have explored the issues faced by those ageing with a learning disability (see, for example, Ward 2012), research with those ageing with physical impairments is also evident. The first major UK study undertaken by Zarb and Oliver (1993), which explored the experiences of those ageing with a variety of physical impairments, and the four studies by Jeppsson Grassman et al. (2012) are examples of such work.

Putnam (2002) argues that the experience of disability throughout the life course will inevitably impact upon older people's experience of ageing; the research has certainly evidenced some important differences between those ageing into and those ageing with disability. Indeed, in later work, Putnam (2012: 92) suggests there is a 'uniqueness to ageing with disability'. Research with those ageing with disability has identified shared experiences among this population: ongoing life changes, related to both impairment and ageing; the effects of ageing being experienced as 'second disability'; and anxiety related to threats to independence. Social workers should pay particular attention to the experience of anxiety around the maintenance of independence. Some of this anxiety may be linked to the development of additional impairments in later life; indeed, Jeppsson Grassman et al. (2012) found that a life lived with impairment did not make it easier for people to face further impairment or ill health. However, anxieties may also be linked to social care provision. In earlier life, those with physical impairments may have received support from disability services, which are often underpinned more clearly by the notion of independent living, choice and control (see chapter 9). However, as the person ages, a transfer to services for older people becomes inevitable; such services may reflect a medical model, and those interviewed in Zarb and Oliver's (1993) study reported receiving services which were less empowering once their care had been transferred. There was also evidence that service users' support packages were reduced, leading to a focus on immediate personal care needs rather than wider social needs.

Social workers will need to consider the appropriateness of the theories of old age informing their practice when working with those ageing with disability. Putnam (2002) notes that many theories of ageing do not examine the impact of lifelong experience of disability, and the usefulness of ageing theories for work with older disabled adults has been subject to debate. For example, the 'successful ageing' paradigm, with its emphasis on the avoidance of disease and disability and the maintenance of physical function, is clearly problematic from a disability perspective (Minkler and Fadern 2002). Social work practice informed by this concept may be oppressive to those ageing with disability, fostering a positive view of neither disabled adults nor old age. Baltes and Baltes' (1990) concept of 'optimal ageing', with its consideration of the importance of making changes to social and physical environments, may prove more useful, as practitioners are required to consider the disabling impact of such factors rather than focusing on individual impairment. This concept requires the social worker in Muriel's case to explore changes that could be made, for example, to her home, reading material format and social circles: adaptations to the home may improve her mobility, and reading material provided in large print or a tactile format (braille or moon) may enable her to re-engage with this once enjoyed hobby.

While social workers should also consider how the social model of disability could be adopted in work with older people, some gerontologists, academics and commentators have questioned its usefulness, suggesting that it may reinforce the perception of old age as a time of inevitable decline (Oldman 2002). However, with its emphasis on disabling physical, social and attitudinal barriers rather than on the individual, Oldman argues that the social model avoids any construction of old age. As such, its adoption in work with those ageing with disability encourages social workers not to problematize old age but, rather, to focus on barriers to independent living, such as poor housing, low incomes and inadequate transport. Recognition of the significance of such environmental factors in the experience of disability as people age should lead to social work interventions based on the adaptation of living environments rather than on interventions influenced by the medical model that seek individual adjustment (Putnam 2002).

Although it is important to recognize differences between those ageing into disability and those ageing with disability, Verbrugge and Yang (2002) suggest that such a distinction can be simplistic. They argue that disability and ageing interweave throughout the life course, and that it is essential to view them as intertwined. Disabled older people are undoubtedly disadvantaged, irrespective of whether they are ageing into or with disability, and there are a number of issues for all of them which should be of concern to social workers:

- older disabled people are at higher risk of mental health problems and cognitive impairment than younger disabled people
- as members of two stigmatized and marginalized groups, older disabled people may experience higher levels of social exclusion
- the experience of poverty in old age may impact on disabled older people's ability to purchase aids, adaptations, equipment and services which support independent living and enhanced quality of life (Phillips et al. 2010).

The end of life: death and dying

Exploring the end of life from a disability perspective raises complex and controversial issues, much in the same way as pre-birth choices do. Policies and practices such as the extermination of disabled people under the T-4 programme in Nazi Germany, the sterilization of disabled women in Scandinavia, the USA and the UK, and physician-assisted suicide in Europe have made disability a life and death issue (Reeve 2008). Central to the legitimization of such practices, and core to the debate about the killing of disabled people, are value judgements about the 'quality' and 'worth' of disabled lives (Priestley 2003a). Gill (2006: 5) argues that both the medical profession and the wider public make assumptions about 'how awful it is to have incurable impairments'; such assumptions, combined with normative approaches to average life expectancy informed by epidemiological statistics, have undoubtedly contributed to the devaluing of disabled lives (Priestley 2003a). Furthermore, public interest in, and campaigns for, assisted dying remain; disability is a significant feature in such campaigns, as it is most often those whose impairments affect their ability to commit suicide who are at the centre of complex ethical and legal debate.

While Switzerland, the Netherlands, Luxembourg, Belgium, and three American states have made legal provision for assisted dying, it is an offence in England and Wales under the Suicide Act 1961 to encourage or assist suicide. Scotland has no specific statutory provision concerned with assisted dying, though those assisting may be prosecuted under existing homicide law. Despite, or perhaps because of the legal position in the UK, a number of British citizens have travelled to Switzerland for accompanied (assisted) suicide provided by the Dignitas organization, established in 1998. The first of these, in 2002, was a British man with terminal cancer. A year earlier, Diane Pretty, who had motor neurone disease, challenged the legal position in England on human rights grounds. While her legal challenge failed, attempts to change the legal position in the UK have continued, including one brought by Debbie Purdy, a woman with multiple sclerosis. In February 2010, as a result of her High Court case, the then director of public prosecutions, Keir Starmer, clarified the factors that would lead towards a decision to prosecute those who assisted suicide. The cases of Tony Nicklinson (a man who experienced locked-in syndrome as a result of a severe stroke, who has since died) and Paul Lamb (who was paralysed from the neck down following a car accident) continued the legal challenge. In May 2013, Lord Falconer introduced a private members' bill, the Assisted Dying Bill, to Parliament. This Bill sought to enable capacitated terminally ill adults to have assistance to end their lives; it made progress through the House of Lords but ran out of time before the 2015 general election. A similar Bill was debated in the Scottish Parliament. In June 2015, the Labour MP Rob Marris tabled another Bill in the House of Commons, continuing the debate.

Alongside such legal challenges, disability organizations have engaged in right-to-life campaigns, protesting against assisted suicide and euthanasia. The disability movement has challenged the 'death with dignity' rationale for assisted suicide and euthanasia, arguing that disabling barriers such as inadequate and underfunded support services are the real threat to dignity (Priestley 2003a). However, disability organizations are not the only groups who have sought to challenge any proposed changes to the law; the medical profession has also expressed concern about assisted suicide. Indeed, Hendry et al. (2013) note a number of systematic reviews of the research evidence concerned with the opinions of medical professionals which indicate opposition to legalizing assisted suicide. While ethical or individual moral grounds often underpinned such views, enabling assisted dying was also viewed by some as a failure to provide good-quality palliative care services.

Research findings of the views of disabled people themselves appear somewhat ambiguous. While the 2007 British Attitudes Survey records that 75 per cent of disabled people supported assisted dying, the first systematic review of international literature on the opinions of patients, carers and the public found that such support was lowest among disabled people (Hendry et al. 2013). Furthermore, a poll commissioned by the disability charity Scope identified that 55 per cent of the 1,005 disabled people surveyed considered the current law necessary to protect disabled people from pressure to end their own lives (Scope 2014a). The qualitative research

undertaken by Bazalgette et al. (2011) possibly offers an explanation for such dispar-
ity. This study identified that, although the majority of disabled people supported
assisted dying for those who are terminally ill, there was far less consensus on
assisted dying for those with non-terminal conditions. This is an important distinction to make, particularly as many disabled people note that the public often confuse
'incurable' with 'terminal' and therefore link disability with terminal conditions (Gill
2006).

Reeve (2008: 232) suggests that social workers must recognize that public debates
on assisted suicide, particularly at a time of welfare reform and cuts to public services,
have made the lives of disabled people 'precarious'. In addition to being informed
about the legal position related to assisted dying, social workers should acknowledge
the impact that negative assumptions about quality of life and the equating of terminal illness and impairment have on disabled people. Furthermore, representation
of the right to die at a time of one's choosing as solely a consumerist personal choice
should not be accepted uncritically. Priestley (2003a) notes that the social environment and level of family and formal support may be key factors in people's end of life
decisions; he goes on to argue that informed and voluntary choice regarding such
decisions is highly compromised in a context of devalued lives and increasingly high
eligibility thresholds for social care support. Social workers must therefore assess
these factors when working with disabled people, particularly those exploring end
of life decisions. They must also be alert to any safeguarding concerns highlighted
by such discussions. Indeed, disabled participants in a number of studies concerned
with end of life decisions raised concerns about coercion, being made to feel a
'financial burden', and being offered reduced options for life-sustaining treatments
(Hendry et al. 2013). Finally, promoting self-directed support (see chapter 9) is a way
social workers can demonstrate their commitment to valuing disabled lives, where
such support enables disabled people to make choices not only about death but also
about living meaningful lives.

Conclusion

Disability is experienced differently in childhood, youth, adulthood and old age.
Social workers can therefore learn much about the relationship between disability,
policy and practice by exploring it through a life course lens. Such a perspective not
only considers the experience of disability during core 'stages' of life but also examines life transitions and raises complex and controversial issues relating to pre-birth
and end of life decisions. While much can be learned from the life course perspective,
valuing diversity is essential if social workers are to avoid associating disability with
'deviance' from a 'normal' life course trajectory. The pervasiveness of notions of a
'normal' life course, centred on an idealized independent adulthood, results in the
devaluing of disabled children and adults and the potential to overlook the impact
of impairment and disability in old age. Social workers have a key role to play in
challenging the devaluing of disabled people's lives, particularly at a time of welfare
reform and cuts in social care services. At a practice level, this involves ensuring full
access to information for those facing difficult pre-birth and end of life decisions,
distinguishing between impairment- and/or disability-related difficulties and life
stage-related difficulties, facilitating the use of services which promote choice and

control, and working alongside the disability movement in redefining the notion of the 'normal' life course.

Key messages

- Much can be learned about the experiences of disability and their relationship with policy and social work practice by exploring them through a life course lens.
- Considering pre-birth choices and end of life decisions from a disability perspective raises complex and controversial debates about the value society places on disabled lives.
- Disabled children value the same things as other children and want the same opportunities.
- Disabled young people encounter the same issues as all young people, but they also experience numerous barriers in their move towards adulthood. Social workers should work collaboratively across agencies and enable disabled young people to control the transition process, focusing on what is important to them.
- The disability movement has challenged dominant notions of 'independence' that serve to undermine disabled people's claims to adult status. While this has contributed to the development of direct payments, barriers to accessing two key markers of adult status remain: parenting and paid employment.
- While the majority of disabled people are over sixty-five years of age, social workers should avoid normalizing impairment in old age.

Activities

- Reflect on whether you think social workers have a role in contributing to and supporting people with pre-birth choices and issues related to assisted dying. How do your thoughts fit with your own perceptions of disability or impact on your approach to practice?
- How would you ensure Giselle's aspirations for adulthood inform her transition process?
- Locate the disability organizations in your area and learn more about the work that is being undertaken in the areas of paid employment and parenting and how social work can support this work.
- How would the adoption of a social model of disability inform intervention with Muriel?

Suggested further reading

Department for Children Schools and Families and Department of Health (2008) *Transition: Moving on Well: A Good Practice Guide for Health Professionals and their Partners on Transition Planning for Young People with Complex Health Needs or a Disability*. London: Department of Health.

Priestley, M. (2003) *Disability: A Life Course Approach*. Cambridge: Polity.

Putnam, M. (2012) Can aging with disability find a home in gerontological social work?, *Journal of Gerontological Social Work*, 55(2): 91–4.

4 The Legal and Policy Perspective

Issues considered in this chapter:

- The relationship between disabled people's lived experience and disability policy
- The historical context of disability policy and the reasons why this is still important
- A critical discussion of current disability policy, specifically social care policy
- Current legislation and policy for social work with disabled people

Introduction

Social care policy for disabled people has its origins in the nineteenth century and its legislative basis in welfare reforms introduced after the Second World War. Until recently, new legislation for adult social care has modified rather than replaced existing statutes, making change incremental. This has made the legal framework complex: 'Care and support law is opaque, complex and outdated. Over the past 60 years, a patchwork of legislation has evolved, but without fundamental reform ... The net result is confusion – for those providing services, for those who use services and for the public' (DoH 2012a: 2).

Now new legislation, the Care Act 2014 (in England) and the Social Services and Well-Being (Wales) Act 2014 (in Wales), consolidates existing adult social care measures into one statute, offering simplification and clarity in relation to entitlements to assessment and care and support. This simplification will be welcomed by social workers. However, there are dangers in ignoring the past, in particular the past experience of disabled people themselves. This lived experience has been affected by policies and service contexts and has also played a part in initiatives to reshape policy and patterns of service delivery. For this reason, the chapter begins by revisiting Helen's experiences described in chapter 1.

Case profile: Helen

I have to say I really started to notice changes after the Disability Discrimination Act (DDA) came into force. People may think of parking and accessible toilets, but for me it was transport ... Later in life I began delivering training on the DDA. I had great hopes for the Act and thought it would help bring down barriers. I also thought it would help me find a job and receive realistic welfare benefits; however, it hasn't done any of that. It is the cheap and the superficial that has been addressed, not the majority of barriers. As a wheelchair user, I still can't get into half the shops in my town. I'm so disappointed, because I really had big hopes.

Helen's experience has been determined by a number of factors, including her impairment, her gender and the attitudes of others. However, policy and legislation have also had an impact. While there have been some positive changes as a result of legislation, noted by Helen, a range of factors have conspired to restrict her opportunities and her ability to make choices about her own future. They have also had a negative impact on her self-confidence and self-image, which has made it less likely that she would challenge the position in which she found herself. This situation is sometimes referred to as 'internalized oppression' (Young 1990; Mason 1992) or as one of the psycho-emotional effects of disability (Reeve 2002). It is evident that both lived experience and professional practice can be affected by policy and service contexts.

The experience disabled people have had of social care services, particularly residential care, has contributed to the development of the social model of disability (see chapter 2). This in turn has had an impact on policy, but it would be misguided to assume that all current policy and practice is informed by the social model and that the problems caused by poor services and professional practice are now history. Oliver et al. (2012) suggest that the social model has exerted less influence on social work practice than disabled activists had hoped. There are also tensions and limitations built into current policy which affect the work of professionals – in particular, the requirement to square limited resources with service users' needs and rights.

Life course issues are also linked to policy and legislation (see chapter 3) and have become increasingly important in recent years; Roulstone and Prideaux (2012: 2) refer to 'the increased compartmentalisation of policy by age group at the expense of holistic family policy'. This has been most significant in the demarcation between adults and children in social care legislation and service provision. Although there has been separate legislation governing social work with children since the 1940s, this did not specifically address the support of disabled children and their families. Until the Children Act 1989, generic disability legislation was utilized to access services for both children and adults, and disabled children may still be eligible for services under the Chronically Sick and Disabled Persons Act 1970. Other services for disabled children were provided by the NHS and education authorities. However, since the 1990s, disabled children have been regarded as 'children first' (Clibbens and Sheppard 2007), and their social services have been provided by teams working with children and families.

Within social care services for disabled adults, there is a distinction drawn between older adults and those of working age, the assumption being that the former need less in terms of resources (Clark et al. 2009; SCIE 2010a). This has been reflected in the funding of care packages, as a recent practice guide highlights:

> The allocation of local authority social care budgets between older people and working-age disabled groups often reflects historical spending patterns, rather than relative needs ... The unit cost paid by a council for a residential placement for an older person tends to be substantially lower than a placement for someone of working age. (SCIE 2010a: 5)

Priestley (2000) argues that social policies have played an important part both in reproducing culturally constructed ideals of independent adulthood and in the exclusion of disabled adults from this status and from the responsibilities of paid work (see chapter 3). However, present welfare policies present a challenge to previous assumptions about disabled adults, who are now increasingly treated as 'adults first' with responsibility to support themselves financially. Access to paid work can still be problematic (Roulstone and Barnes 2005; Parekh et al. 2010), and this is also the case in respect of accessing other rights and responsibilities associated with adulthood (Pascall and Hendy 2004). Therefore disabled adults have to negotiate conflicting expectations about their behaviour, status and rights.

Social workers need to comply with the policy and legislation that directly affects their day-to-day work. The Professional Capabilities Framework (4.1), the HCPC Standards of Proficiency (6.1), the Scottish Codes of Practice (1.5) and the Code of Practice for Social Care Workers in Wales (1.5) require social workers to understand and apply principles of social justice, inclusion and equality. Recent developments in social care policy have been influenced by the social model of disability, which has drawn on the lived experience of disabled people. Professional practice and the way services are organized have helped to shape this lived experience. A more critical approach to policy will also enable social workers to question the taken for granted assumptions on which policy is sometimes based – for example, assumptions about the life course. Awareness of this can alert social workers to the need to develop practice which ameliorates any consequences that disadvantage service users. An understanding of the contested nature of some of the concepts that underpin policy can also foster a more critical approach to practice which goes beyond simple acceptance of current rhetoric. An example would be *independence*, which is used by disability activists to signify control over one's own life (Barnes and Mercer 2006) rather than being able to do everything without assistance, with very different implications for social work practice. The concept of *social inclusion* is similarly contested (Levitas 2005) and has particular relevance for the discussion of current welfare policy below. In times of austerity, we may hear less about the *rights* of disabled people, as identified in the Equality Act 2010 and the UN Convention of the Rights of Disabled People (UNCRDP), and more about their duties and the costs of benefits and services. Social work agencies are not immune from the impact of austerity measures, and social workers will need to be 'policy and legally literate' in order to advocate for and with disabled service users (PCF 4).

The historical development of policy

Since the nineteenth century, disability policy has developed from having a primary focus on institutional care to the present-day concerns with social inclusion and citizenship. Within this long history are several recurring themes. One of these is the paradox between the development of a unified disability policy and the creation of services for people with particular impairments. Access to the latter was often determined through medical assessment, and services were focused on the nature of the impairment rather than on the social and environmental barriers that people faced. For example, self-contained residential 'colonies' were set up for people with epilepsy and for people with learning disabilities, and specialist residential schools were founded for 'crippled', blind and deaf children (Borsay 2005). In general, these services were informed by the medical model of disability (see chapter 2).

A second important policy theme is the distinction between those regarded as 'deserving' of assistance from the state and those who are 'undeserving'. This distinction originated with the Poor Law. When a unified disability policy emerged following the Second World War, this distinction was an important part of the infrastructure onto which the new policies could be mapped (Roulstone and Prideaux 2012: 5). In practice it is closely related to where the boundary between disabled and non-disabled people should lie, and therefore crucial to policing access to welfare. The historical assumption that significant impairment results in an inability to work has been challenged by supporters of the social model of disability, who have emphasized the social barriers to employment rather than individual impairment (Oliver 1990, 2012). This leads to another key theme in the narrative: the apparent success of social model arguments in persuading governments that disabled people have a right to work. This has had some benefits, in particular the introduction of anti-discrimination legislation, but it has also led to the raising of the threshold for access to disability benefits, with decisions still based on medical scrutiny of claimants' impairments.

Drake (1999) identifies four kinds of objective which have guided disability policy since the nineteenth century: *containment and segregation*; *compensation*; *welfare*; and *citizenship*. Although these objectives came to the fore consecutively, they have overlapped, and each continues to exert an influence.

Containment and segregation, as the name suggests, aims to keep disabled people away from the mainstream of social life, often in institutions built for congregate living, and has its origins in the nineteenth century. While the most immediate need for social workers is knowledge of current policy and legislation, recent events have emphasized the importance of learning from history.

In June 2011, a BBC Panorama programme showed covert film of life in Winterbourne View, a privately owned hospital for people with learning disabilities and autism. Patients were abused and segregated from the local community, and many were a long distance from their families. They had little opportunity to draw anyone's attention to their plight and no choice in the way they lived their lives. Staff members who were concerned about the treatment of patients found they could make no headway in eliciting action, either from the managers of the hospital or from external authorities. There was widespread public condemnation of the abuse suffered by patients in this setting, and there have since been criminal prosecutions of staff. Winterbourne View is now closed.

Although initial public reaction focused on the abuse of patients and the repeated failings of the systems which should have protected them, the government response has gone beyond this in identifying the inappropriateness of in-patient hospital care for people with learning disabilities and 'challenging behaviour'. The final report responding to the scandal stated that 'the assumption should be for services to be local and that people remain in their communities' (DoH 2012b: 59). In fact, this has been the assumption for a long time; the government embarked on a programme of closure of its own long-stay learning disability hospitals as long ago as the 1980s. However, hospital care for patients at Winterbourne View had been commissioned from a private company by the NHS. The assumptions which underpin the commissioning of institutional care of this type have their roots in history. For people with learning disabilities, particularly those regarded as having 'challenging behaviour', long-stay hospitals were the major source of service provision until the 1980s. It is well documented that quality of life in these institutions was very poor (Ryan and Thomas 1987).

This system of 'care' originated in the Victorian era, when disabled people could be placed in workhouses, prisons or asylums. According to Finkelstein (1980), the explanation can be found in the rise of industrial society and changes in the nature of work. In pre-industrial society, some disabled people were able to contribute to small-scale rural and home-based production, but the advent of the factory system meant that they were no longer in demand as workers.

Initially disabled people were likely to be placed in general workhouses. As the nineteenth century progressed, specialization developed. Large asylums and 'colonies' established strict systems of rules which mirrored the discipline and surveillance of the factories (Drake 1999). Later, the 1913 Mental Deficiency Act provided a legal basis for the segregation of people who would now be described as having learning disabilities. This reflected the fears of the eugenics movement about the prevalence of 'feeble mindedness' and the risk this posed for the degeneration of the 'race'. The Mental Deficiency Act was drafted sufficiently broadly that a wide group of people were incarcerated, including some women who had given birth outside of marriage. Scull (1979: 252) maintains that the asylums and 'colonies' became 'a dumping ground for a heterogeneous mass of physical and mental wrecks' who were committed because of their inability to conform to the discipline of paid labour.

The historical legacy of institutional care also affects people with sensory and physical impairments. Drake (1999) refers to the founding of schools for children with particular impairments and points out that the objectives of this went beyond containment, to philanthropy and rehabilitation. By developing the skills of disabled children, it was hoped that they would be better able to support themselves in adult life and therefore be less likely to be a 'burden' on the state (Borsay 2005: 106). However, this led to segregated residential schooling.

From the late nineteenth century, policies of segregation continued alongside others that were informed by the principle of *compensation*. These aimed to compensate disabled people for their lack of access to paid work. Initially this was restricted to those disabled as a result of accidents at work or injury during military service. However, an exception can be found in the progress made by blind people, who successfully campaigned for legislation by marching on London. Policies of compensation were expanded in the face of mass casualties in the First World War.

Following the Second World War, more comprehensive welfare legislation came into force. The rise of the *welfare* principle led to more intensive professional interventions in the lives of disabled people (Drake 1999) and the growth of new welfare professions such as social work. The new policy of community care coexisted with continuing policies of 'compensation' and 'containment'. With those injured in the Second World War in mind, firms were required to employ a 'quota' of disabled people. A more comprehensive system of social security benefits was introduced. There was also continued use of hospital care, with the NHS taking over the long-stay hospitals previously run by local authorities and voluntary organizations. Local authorities were required by the National Assistance Act 1948 to provide residential services for older and disabled people. The experience of institutional living has been described in autobiographical accounts produced by former residents of the long-stay hospitals (Atkinson et al. 1998), and these testify to the rigidity of daily regimes. Enquiries into abusive treatment in the hospitals contributed to the shift in policy towards community care.

As community care services were slow to develop, in the 1960s many people with physical and sensory impairments experienced residential care, some of which was provided by local authorities and some by voluntary organizations. This affected children as well as adults, and parents giving birth to babies with significant impairments were often being advised not to take their babies home with them. Alison Lapper describes her mother's experience in 1965: 'she plucked up enough courage to ask the doctor about me. His response was very direct and to the point. He told my mother that it would be best if I were looked after by the state and that she should put me out of her mind' (Lapper 2005: 16).

Sally French (2004a: 83) writes of the regimentation of life in one of her residential special schools for blind children and comments: 'Such was our isolation at this school that issues of how to behave in the "normal" world were rarely addressed.' At her next school, much more attention was paid to the demands of the outside world, but at both schools there was a normalizing ethos:

> He [the headmaster] liked us to regard ourselves as sighted and steered us away from any connection with blindness; for example, although we were free to go out by ourselves to the nearby town and beyond, the use of white canes was never suggested, although many of us use them today ... there was never any suggestion that the world could adapt, or that our needs should be accommodated. The underlying message was always the same: 'Be superhuman and deny your impairment and disability.' (Ibid.: 82–3)

It was from within care homes run by the Leonard Cheshire Organization that disabled people began to speak out for themselves. Paul Hunt (1966a: 1) had spent all of his adult life in 'institutions among people who, like myself, have severe and often progressive physical disabilities'. Although residential homes run by Leonard Cheshire were smaller than the old long-stay hospitals, there remained a controlling ethos, as Paul's experience indicates.

> In the hospitals and homes I have lived in one rarely sees any physical cruelty. But I have experienced enough of other kinds of subtly corrupting behaviour. There are administrators and matrons who have had people removed on slight pretexts, who try to break up ordinary friendships if they don't approve of them. There are the staff who bully those who cannot complain, who dictate what clothes people should wear, who switch the television off in the middle of a programme, and will take away 'privileges' (like getting up for the day) when they choose. (Ibid.:12)

This indicates that policies of containment and segregation continued alongside other more progressive principles well into the second half of the twentieth century. This was a key rationale for the founding in 1974 of the Union of Physically Impaired Against Segregation, of which Paul Hunt was a member. From then onwards, the focus moved from welfare to rights, as reflected in a new definition of disability, which was consistent with the social model of disability: 'the disadvantage or restriction of ability caused by a contemporary social organization which takes little or no account of people who have physical impairments and thus excludes them from participation in the mainstream of social activities' (UPIAS and Disability Alliance 1976: 14).

Although it was grounded in meeting 'needs' rather than rights, the 1970 Chronically Sick and Disabled Persons Act was an important landmark in the development of community services. Among services that councils were required to provide were practical support in the home; meals; assistance to obtain radio, TV, library or other recreational services; recreational and educational activities outside the home; help with travel; and aids and home adaptations.

The introduction of market principles into social care through the National Health Service and Community Care Act 1990 was in part an attempt to contain spiralling costs and introduce a mixed economy of care provision (Powell 2007). It was also a response to critiques of inflexible services and professional power. The new legislation was hailed by politicians as an opportunity to increase service-user involvement in assessment and care planning and, in contrast to the previous service-led system, to create needs-led packages of care. It did lead to more intensive packages of personal care for people in their own homes. However, the power of local authorities, the control exerted by the 'disabling professions' (Illich et al. 1977) and the way services were 'isolated from the congress of everyday life' (Drake 1999: 54) became key issues for the disabled people who campaigned for rights, citizenship and independent living. Professional assessment of need and control of funding (which was, in any case, limited) meant that promises of greater service-user empowerment were not fulfilled. In response to a legal challenge in 1997 known as the 'Gloucestershire Case', it was ruled that local authorities with insufficient funds could not be compelled to meet every need.

Citizenship and current policy

There is a tension in recent policy between collectively inspired policies emphasizing citizenship, equality and rights and the neo-liberal market-based approaches to service-user empowerment that have shaped both New Labour and the Conservative–Liberal Democrat coalition government policies. Governments have emphasized service-user control, but also individualism, responsibility and (in social security policy) conditionality. This has been a challenge to previous conceptions of disabled people as passive recipients of benefits and services.

Organizations of disabled people have continued to campaign for the right to independent living and control over their own lives. Campaigning has also focused on the need for anti-discrimination legislation in respect of disability. This reflects what Paul Hunt wrote back in the 1960s: 'We are challenging society to take account of us, to listen to what we have to say, to acknowledge us as an integral part of society itself. We do not want ourselves, or anyone else, treated as second-class citizens and put away out of sight and mind' (Hunt 1966a: 16)

Campaigners have had notable successes in influencing governments. Although it took many years to overcome government reluctance to acknowledge the existence of disability discrimination, a Disability Discrimination Act was eventually passed in 1995. This was weaker than activists had hoped but has since been strengthened. Potential complainants had first to establish that they were disabled under the terms of the Act, which defined a disabled person as someone with 'a physical or mental impairment which has a substantial and long-term adverse effect on his [*sic*] ability to carry out normal day-to-day activities.' This definition emphasized individual functional abilities rather than any social or environmental barriers to participation in society, and in this respect it did not offer a fundamental challenge to medical and individualized approaches to disability (see chapter 2). Furthermore, the definition of disability contained in Section 29 of the National Assistance Act 1948 remained key to accessing assessment and community care services until the Care Act 2014 became law. This defined disability in terms of types of impairment: 'persons who are blind, deaf or dumb, and other persons, who are substantially and permanently handicapped by illness, injury or congenital deformity or who are suffering from a mental disorder within the meaning of the Mental Health Act'.

However, the very existence of the Disability Discrimination Act represented progress. The duties imposed by this legislation to make adjustments to facilitate the participation of disabled people in employment and education and to promote access to goods and services reflect an approach based on rights, though limited by the requirement that such adjustments must be 'reasonable'. The Disability Discrimination Act 2005 introduced the disability equality duty, which required public authorities, including government departments, both to consider how their policies and practices affect disabled people and to promote equality of opportunity. The New Labour government also announced the intention that, by 2025, disabled people would be equal members of society (PMSU 2005). A working group, Equality 2025, was set up to carry this forward within government, and in 2009 the UN Convention on the Rights of Persons with Disabilities was ratified. Disability discrimination legislation has now been subsumed within the Equality Act 2010, which has provided a more consistent approach to combating discrimination across all protected characteristics. Reminding public authorities of their duties under the Equality Act 2010, and also the Human Rights Act 1998, has proved key to successful challenges of central government and local authority decision-making. For example, in 2013, central government's decision to close the Independent Living Fund was quashed by the Court of Appeal, when five disabled people referred to a failure by the minister for disabled people to take into account the public-sector duty to advance equality. (However, a legal challenge to a later government decision to close the Independent Living Fund was unsuccessful.)

Disability campaigners have had to engage with the political discourse of governing parties in order to promote their aims (Morris 2011b). For example, the language used by disabled activists in arguing for direct payments (discussed below) fitted well with the individualist agenda of the Conservative government of the time. However, Morris also maintains that governments have 'colonized and corrupted' some of the concepts developed by the disability movement, such as 'independent living' and 'user involvement', in ways that have disadvantaged disabled people. These have tended to be used in support of the neo-liberal agendas of Conservative, New Labour, and coalition governments who have been intent on reducing the role of the state, encouraging the development of markets in service provision, and reinforcing the responsibility of citizens to be self-supporting. Although disabled people have made gains in respect of the civil and political rights of citizenship, there has been an attack on the social rights that underpin their ability to exercise control over their own lives. As Morris writes:

> The current political agenda is dominated by a widely-held belief that there are two problems facing the welfare state: increasing and unsustainable expenditure; and the creation and maintenance of 'dependency' among those who rely on its cash benefits and/or services.
>
> The undermining of the welfare state has a particular impact on disabled people in the context of both welfare reform and changes to the adult social care system. (2011b: 5)

In respect of welfare reform, there have been policies of social inclusion through paid work since the election of the New Labour government in 1997. This was presented positively by New Labour as 'empowerment' (DWP 2006) and has been associated with the rhetoric of the social model of disability. Similarly, the Green Paper outlining plans to transfer a million people from incapacity benefit to paid work was entitled *No One Written Off* (DWP 2008) and argued its case in terms of social inclusion. However, this has been combined with suspicion of benefit claimants and the stigmatization of 'dependency'. Newspaper headlines have sometimes emphasized the fraudulent nature of some claims for disability benefits – such as the following in the *Daily Express*: 'Benefit cheat who claimed thousands pretending to be disabled caught lifting furniture' (4 November 2013).

A distinctly medical model approach has been evident in the way the boundary between disability and 'ablebodiedness' has been policed. Despite the existence of anti-discrimination legislation, greater emphasis has been on the workless individual rather than the barriers to participation in employment. The welfare reforms of the current government have a similar focus on reducing 'dependency', and the coalition continued with the implementation of New Labour's policy to replace incapacity benefit with employment and support allowance. The Work Capability Assessment, intended to distinguish between those who are capable of work and those whose impairments preclude this, has been made more rigorous. A new classification has been added: that of people who are deemed capable of 'work-related activities', and who can be sanctioned by Job Centre Plus if they do not complete the activities they have been allocated. Under this system, access to the support group, in which benefit will be paid without requirement for activities, has become much more restricted, reflecting the current emphasis on the responsibility to self-support and the old distinction between 'deserving' and 'undeserving'.

In arguing the case for anti-discrimination legislation, disabled activists had challenged the assumption that disabled people were unable to work. Unfortunately this has appeared consistent with the suspicions of politicians that many benefit claimants are not 'really' ill or disabled (Morris 2011b). Since the introduction of the new Work Capability Assessment, the government has been keen to advertise the success of this process in detecting malingerers, although critics have questioned the accuracy of assessments, as evidenced by the number of successful appeals (House of Commons Public Accounts Committee 2013).

Similar suspicion has been raised about the recipients of disability living allowance, a benefit which provides the resources for disabled people to decide for themselves how to meet the additional costs associated with disability. The coalition government decided to replace this with the personal independence payment, the aim of which is to reduce the number of people who qualify (DWP 2010).

Adult social care

The focus of recent adult social care policy has been towards greater self-direction, control and choice for service users. This is something that disabled people have campaigned for, and early initiatives were characterized by collective civil rights and equal opportunities approaches supported by user-led organizations such as Centres for Independent Living. Subsequently the approach to service-user empowerment has been essentially an individualized market-based one, with individuals being allocated funding with which to purchase services to meet their assessed needs. Although markets had already been introduced into social care following the NHS and Community Care Act 1990, this had not resulted in a significant shift in power between professionals and disabled people (Priestley 1998b). From the late 1990s, the introduction of direct payments achieved a transfer of purchasing power to service users, which provided the flexibility and control that disability activists had demanded. By 2007, these principles had been developed as *personalization*, the concept that informed the policies of both New Labour and coalition governments.

The earliest example of the provision of direct funding for social care is the founding in 1988 of the Independent Living Fund (ILF), which was a response to the withdrawal of a social security benefit for people who needed help with domestic tasks. It proved extremely popular with disabled people, as for the first time it provided cash for support services which they could control themselves. ILF gave some disabled people the experience of controlling their own funding for care and demonstrated the benefits in terms of quality of life (Morris 1993b). However, the eligibility criteria tightened over the years, and most often payments from the fund were used to supplement payments for services provided by local authorities. The fund closed to new applications in June 2010, and, following unsuccessful legal challenge, the decision by government to close it completely by June 2015 was realized. As a result of campaigns for the introduction of direct payments into social care more generally, the Community Care (Direct Payments) Act 1996 was passed, giving local authorities the power to fund younger disabled adults to purchase their own services.

The policy of the New Labour government was set out in the White Paper *Modernising Social Services* (DoH 1998b). This emphasized the independence of disabled people and argued that they should be at the centre of decision-making within a system that was more responsive. In 2003, regulations passed under Section 57 of the Health and Social Care Act 2001 made it mandatory for direct payments to be offered to all eligible adult service users. In England, this duty has since been consolidated and expanded in sections 31 to 33 of the Care Act 2014. Similar provisions can be found in the Social Services and Well-Being (Wales) Act 2014 and the Social Care (Self-Directed Support) (Scotland) Act 2013. The Green Paper *Independence, Well-Being and Choice* (DoH 2005a), followed by the White Paper *Our Health, Our Care, Our Say* (DoH 2006), had previously argued for the joint commissioning of services and for greater use of direct payments and individual budgets. Both advocated a broader approach to independence, well-being and quality of life and emphasized the use of community resources and universal services for the purpose of prevention, to supplement social care support, and for disabled people to be able to make a contribution to society. The concept of 'individual budgets' first appeared in *Improving the Life Chances of Disabled People* (PMSU 2005), the government's overall disability strategy, and involved the merging of payments from a number of funding streams into an integrated budget.

While there have been pilot projects on individual budgets, these have not as yet been introduced on a national basis. However, budgets for social care services, known as personal budgets, are a feature of current national policy (see chapter 9). They are the specified funds allocated to meet the support needs of individuals and can be paid fully or partially as a direct payment or managed by a third-party provider (an Individual Service Fund) or the local authority. Whichever option is chosen, the priority is that service users know how much money is available to them and have control over how it is spent to meet their support needs. The Care Act 2014 puts personal budgets on a statutory footing, creating a legal entitlement to them for those with eligible needs. The flexibility and control that personal budgets seek to achieve is further reflected in the Care Act's move away from placing duties on local authorities to provide specific services (such as those contained in the 1970 Chronically Sick and Disabled Persons Act); instead, the Care Act includes the broader duty on local authorities to meet assessed eligible needs, as does the Social Services and Well-Being (Wales) Act 2014.

Personalization

Policy themes that have been consistent across both New Labour and coalition governments were personalization and self-direction. These are not new principles, being evident in the emphasis on choice and service-user involvement in community care policy since 1990, but there is now a clear attempt to incorporate the principles of the independent living movement, in particular the capacity for disabled people to control their own support services and to participate fully in society (Roulstone and Prideaux 2012). The first use of the term 'personalization' in national social care policy occurred in the concordat *Putting People First: A Shared Vision and Commitment to the Transformation of Adult Social Care* (DoH 2007b). The origins of the term are in information technology, with the application to social care resulting from the work of Leadbetter (2004: 19) situated within the thinktank Demos: 'by putting users at the heart of services, enabling them to become participants in the design and delivery, services will be more effective by mobilising millions of people as co-producers of the public goods they value.'

Personalization has been described as 'ensuring that people who receive support remain central to and in control of the process by which they receive it; the aim is to enable them to live their lives as they choose' (Leece 2012: 10). This is consistent with the use of personal budgets and direct payments. However, the concept of personalization is broader than this. Service users are to be 'co-producers' of services. Prevention and early intervention are also emphasized, with the aim of avoiding or delaying the need for more intensive health or social care provision. Investment in universal services such as leisure, transport and adult education is also to be part of the strategy, as is the development of social capital through volunteering and the co-production of services. In addition, the personalization agenda is about promoting the desired outcomes of service users and enabling their full participation and contribution within society. It is therefore a challenge to previous modes of service delivery, in which service users had been passive recipients and were absolved from responsibilities to others. This reflects the sentiments expressed in *Improving the Life Chances of Disabled People*, which maintained that

> policies and practice do not pay enough attention to enabling disabled people to be active citizens, or to supporting disabled people to help themselves ... Responses to needs are often more likely to create dependency than enable people to participate in their local communities, fulfil family responsibilities or be economically active. (PMSU 2005: 72)

In 2008, the government allocated a three-year development grant for local authorities to help defray the costs of transforming the social care system, anticipating that 30 per cent of service users would be receiving a personal budget by 2011 and 100 per cent by 2013.

The approach of the coalition government had much in common with the previous New Labour government, as evidenced in the Green Paper *A Vision for Adult Social Care: Capable Communities and Active Citizens* (DoH 2010d). However, the emphasis on strengthening communities and reducing dependence on the state is perhaps even stronger, as well as being consistent with the 'Big Society' policies of the Conservative Party. The Green Paper committed the government to further integration of health and social care, the extension of personal budgets, and the improvement of respite care. The stated principles on which it was based were prevention, personalization, partnership (particularly between health and social care), plurality (diversity of provision), protection, productivity and people (a skilled workforce). This indicates that social workers will have to continue to adapt to new organizational contexts and interprofessional partnerships (PCF 8.1, HCPC SoP 14.8). The foreword to the Green Paper sets out the values of the government, which have informed what follows. These are 'freedom', 'fairness' and 'responsibility'. The first is linked to service-user control of support, and the last to the role of the wider community to build networks of support. 'Fairness' related to two issues which still required resolution: how social care is to be paid for and the need for a clear legal framework. Enactment of the Care Act 2014 in England and the Social Services and Well-Being (Wales) Act 2014 in Wales seeks to resolve the latter.

The three-year *Putting People First* programme was replaced in 2011 by Think Local, Act Personal, a partnership between a range of organizations involved in social care with the remit of supporting the transformation to a personalized system. This demonstrates the developing consensus across both the social care sector and political parties about personalization. This direction of travel was confirmed by the White Paper *Caring for our Future: Reforming Care and Support* (HM Government 2012). This was based around the principle of promoting people's independence and well-being in order to minimize the need for formal care, the promotion of service-user control through personal budgets and, as a result of providing better access to information and advice, enabling individuals to self-assess and develop their own support plans. These developments appear to address many of the issues raised by disability campaigners and to represent progress in tackling some long-standing problems within the social care system. However, they have taken place in the context of significant budgetary constraint and the tightening of eligibility criteria which have excluded many people who formerly received services. The Commission for Social Care Inspection (2008) noted that local authorities were funding only those in higher categories of need and expressed concern that some people who required support were being ruled ineligible. There are clear indications that this trend has continued beyond 2008.

Case profile: Mark

Mark is in his sixties. He has a partner, and both his adult son and daughter live in the same town. He was involved in a road traffic accident in his late teens in which he suffered multiple fractures, and he has had significant mobility problems ever since. In recent years he has developed arthritis in many of his joints. This is very painful, has restricted the distance he can walk, and has made it difficult for him to use his hands. He had to take time off work and eventually received incapacity benefit. The family budget is very tight, although his partner has a job. Money worries have put their relationship under strain, and Mark's partner has seen her GP for help with depression. Their stress has increased recently as Mark has had to apply for employment and support allowance and was told that he is fit for work. His benefit is now much reduced, which has exacerbated their financial problems; one of his creditors has threatened County Court action. His partner left the family home after a heated argument, and Mark is having difficulty carrying out basic household tasks on account of his impairment. Recently he has had difficulty using stairs and has taken to sleeping downstairs on the sofa. His GP has referred him to adult social care but is not sure whether he will be eligible.

The Community Care Statistics for 2012–13 (Health and Social Care Information Centre 2013) show that the number of people receiving services had fallen by 9 per cent from the previous year and by 25 per cent from 2007–8. Brawn et al. (2013) observe that, in relation to disabled adults of working age, the number of people using care and support services has fallen by at least 90,000 since 2008. The emphasis on prevention in *Putting People First* (DoH 2007b) made this problematic. As a result, guidance on eligibility was updated (DoH 2010b); this attempted to square the eligibility criteria with prevention by advocating fuller use of universal services, the use of the wider community and voluntary provision, and signposting people to other sources of support. The Care Act 2014 takes this further, requiring local authorities to consider the potential of preventative, universal and local services when completing assessments of need (Section 2). It also requires local authorities to provide or arrange services that help prevent or delay the need for ongoing care and support. Furthermore, the Care and Support (Eligibility Criteria) Regulations 2014, made under Section 13 of the Care Act 2014 to replace the 2010 policy guidance, outline the national eligibility criteria with which all local authorities in England must comply. As such, the Care Act 2014 has introduced a national minimum threshold for social care for the first time.

Given the severity of the public spending cuts and the coalition government's promise to protect health and education, Duffy (2011: 17) maintains that expenditure on disabled people is an obvious target – an example of 'Robin Hood in reverse'. However, referring to the limitations of personalization in delivering a fair society, he points to the weakness of disabled people's entitlement to services, 'super taxation' resulting from charges for services, 'deep poverty traps' caused by means tests for benefits, and over-reliance on unpaid care by families – all features of the policies of both recent governments. In chapter 9, critiques of personalization are explored in terms of the *mechanisms* that affect practice, in particular resource allocation systems. Ferguson (2012) has also argued that the neo-liberal agenda that underpins personalization is incompatible with social justice and that government rhetoric has conflated this 'market-consumer' discourse with the more progressive agenda of the disability movement. It has been asserted that collective action on the basis of this progressive agenda will be more effective in addressing powerlessness than the market-based solutions of personalization (Ferguson 2007; Morris 2011b).

Personalization may also lead to insecurity for service providers and the closure of traditional services such as day centres without adequate replacement (Beresford 2009). This may in itself restrict choices. Beresford also sees the campaign for direct payments as grounded in collectively inspired support for rights and liberation but points out that this ran in parallel with government policies promoting choice through markets and privatization. For governments, the term 'service-user involvement' has meant a consumerist model, contrasting with the democratic model of collective user movements.

Overall there has been some progress in increasing the flexibility of services and the degree of control that disabled people are able to exercise over those services. However, this has been counterbalanced by increased demands and responsibilities, which have been critiqued as the 'privatization of risk' (Ferguson 2007). Although there is evidence that personalization policies have improved outcomes for some service users, this has not been the case for all (Glendinning et al. 2008). Furthermore, while the Care Act 2014 seeks to embed personalization policies in legislation, with the legal entitlement to personal budgets, an expansion of direct payments, and a 'continuity duty' enabling disabled adults to move to a new local authority area and continue to have their needs met pending assessment, disability activists and organizations have observed that it contains no reference to a right to independent living. Calls to expand the statutory well-being principle (a duty on local authorities contained in Section 1 of the Care Act 2014 to promote an individual's well-being when exercising their care and support functions) to include a duty to promote well-being *and independent living* were not heeded. While the statutory guidance notes that 'the concept of independent living is a core part of the well-being principle' (DoH 2014: 1.18), care and support services remain grounded in principles of welfare rather than being enforceable statutory rights (Collingbourne 2014).

However, social workers should be alert to the potential of the United Nations Convention on the Rights of Persons with Disabilities (UNCRPD) and not focus solely on domestic legislation. As noted earlier, the UNCRPD was ratified by the UK in 2009. It contains, *inter alia*, rights to choice and independent living, and, since ratification, the UK government is responsible for ensuring local authorities take action towards its implementation. The UNCRPD is not part of domestic law in the UK, so disabled adults who believe their convention rights have been breached are unable to challenge a public body or the UK government in a domestic court. However, it can be referred to in order to strengthen claims made under the Equality Act 2010 or the Human Rights Act 1998, as well as ombudsman, Care Quality Commission and local authority complaints. Indeed, the convention was referred to by Baroness Campbell of Surbiton in her campaign for the portability of care and support packages for disabled people and the 'continuity duty' referred to above. In practice, social workers may also refer to it when seeking public funding for care and support packages that facilitate independent living at home, and they can also raise awareness of its potential among disabled adults, groups, organizations and the local authority with whom they are working (PCF 4.3, HCPC SoP 2.2, 2.7). Visit the website of the European Convention on Human Rights (ECHR) to find some further examples of how it can be used by practitioners.

Policy for disabled children

In addition to equalities legislation, which offers protection to people of all ages, there are two significant areas of policy for disabled children. These are social care and education.

Social care policy

Disabled children have been on the fringes of children's social care policy until recently, 'often forgotten or tagged on as an afterthought' (Marchant and Jones n.d.). They have become the responsibility of children's services only since the 1989 Children Act, and their marginal status is demonstrated by the fact that no specific mention is made of disability in the Green Paper *Every Child Matters* (DfES 2003). However, the five outcomes specified there are equally relevant for all children: being healthy; staying safe; enjoying and achieving; making a positive contribution; and economic well-being. The fact that disabled children are more likely to be economically disadvantaged than other children (Children's Society 2011), as well as at greater risk of neglect and abuse (OFSTED 2012), makes the five outcomes in *Every Child Matters* even more important for them. As 'children first', under the Equality Act 2010 they should have access to all the services available to other children. However, while this requires that mainstream services should be made more accessible, there has also been an approach of continuing to provide some 'special' or targeted services.

Disabled children and their parents became eligible for direct payments for social care services as a result of the Carers and Disabled Children Act 2000, and these can be paid directly to a young person once she or he reaches the age of sixteen. Personal budgets and the personalization agenda more generally have become important in children's services, as demonstrated by the Children and Families Act 2014. This is discussed below, particularly in relation to education policy, but it also has salience for social care and health.

The definition of disability in the Children Act 1989 is closely aligned with that of the now repealed 1948 National Assistance Act and refers to a disabled person as someone who is 'blind, deaf or dumb or suffers from mental disorder of any kind or is substantially and permanently handicapped by illness, injury or congenital deformity or such other disability as may be prescribed' (Section 17, Subsection 11). This definition is outdated in its language and is based on impairment rather than disability. However, it has the benefit of being broad and, therefore, inclusive of a wide range of impairments.

Key legislation for disabled children's social care is the Chronically Sick and Disabled Persons Act 1970 and the Children Act 1989. The 1970 Act, which applied to disabled people of all ages (though, following the Care Act 2014, it no longer applies to disabled adults), imposes a duty on the local authority to provide many services for disabled children where a need has been established. Broach et al. (2010) maintain that the duty to provide a service is more enforceable under the Chronically Sick and Disabled Persons Act than under the Children Act. Services specified in Section 2 of the Chronically Sick and Disabled Persons Act have been described earlier. Here it is relevant to point out that they can include home-based short breaks, such as sitting services and befriending, but not residential short breaks (previously known as respite). However, the Children and Young Persons Act 2008 places a duty on local authorities to provide short break services for disabled children and their families.

Disabled children are automatically treated as 'children in need' under Section 17 of the 1989 Children Act, and supportive services for children and families can also be offered under these provisions. Statutory guidance (DCSF 2010a) about short breaks has also been produced. These can be provided under Section 17 of the Act as a service for children in need, and in this case the child does not become a 'looked after child'. However, Section 20(4) of the Act must be used if the child has a substantial package of short breaks, sometimes in more than one place, and if the family is less able to monitor the quality of care a child is receiving while away from home. Full 'looked after children' regulations apply if any short breaks last for more than seventeen days, if short breaks are with more than one provider, or if a child spends more than seventy-five days in short break accommodation in one year. This includes the duty to make a care plan and appoint an independent reviewing officer. For children accommodated under Section 20(4) for shorter periods of time and in the same place, longer-term planning remains with the parents. In these cases, the local authority must make a more limited plan covering the safe care of the child during short breaks. However, in all these cases the parents retain parental responsibility.

From 2005 onwards, the New Labour government began to address policy for disabled children more seriously. The *Improving the Life Chances of Disabled People* report highlighted their needs specifically (PMSU 2005). Following pressure from those who had campaigned under the banner of *Every Disabled Child Matters*, the government published *Aiming High for Disabled Children* (HM Treasury and DfES 2007). This describes plans to improve services and funding, including better access to information; individual budgets; responsive services; and improving service quality and capacity, particularly for short breaks and accessible childcare. The aim was expressed in terms of equality of opportunity: 'ensuring that every disabled child can have the best possible start in life and the support they and their families need to make equality of opportunity a reality, allowing each and every child to reach their potential' (ibid.: 3)

Education policy

The above aim cannot be realized without reference to the education of disabled children. Not all disabled children have difficulty with learning at school. Some, however, would have difficulties in mainstream schools without additional resources or 'reasonable adjustments'. This could be as a result of a sensory or physical impairment that makes it hard to access the curriculum in the way that has been designed for non-disabled students. It could be because of a behavioural or emotional problem that makes prolonged concentration difficult or a 'specific learning difficulty' such as dyslexia. In none of these cases is the difficulty caused by limited intellectual ability. However, there are also children who have generalized difficulties in learning unrelated to any physical impairment. Some of these children would also be regarded as having learning disabilities by professionals in health and social care. A social model approach would focus on the social and environmental barriers that impede learning, the argument being that schools should adapt to accommodate the needs of a more diverse range of students.

The term that has been used to describe this need for adjustments, or additional or different type of support, is 'special educational needs'. Its meaning is not identical with that of disability, but there is an overlap. Inevitably, 'special' has been conceived as anything that varies significantly from the standard provision for non-disabled students. The term 'special educational needs' was introduced by the 1981 Education Act, which enacted the recommendations of the Warnock Report (Department of Education and Science 1978). This was a landmark piece of legislation in that it marked a break with the exclusionary provisions of the 1944 Education Act, under which children were classified in medical terms and many were considered to be uneducable. However, the 1981 Act has itself been criticized for creating a group of students who are classified as 'special' in opposition to the majority of students who are not. It introduced 'integration' on the basis of common educational goals for all children. Although special schools remained, some children with special needs could be educated in mainstream schools with support. Access to this support and to places in special schools came through a system of assessment by a range of professionals, resulting in a Statement of Special Educational Needs.

Since then, the trend has been away from categorizing children with special educational needs as separate. Throughout the 1980s and 1990s there was an increase in the percentage of students identified as having special educational needs but a decline in the number of children in special schools. This trend was confirmed by the 1997 Green Paper *Excellence for All Children: Meeting Special Educational Needs* (DfES 1997). This supported the United Nations statement on special needs education (UNESCO 1994), which called for inclusion and an expansion of the capacity of mainstream schools to provide for all children. Subsequently, the Special Educational Needs and Disability Act 2001 strengthened anti-discrimination legislation relating to education and the right to a place in a mainstream school. Action to improve early identification and embed inclusive practice was emphasized in the government's five-year strategy *Removing Barriers to Achievement* (DfES 2004).

While the reduction in use of segregated education has been welcomed by many disability activists, the reaction of the Deaf community is less enthusiastic. Deaf activists fear that their language and culture is under threat as a result of the closure of specialist schools (Ladd 2003). The historical legacy of 'oralism' in education, whereby Deaf children were 'normalized' by not being allowed to sign, has had an impact on the response of some in the Deaf community to the inclusion of Deaf children in mainstream education. There has been ongoing dialogue between disability activists and Deaf people, who argue that the retention of segregated provision is a necessary means of valuing linguistic and cultural diversity.

The general direction of travel has been for mainstream schools to be made more inclusive, increasing their capacity to meet a diverse range of learning needs and to make 'reasonable adjustments' under the equalities legislation. There have also been initiatives to reduce the number of children who have a Statement of Special Educational Needs and give schools rather than local education authorities the task of assessing and providing for students whose needs are more moderate. The 'statementing' process has been a source of conflict between parents and local authorities and has been criticized both as leading to an inequitable distribution of resources and as failing to support inclusive practice (Audit Commission 2002). This is an example of the tension between developing inclusive environments and legally enforceable provision for individual children, the option favoured by some parents.

This has taken place alongside a broadening of the range of impairments being identified within schools. In particular, there has been a significant increase in the numbers of children diagnosed with autistic spectrum conditions and social, emotional and behavioural difficulties (House of Commons Education and Skills Committee 2006; Baron-Cohen et al. 2009). This has represented a challenge for mainstream schools. It has also been a factor in campaigns by parents against the closure of special schools. Further impetus for these campaigns resulted from Mary Warnock's (2005) pamphlet, which expressed strong reservations about the closure of special schools and fears that vulnerable children could become isolated in mainstream schools. In particular, she questioned treating students with special educational needs as a unified group who all need the same policy. As the person who had originated the current system, her apparent change of heart attracted a great deal of media attention. The House of Commons Education and Skills Committee investigation into special educational needs became a focus for the discontents of parents, voluntary organizations and others with the current situation, and the committee concluded that this was at least in part a result of confusion about the meaning of 'inclusion'. Its comments about inclusion give an indication of the issues that had caused public discontent: 'There is nothing in the word inclusion itself to cause offence but it has become associated with blanket policies of forced inclusion or exclusion from particular schools or access to resources. Associations with such needs-blind policies have raised passionate opposition' (2006: 22). The committee reviewed several definitions of inclusion, many of which were not about the type of school children attended. While the government assured the committee that the closure of special schools played no part in its inclusion policy, its five-year strategy urged local authorities to reduce the percentage of children attending special schools.

It is not surprising that the discontent of an articulate group of parents was noted by the Conservative opposition and that, following the election of a Conservative–Liberal Democrat coalition government in 2010, a change of policy was announced giving more emphasis to parental choice and the need to avoid unnecessary closure of special schools (DfE 2011). This caused concern among the supporters of the social model of disability and inclusive education, who understandably fear a reversal of the gains made in achieving access to the mainstream (Runswick-Cole 2011). The code of practice accompanying the Children and Families Act 2014 states that 'the majority of children and young people with SEN will have their needs met within local mainstream early years settings, schools or colleges' (DfE and DoH

2014: 142). At the time of writing, 2.8 per cent of pupils in schools in England have a Statement of Special Educational Needs and, of those, 44.4 per cent are attending special schools (DfE 2014b). This would amount to less than 1.3 per cent of all pupils in English schools. The effect of greater parental choice on this figure is difficult to predict accurately, but the fears of supporters of inclusive education are that the percentage could increase.

Some key provisions of the Children and Families Act 2014:

- replacing Statements of Special Educational Need with Education, Health and Care Plans, which will be issued when the local authority considers that the special educational needs of the child cannot be reasonably met with the resources normally available to mainstream organizations;
- joint commissioning by local authorities and the NHS;
- the duty of local authorities to set out a 'local offer' of services available;
- statutory protection for young people is extended to the age of twenty-five;
- parents and young people will have the right to a personal budget to purchase support specified in the Education, Health and Care Plan.

This legislation reflects several wider policy trends. The introduction of personal budgets as a means of increasing choice and control reflects developments in social care more generally, and there is also an emphasis on joint commissioning and the integration of services. If these reforms go ahead on the basis of the current timetable, the merging of funding streams through personal budgets will have progressed faster than it has in adult services.

Conclusion

Recent policy has focused on promoting the independence and autonomy of disabled people and better access to community-based support. The aims of policies have gone beyond care and have addressed overall well-being, quality of life and capacity to participate fully in the community. Better coordination of services has also been an ongoing theme, and in some instances this has resulted in the integration of formerly disparate services. Service-user empowerment has been promoted largely through market-based solutions such as direct payments and personal budgets, and these are now on a statutory footing. It is anticipated that these mechanisms will enable service users to access and control support that is integrated and flexible, though research findings thus far are mixed.

Personalization, the dominant theme in current policy, emphasizes individualism, independence, responsibility and co-production. Wider social policies have equated social inclusion with paid work, and the boundary of the disability category has shifted accordingly. However, the historical legacy of institutional care and social exclusion has continued to influence provision, and this has sometimes been exacerbated by financial pressures. The same financial pressures have restricted eligibility for social care. As a result, people with 'lower-level needs' have become more dependent on informal and community resources. Those who fall below the eligibility threshold will not be able to access social care services unless they are in a position to self-fund. This could be a source of widening inequality in the future.

For social workers, these developments have led to service integration, interprofessional working, greater service-user involvement in support planning, and an increased focus on the potential of universal services and community resources in meeting needs and aspirations. In meeting these challenges, social workers are likely to need an extended range of skills.

Key messages

- Policies based on segregation have proved remarkably resilient, and there is a danger of these being 'reinvented' within a privatized care market.
- Since the 1960s, policies have emphasized community rather than institutional care.
- Recent policies to promote service-user empowerment have been market based and individualized. Personalization has been the main guiding principle, and this has emphasized responsibility, participation and co-production of services. This has been extended from adult to children's social care, where it may be leading the way with Education, Health and Care Plans.
- Eligibility criteria in adult care have meant that expenditure has been focused on people with the greatest support needs. Policies to develop prevention are being pursued mainly through the use of universal services and informal and community activity.
- The trend in education policy has been for the inclusion of a greater number of disabled children in mainstream schools. There are fears that this trend may stall as a result of present policies.
- Social workers will need to extend their range of skills in order to meet the challenge posed by recent policy developments.

Activities

- Why do you think the Disability Discrimination Act failed to tackle the barriers that were important to Helen?
- To what extent can policies of personalization deliver equality for disabled people?
- Referring to the Care and Support (Eligibility Criteria) Regulations 2014, do you think Mark will be eligible for adult social care?
- How do you think the Care Act 2014 and the Social Services and Well-Being (Wales) Act 2014 will change the way disabled people experience care and support?
- Is it possible to offer both parental choice and inclusion for disabled children in education?

Suggested further reading

Barnes, C., and Mercer, G. (2004) *Disability Policy and Practice: Applying the Social Model of Disability*. Leeds: Disability Press.

Borsay, A. (2005) *Disability and Social Policy in Britain since 1750: A History of Exclusion*. Basingstoke: Palgrave MacMillan.

Broach, S., Clements, L., and Read, J. (2015) *Disabled Children: A Legal Handbook*. 2nd edn, London: Legal Action Group.

Roulstone, A., and Prideaux, S. (2012) *Understanding Disability Policy*. Bristol: Policy Press.

PART II

DIVERSITY, INEQUALITY AND DISABILITY

5 Inequality, Oppression and Disability

Issues considered in this chapter:

- Evidence of discrimination and disadvantage experienced by disabled people
- Links between these experiences, the concept of oppression and models of disability
- The place of social work in challenging discrimination and oppression

Introduction

Given the diversity that exists among disabled people, knowledge of the inequality and oppression they experience in general is bound to provide only a partial picture. There have been challenges to approaches that simply contrast the experience of 'disabled people' with that of non-disabled people. For example, some writers have stressed that disability is something that affects all of us at some point in our lives to a greater or lesser extent – in fact, that it is universal (see chapter 6); 'What we need are more universal policies that recognize that the entire population is "at risk" for the concomitants of chronic illness and disability ... without such a perspective we will further create and perpetuate a segregated, separate but unequal society' (Zola 2005: 1).

A similar point was made in chapter 2, which cites the argument by Depoy and Gilson (2008) that disability should be viewed as a lack of fit between people and their environments, and that social work should be concerned with the 'advancement of human rights for the full range of human diversity'. This presents a challenge to 'them and us' conceptions of disability and appears to undermine the value of analysing the experience of disabled people as a discrete 'group'. In terms of remedies for inequalities, Nancy Fraser (1997: 16) maintains that affirmative action based on group identities can even lead to the stigmatization of the disadvantaged group and 'mark [them] as inherently deficient and insatiable, as always needing more and more'. She observes that reliance on simple group identities can overlook the complexities of people's affiliations and argues instead for parity of status for all individuals. It is certainly the case that disabled people can have a range of other affiliations and experiences of oppression, including those linked to ethnicity, gender, sexuality and social class. This intersectionality is explored in chapter 6.

However, Young (1990: 47) maintains that social justice 'requires not the melting away of differences, but institutions that promote reproduction of and respect for group differences without oppression.' This chapter argues that there *is* value in developing knowledge and understanding of the experience of disabled people as a group, and that an exclusive focus on diversity may obscure the structural oppression of disabled people (Roulstone 2012). As Linton (1998: 13) argues: 'I'm not willing or interested in erasing the line between disabled and nondisabled people, as long as disabled people are devalued and discriminated against, and as long as naming the category serves to draw attention to that treatment.' Although there is also a need to acknowledge the progress made over the past twenty years (Shakespeare 2014), the premise here is that disability is a form of oppression. The chapter is grounded in a social relational model of disability in which disability is defined as 'a form of social oppression involving the social imposition of restrictions of activity on people with impairments and the socially engendered undermining of their psycho-emotional wellbeing' (Thomas 1999: 60). In later writing, Thomas (2007) has referred to 'disablism' rather than 'disability', which clarifies better the social relational character of this definition.

If disability is defined in this way, arguments about the relative impact of impairment and disability on activities become less relevant. However, this does not necessarily mean that impairment can be consigned to the purely biological, as Abberley (1987) states that it is also part of the oppression. He has identified the impact of social disadvantage on the distribution of impairment and argues that the effects of biological factors are only apparent in real social and historical contexts. For example, in relation to his own experience of childhood polio, he maintains: 'had I been born a few years earlier, before the development of respiratory support systems, I would have died; a few years later and the advent of effective vaccination techniques would have made my contraction of the disease improbable' (ibid.: 6).

As well as being biological variations, impairments are markers for discrimination. Tremain (2001) has argued that the classification of an atypical biological characteristic as an impairment is therefore part of the social process of disablement. It is apparent that biology alone is insufficient to explain why *some* variations rather than others are regarded as impairments; the recent medicalization of shyness and the demedicalization of homosexuality are examples of the influence of social environments on the way that human variation is conceptualized. This is partly a matter of changing attitudes in society. However, there can also be changes in the demands and expectations placed on people over time. For example, the recognition of dyslexia as an impairment reflects greater demands for literacy among the population and resulting social disadvantages for those who cannot achieve this (Riddick 2001). Therefore Abberley (1987: 13) takes issue with the view that impairment is universal, arguing that this cannot be reconciled with the fact that only some people are labelled 'impaired' or 'disabled', and that it 'separates the human condition from the social and historical conditions of its production'. Although Shakespeare (2014) asserts that impairment is 'real' and exists independently of its labelling and diagnosis, he also acknowledges that diagnoses affect the way conditions are understood and how people are treated.

A social relational approach to disability also grants space to oppression in the private sphere, where disablism can have significant consequences, and broadens the impact of disablism to include not only activity, or what people can *do*, but also psycho-emotional well-being. This restricts what people can *be* (Thomas 1999) and is particularly important in the light of literature linking psycho-emotional disablism and internalized oppression (Reeve 2014).

What is oppression?

Case profile: Gail

Gail is a lone parent of two children without a close network of support from friends or family. She has multiple sclerosis and has found it difficult to keep up with household tasks and childcare. She has also dropped out of the college course she was taking since developing problems with her vision associated with her MS. Following concerns raised by the children's school about their unkempt appearance and irregular attendance, a social worker has visited Gail and said that her children are officially 'in need' as a result of her disability and that she must guard against their becoming 'young carers'. The social worker is to return shortly to carry out an assessment. She has advised Gail to phone her if she feels unable to cope in the meantime. Gail was worried, as she associates social workers with removing children from home, and was determined to show the social worker that she could manage. One day she felt so ill that she didn't want to get out of bed. However, she did her best to carry on because she didn't want the social worker to think she couldn't cope. By the end of the day she felt completely exhausted.

Gail is clearly afraid of the power of the social worker to judge her an inadequate parent and to remove her children. The social worker meant to be supportive and may not be aware of the impact her remarks have had. It is her job to focus on the welfare of the children, and she has identified the potential problem of the children having to support their mother. Gail feels that she has no option but to show that she can operate 'normally' as a parent, which means doing everything without assistance.

The social worker's concern about the children possibly becoming 'young carers' is understandable. However, by constructing the problem in these terms alone, she has made a preliminary judgement of Gail's parenting capacity based on her disability. This has affected Gail's self-image, and she also fears that decisions about her children will be taken out of her hands. It is not clear how the social worker intends to respond to Gail's situation in the longer term, but her initial response appears to be informed by an individual model of disability. If the situation was interpreted on the basis of the social model, the problem would be a lack of support for a disabled adult to undertake her parenting responsibilities. Gail is eligible for an assessment under adult social care legislation; this should include needs relating to her role as a parent (see chapter 9).

Mullaly (2007: 253) points out that '[n]ot everything that frustrates or limits or hurts a person is oppressive.' Oppression occurs when this happens purely because someone is a member of a particular group or category of people (PCF Domain 4). This is reflected both in Dominelli's (2002) definition and, in relation to disability, in the conditions set out by Abberley (1987).

> Oppression involves relations of domination that divide people into dominant or superior groups and subordinate or inferior ones. These relations of domination consist of the systematic devaluing of the attributes and contributions of those deemed inferior, and their exclusion from the social resources available to those in the dominant group ... oppressive relations are about limiting the range of

options that subordinate individuals and groups can readily access. (Dominelli 2002: 8–9)

> To claim that disabled people are oppressed … is to argue that on significant dimensions disabled people can be regarded as a group whose members are in an inferior position to other members of society because they are disabled people. It is also to argue that these disadvantages are dialectically related to an ideology or group of ideologies which justify and perpetuate this situation. Beyond this it is to make the claim that such disadvantages and their supporting ideologies are neither natural nor inevitable. Finally it involves the identification of some beneficiary of this state of affairs. (Abberley 1987: 7)

Young (1990) defines oppression as processes that prevent people from learning, developing their capacities and communicating their perspectives in situations in which others will listen; these are constraints on self-development. Domination involves constraints on self-determination. Young argues that oppression usually includes domination, as oppressed people are often constrained by rules set by others.

Oppression does not always result from the conscious and intentional actions of powerful individuals and groups. There are certainly examples of deliberate and conscious oppression, with the Apartheid system in South Africa being one of the best known. However, Young (1990: 41) stresses that oppression is 'embedded in unquestioned norms, habits and symbols, in the assumptions underlying institutional rules and the collective consequences of following those rules.' It can also be maintained through cultural imagery and stereotypes. Although oppression involves relations between groups, it does not necessarily involve one group *intentionally* oppressing another. Oppression is reproduced by many individuals who may or may not be direct beneficiaries of the situation, but often this is through 'the normal processes of everyday life' or through 'simply doing their jobs' (ibid.: 42). This can apply to social work, in which '[t]he very language of "care", "local authorities", "services" and "entitlements" emanates from the power of affordances that state professionals are invested with' (Roulstone 2012: 148–9). However, there are also examples of more positive rhetoric. The Association of Directors of Adult Services and the Department of Health (2010: 3) stated that the outcomes social work should aim to achieve with disabled adults are choice and control; dignity and respect; economic well-being; improved quality of life; health and emotional well-being; making a positive contribution; and freedom from discrimination and harassment. This indicates that social work has a role in addressing the types of oppression discussed in this chapter. As Oliver et al. (2012: 160) assert: 'What is required is a form of professionalism that is capable of asserting itself in the face of oppressive social policies, but which does so with disabled people rather than for them.'

Types of oppression

Abberley (1987) explains that use of the term 'oppression' has developed as complementary to *exploitation*, a term associated with Marxist analysis of social class. *Exploitation* has a specific and limited meaning, which cannot account for the experiences of all subordinate groups. It can be regarded as just one type of oppression, which is a broader concept.

In this chapter, the experiences of disabled people will be considered primarily through the lens of the 'five faces of oppression' identified by Young (1990), but it also draws on a similar framework developed by Deutsch (2005). Young (1990) has argued that a group should be regarded as oppressed if its members suffer the consequences of any one of these five processes: exploitation, marginalization, powerlessness, cultural imperialism and violence. Each of the 'five faces of oppression' has some relevance for disabled people.

Exploitation

Marxist analysis draws on the *labour theory of value* to explain exploitation as the gap between the cost to an employer of the labour necessary to add value to a product and the amount that product can fetch in the market. This may appear complex and abstract, but Davis (1993: 5) has defined it in a very accessible way:

> If you work for such and such a time to produce goods which are worth so much money, for this you are paid by the hour, and the time you spend producing, converted into cash, is less than the value of the thing produced. If the spare cash is collected by someone else, then your labour is being exploited.

Although, as later sections of this chapter show, disabled people are less likely to be employed than others, and *some* disabled people may not be able to work at the same rate as non-disabled people, this does not mean that they cannot be exploited. Disabled workers tend to be more poorly paid, and low pay can be an indicator of exploitation (Davis 1993).

There is evidence of the low pay of disabled workers. For example, Burchardt (2000) found that the work available to disabled people leaving the benefits system was often poorly paid. Evidence published in 2010 indicates that the hourly pay rate of disabled people was slightly less than a pound lower than that of non-disabled people, and that there was a gap of almost 7 per cent between the pay of disabled and non-disabled people who achieved 'higher level employment' (Riddell et al. 2010). This gap had increased to £1.10 by 2012 (Hansbro et al. 2013), with only 49 per cent of disabled people earning more than £10 per hour, compared to 55 per cent of non-disabled workers (Coleman et al. 2013a).

However, Davis (1993: 5) also takes a broader view of the exploitation of disabled people: 'Just as oil is taken from the earth to provide fuel and make plastics, disabled people have provided the fuel for the careers of millions of able-bods, all concerned with taking care of disabled people.' He goes on to point to the predominance of non-disabled people in these roles, as well as their tendency both to 'know best' and to see disability as an individual problem. The ideological justification for this situation is that disabled people are *dependent* on non-disabled people because of their impairments. This may explain why disabled people are under-represented in social work; for example, in 2011 in adult services, 10 per cent of social workers were disabled as defined by the current equalities legislation and 7 per cent where the disability had also been defined as 'work limiting' (Skills for Care 2012). These figures can be compared with the proportion of the working-age population who were disabled in 2011/12 according to the Family Resources Survey, which was 16 per cent. Barriers faced by those who do enter the profession are noted in chapter 6.

Disabled people are also under-represented in other professions, which leads to the next category of oppression: *marginalization.*

Marginalization

According to Young (1990: 53), this is 'perhaps the most dangerous form of oppression. A whole category of people is expelled from useful participation in social life and thus potentially subjected to severe material deprivation and even extermination.' Deutsch (2005) links material deprivation to injustice in the distribution of material and social goods and identifies several types of 'capital' that oppressed groups may lack. This includes 'consumption capital', which concerns income and standards of living. Access to employment is likely to be an important factor in determining standard of living. There is a gap of about 30 per cent in the employment rates of disabled and non-disabled people (Riddell et al. 2010). Labour Force Survey figures published in 2012 show that 46.3 per cent of disabled people of working age were employed in comparison with 76.4 per cent of non-disabled people (cited by Hansbro et al. 2013). Although there is evidence of this gap narrowing over time (Shakespeare 2014), there is survey evidence that significantly more disabled people feel that they have been discriminated against when seeking work (Department of Communities and Local Government 2010).

Disabled people are under-represented in what Riddell et al. (2010) refer to as 'higher level jobs', which include management and professional occupations. Unfair treatment at work may be partly responsible for this, as Coleman et al. (2013a) have identified a variety of discriminatory practices reported by disabled people. These included the type of work disabled people were given, often with less responsibility than they would have liked; being ignored; and unfair assessment or appraisal.

Being disadvantaged in the labour market is only one factor that makes disabled people susceptible to poverty and debt. Although MacInnes et al. (2014) state that the poverty rate for disabled people, at 23 per cent, is only slightly higher than that for non-disabled people (at 21 per cent), this does not take into account the additional costs of disability. Brawn (2014) estimates that, in order to achieve a reasonable standard of living, disabled people will incur additional costs of up to £550 per month. MacInnes et al. (2014) argue that disability benefits such as disability living allowance should be discounted when calculating income, as they are supposed to cover such extra disability-related costs. Recent welfare reforms threaten this funding and therefore put the independence and participation of disabled people at risk. Disabled people are already unable to save for contingencies and are more likely to be in debt (Balmer et al. 2006; Brawn 2014). This has a cumulative effect resulting in smaller pensions, lower rates of saving and fewer assets in retirement.

Among debt clients at Citizens Advice, disabled people generally had lower levels of debt, but they were more likely to use high-cost credit and to have mail-order debts (Tutton et al. 2011). Reasons given by disabled clients for their debts included problems with budgeting, long-term low income, problems with benefits, and the additional costs of disability, including fuel costs. Disabled clients also faced additional problems when service providers failed to make reasonable adjustments or to follow agreed standards. Some clients had difficulty telling creditors about their impairments, and this was sometimes due to inflexible communication methods. For example, in the case of a woman who was deaf and could not use the phone, the creditor insisted that she must answer a series of security questions without the adviser acting as an intermediary. Other clients were unaware of the extent of their debts because creditors failed to send information in accessible formats. In some instances, the researchers found that unfair business practices continued even after the creditor had been informed about a client's disability.

Harris and Roulstone (2011) observe that the higher profile of paid work for disabled people in recent policy has a number of implications for professionals. Social workers can help to facilitate access to paid work by fully appraising themselves and disabled service users of the support available, including supported employment schemes and specialist services provided by Jobcentre Plus. This may involve referral to a specialist disability employment adviser and use of Access to Work funding to offset the costs of any adjustments or equipment required in the workplace.

By working with disabled people to facilitate access to employment, social workers will be assisting them to achieve both economic well-being and the ability to make a positive contribution. Access to skilled advice about benefits and debt is also relevant to economic well-being, and social workers should be knowledgeable about local advice agencies and be prepared to support disabled people in accessing their services (PCF domain 5.12, SOP 1.1).

Both education and what Deutsch (2005) refers to as 'skill capital' are crucial in obtaining higher status and better paid employment. Disability studies scholars and campaigners have long argued that the segregated 'special education' provided for disabled children 'perpetuates their exclusion and marginalization from mainstream society' (Benson 2014: 50). Article 24 of the UNCRPD states the right to an inclusive education, and this has been government policy since the 1980s. However, Moore and Slee (2013) have identified a recent backlash against this policy, with government's preference for parental choice (see chapter 4). They also consider league tables and the current emphasis on attainment as perverse incentives when it comes to the inclusion of disabled children in mainstream education.

Recent evidence of attainment in the *Fulfilling Potential* report (Hansbro et al. 2013) indicates that the gap between disabled and non-disabled children had narrowed at key stages 2 and 4 in 2010–11, but that the rate of improvement was greatest for children classified as having special educational needs (SEN) without a statement. The gap between children without SEN and those with a Statement of SEN had widened to 64 per cent. The same report states that disabled young people are four times less likely than their non-disabled peers to be in higher education. This has an impact on future employment prospects, as it was found that 71 per cent of disabled graduates were in employment compared to only 42 per cent of disabled non-graduates. However, achieving degree-level qualifications was not a guarantee of finding work, as graduate unemployment rates were significantly higher for disabled people. There was also considerable variation on the basis of type of impairment.

There is therefore evidence of marginalization in education and employment, both of which are associated with low income. According to Young (1990), advanced capitalist countries have made some attempt to address material deprivation through their systems of welfare benefits and services. However, any improvements in material circumstances thus achieved have been offset by two types of further injustice.

The first of these concerns welfare itself, which Young considers to undermine the rights and autonomy of its recipients: 'Dependency in our society thus implies ... a sufficient warrant to suspend basic rights to privacy, respect, and individual choice' (ibid.: 54). This has much in common with critiques of welfare from disabled activists. It is not difficult to find examples of a controlling ethos within the social security system, where, as explained in chapter 4, policies have moved in the direction of greater 'conditionality'. However, Wilson and Beresford (2000: 558) have referred to 'the illusion of anti-oppressive practice' and maintain that, '[f]or many service users, social work itself is part of the problem.' Although social work education may subscribe to new models of disability, it often does so 'without orientating students to the harsh realities of the practice environment' (Roulstone 2012: 144). The gap between theory and the practice that students observe on placement can make it difficult for them to apply progressive models. In situations of austerity, progressive policies may be offset by the tightening of eligibility criteria and increased scrutiny of the way people spend their direct payments, with an associated reduction in autonomy and choice.

Marginalization of oppressed groups through diversion to the welfare system is also damaging because it 'blocks the opportunity to exercise capabilities in socially defined and recognised ways' and can lead to 'uselessness, boredom and lack of self-respect' (Young 1990: 54–5). This is partly because people are denied employment, but it also includes decreased access to other productive activities. Such activities can sometimes be accessed through participation in organized volunteering; 52 per cent of voluntary organizations included in a recent survey have reported that disabled people are under-represented among their volunteers (IVR 2004). The same research identified a number of barriers to volunteering, including lack of confidence, the perceived attitudes of colleagues, and the fear of losing welfare benefits. Among practical barriers for disabled volunteers were physically inaccessible environments and the failure of some organizations to pay expenses. Lamb (2005) found that, although many disabled volunteers were having positive experiences, stereotypical assumptions about disabled people were a problem in some areas of the voluntary sector, and that accessibility was more problematic in organizations whose remit was not disability-related. The Institute for Volunteering Research (2004) research found that, where barriers had been overcome, volunteering was reducing feelings of social isolation and was increasing self-confidence and self-worth.

Deutsch (2005: 4) considers marginalization to be a lesser form of what he terms 'moral exclusion'. This applies to groups and individuals 'who are outside the boundary in which considerations of fairness apply [and] may be treated in ways that would be considered immoral if people within the boundary were so treated.' The concept of moral exclusion appears to be a factor in the harassment and violence towards disabled people, discussed later in this chapter. He cites a number of examples of atrocities against minority groups, including systematic extermination. It is salient that disabled people were among those selected for extermination and inhumane experimentation in Nazi Germany and for enforced sterilization in more than one country. Minorities may be at greater risk of unjust treatment, scapegoating and victimization when societies are under pressure and resources scarce (Deutsch 2005). As discussed in chapter 4, recent welfare reforms, taking place in conditions of economic austerity, have raised thresholds for access to benefits for disabled people, reduced the value of some benefits, and encouraged a climate of suspicion of claimants, with disabled people often cast as 'benefit cheats'. Shakespeare (2014: 104–5) refers to 'a savage attack on the living standards of disabled people ... together with a cultural backlash that associates disabled benefit claimants with scroungers'.

Powerlessness

As with exploitation and marginalization, powerlessness is a result of the social division of labour (Young 1990). Although it is elected politicians and the owners of businesses who decide the direction of policy, professionals have a degree of authority over other workers, and sometimes over the users of their services. In contrast to less skilled workers, they have considerable day-to-day autonomy in their work arising from their expertise and are able to command more respect.

For example, Hassenfeld (1987) has identified four sources of power that attach to the social work role: the power of expertise; 'referent power', or persuasion, which arises from interpersonal skills and the ability to develop empathy and trust; 'legitimate power', arising from legislation, policy and organizational procedures; and the power of resources, which arises from social work's gatekeeping role. The case profile of Gail, above, exemplifies the social worker's *legitimate power*, as she is empowered by law to take action to protect Gail's children. She also has access to *resources* which could be helpful for Gail, but access to these is dependent on the result of her assessment. The social worker therefore also has a gatekeeping role. Her role as an assessor implies *expertise*; she is assumed to have the necessary knowledge to identify needs. Harris and Roulstone (2011) identify professional power based on 'expertise' as one of the barriers to choice and control for disabled people and, by implication, as a contributory factor in powerlessness. They argue for practice that is outcome-focused and based on facilitation and advocacy. This approach would have involved Gail in identifying the outcomes she wanted to achieve (PCF 2.5, SOP 9.4) and would have involved the social worker in advocating for Gail and her children (PCF 4.5, SOP 9.4 & 13.4) and facilitating access to resources. The case study suggests that the social worker's use of *referent power* was less effective, as Gail is left feeling fearful rather than trusting.

The greater power of professionals spills over into life outside of paid work. The higher status of professionals means that people in service settings are more ready to listen to them and accede to their requests (Young 1990). This is in contrast to the experience of less powerful groups such as disabled people. Almost a quarter of disabled respondents in a recent survey believed they had been discriminated against in accessing goods and services, and a larger proportion (40 per cent) had experienced difficulties (Gore and Parchar 2010). Although many of the difficulties involved physical accessibility, some respondents had experienced service providers 'talking down to them' or using inappropriate language. The majority of respondents (62 per cent) did not challenge service providers, and, of those who did complain, only 9 per cent reported that the organization had made improvements in its provision of services for disabled people. This tends to exemplify the relative powerlessness of disabled people in their interactions with service providers. Legal channels for redress were felt to be expensive and inaccessible, further exacerbating powerlessness.

Cultural imperialism

This refers to the way that the meanings and culture of dominant groups becomes pervasive and the norm, reconstructing difference as 'deviance and inferiority' (Young 1990: 59).

Reeve (2014) links both cultural imperialism and psycho-emotional disablism with internalized oppression, which involves internalizing dominant stereotypes in a way that restricts who a person can be. Psycho-emotional disablism can be both direct and indirect. The former arises from interactions with others, which may involve being stared at, invasive questions about one's impairment, disablist jokes and being avoided. Indirect psycho-emotional disablism can arise from the emotional response to inaccessible physical environments. As disabled people have to negotiate such environments on a daily basis, there can be a cumulative effect on self-confidence and self-esteem.

Minority groups may have different perspectives on the social world based on shared experience of oppression, and sometimes these are openly and collectively expressed. Examples would be identification with Deaf culture, neurodiversity (Singer 1999) and, especially, the social model of disability. However, the consciousness-raising effects of the social model of disability can in fact result in what Young (1990: 60) calls 'double consciousness' – an internal conflict between dominant and subordinate cultures: 'While the subject desires recognition as human, capable of activity, full of hope and possibility, she receives from the dominant culture only the judgement that she is different, marked or inferior.' The dominant culture can be woven into the procedures and processes of everyday life and also the policies of welfare organizations. For example, applying for benefits can force disabled people to emphasize their deficits rather than their capabilities, which can be distressing. Reeve (2014) argues that this stressful process can exacerbate impairments, particularly for people with mental health difficulties.

Internalized oppression may also be a factor in the decision of some people with invisible impairments to try to 'pass as normal'. There may be costs involved in terms of pain and fatigue, as well as fear of discovery.

Case profile: Harry

Harry was born with moderate to severe hearing impairment. He attended mainstream schools, and as he was bright it was assumed that he would 'cope'. He was encouraged to 'get on with it' rather than seeing himself as disabled. There was no additional support at his school, but he studied hard and achieved good A-levels. He wanted to become a teacher and was eventually accepted at a college. It was on placement that Harry became aware of the difficulties he would have in the classroom. Until then, he had struggled to cope as a hearing person and had always managed to succeed through working harder than others. He found the challenge to his identity quite frightening and became ill with depression. Looking back on the experience, Harry recognizes that neither the college nor the school made proper preparation for his teaching practice. However, he also acknowledges that his strategy of trying to ignore his deafness and perform as a hearing person was a contributory factor.

Harry had eventually encountered a difficulty that could not be tackled by additional effort alone. Certainly his impairment was a factor in this, as a classroom situation in which he would have to respond to children, sometimes several at once, would pose a challenge to a deaf person. However, it was the disruption to the way that he had coped previously, and the resulting challenge to his identity, that caused the most distress. His decision to 'pass as normal', to eschew signing or additional support, was not entirely his own. When he was a child, the views of parents and teachers would have been very influential. However, Harry had internalized this negativity towards disability and deafness, which determined the emotional effect of his failure to 'pass as normal' in this new situation.

Given the emotional distress that Harry experienced, would he have benefited from counselling? Reeve (2004a) points out that counselling for disabled people has often been based on individual models of disability, on theories of loss and on the process of adjustment. This fails to acknowledge social and environmental barriers that disabled people face and presupposes that it is the individual who has to adjust. However Oliver et al. (2012) refer to the use of counselling to raise consciousness and empower disabled people. This can be consistent with the social model of disability, as the low self-esteem characteristic of internalized oppression, often the result of disablism, can become a disabling barrier in itself.

Conversely, people whose impairments are invisible may face suspicion from others who claim that they are not 'really disabled'. This can be a major factor in the experience of disabled workers with invisible impairments, who may find the legitimacy of any adjustments made for them questioned by colleagues and managers. For some disabled social workers, this has meant a continued struggle to perform 'normally', often resulting in pain and fatigue (Castle 2007).

Violence

Violence against disabled people has featured in the media and has been the subject of several research reports and publications (Quarmby 2011; Roulstone and Mason-Bish 2013). There are strong indications that the cases that come to court are only the 'tip of the iceberg' (EHRC 2011).

Incidents in which the perpetrator is motivated by prejudice or hatred of the victim because of their disability are regarded as disability hate crimes (CPS 2007). Legislation relevant to this offence is described in chapter 10, where there is also a critical discussion of the commonly held assumption that it is impairment alone that makes disabled people vulnerable. Barbara Perry, writing in an American context, argues that 'bias motivated violence' is part of a wider pattern of subordination. She links both vulnerability and hatred to oppression:

> Together, structural exclusions and cultural imaging leave minority members vulnerable to systemic violence ... The former makes them vulnerable targets, the latter makes them 'legitimate' targets. Moreover, violence is very likely to emerge in contexts wherein the formerly disadvantaged challenge the other bases of oppression, as when they seek to empower themselves economically or socially through rights claims. Efforts directed toward empowerment are commonly met with equally steadfast reactionary mobilizations. (Perry 2003: 17–18)

Referring to deinstitutionalization and campaigns for independent living, Jane Campbell reflects on the possible connection between this and the harassment of disabled people: 'I would say that people started taking the gloves off and being nasty about the time when we started becoming visible. And that's when I started to experience hate words or people telling me that we were asking for too much' (cited in Quarmby 2011: 115). This is also consistent with Young's (1990) observation that violence can intersect with cultural imperialism if the oppressed group is thought to pose a threat to the universality of the dominant culture or if they appear to reject dominant meanings and assert their own perspectives.

Several reports have referred to 'harassment', which many disabled people regard as a 'commonplace experience of everyday life rather than as hate crime' (Coleman et al. 2013b). Not all harassment is classified as crime. However, it can be the precursor to serious assault and sometimes murder. Disabled people are also victims of domestic abuse (see chapter 10).

It is not clear how widespread violence against disabled people is. Shakespeare (2014) has commented that research studies have often been based on small self-selected samples. However, research reviews commissioned by the World Health Organization have found that disabled people are 50 per cent more likely than non-disabled people to have experienced violence in the previous year. This amounts to 3 per cent of all disabled people (Hughes et al. 2012). Emerson and Roulstone (2014) have analysed responses from the UK Life Opportunities Survey, which revealed that disabled people were 2.3 times more likely to have been the victim of violent crime and 2.6 times more likely to have been the victim of hate crime than non-disabled people. However, only one in three of those reporting a hate crime attributed it to their disability. Coleman et al. (2013b) maintain that, in the period 2007–8 to 2010–11, an estimated 39,000 adults per year were victims of disability hate crime. Findings from the British Crime Survey 2010–11 (Smith et al. 2012), which is based on the self-reporting of victims, suggested that there were 65,000 disability hate crimes a year in England and Wales. In Scotland in 2013–14, 154 cases were reported, 12 per cent more than in 2012–13. It is considered that this type of crime continues to be under-reported in Scotland compared to other forms of hate crime (Crown Office and Procurator Fiscal Service 2014).

There has been little research into the perpetrators and the causes of abuse and violence directed at disabled people. In his research concerning people with learning disabilities, Gravell (2012) found that 7 per cent of harassment and hate crime was committed by family members, 25 per cent by known people in the neighbourhood, 17 per cent by school children, 11 per cent by strangers in the street, and 13 per cent by 'friends'. Cameron (2014) observes that, in the case of disability hate crime, multiple perpetrators are often involved. Some of the worst cases of exploitation and abuse have involved 'mate crimes' committed by so-called friends (Thomas 2011) (see chapter 10).

Quarmby (2011) attributed the motivations of perpetrators to historically held 'fears and prejudices', as well as more recent stereotypes of disabled people as 'welfare scroungers'. Shakespeare (2014: 234) has suggested causes including carer stress in domestic settings and problems of disaffected youth in some impoverished areas: the 'boredom and anomie of life on the margins'. This appears to link with Emerson and Roulstone's (2014) finding that disabled people living in severe poverty are at significantly greater risk of violence and hate crime. In these circumstances, disabled people can be perceived as 'soft targets' and to have access to benefits which are not available to others. This can cause jealousy and resentment.

In terms of the way forward, there are a number of implications for social work and other professions. There is a need for stronger support for disabled people living independently. This does not necessarily mean that the lives of victims should become more restricted, as disabled people could be assisted to develop stronger networks of friendship and support in the community (Shakespeare 2014) (PCF 7.7, SoP 9.5). In cases where victims have died as a result of harassment and violence, they were often socially isolated and therefore susceptible to exploitation by those who offered 'friendship' (EHRC 2011). Balderston (2013) argues for promoting links with organizations of disabled people, which can integrate people into a circle of support.

Professionals should consider whether reluctance to engage with their services results from intimidation. Under-reporting of abuse may result from both fear of repercussions from the perpetrator and fear of not being believed (EHRC 2011). It is therefore important that social workers and police take seriously any complaints a disabled person may make about harassment or violence, irrespective of whether she or he appears to be a reliable witness.

Incidents sometimes referred to as 'lower-level harassment' should also be taken seriously. Experience has indicated that lack of effective action at this stage can lead to an intensification of abuse or to the victim reaching the end of her endurance. This was certainly the case as regards the death of Fiona Pilkington, who was eventually driven to kill herself and her disabled daughter after experiencing a sustained campaign of harassment (EHRC 2011).

Chapter 10 refers to the need for close liaison and collaboration with criminal justice agencies where appropriate (PCF 8.7, SoP 8.9, 9.6), and Quarmby (2011) also refers to a relative lack of connection between local authority safeguarding processes and reporting of crime to the police in the cases she investigated. Reflecting on failure to protect a victim in his area, one chief constable said:

> He [the victim] was in contact with a lot of authorities, but they just didn't understand that what was happening to him was a risk to his life. There has been a lot of focus on freedom, on the drive to independence, but you don't have to take away someone's freedom to recognise that something is happening that shouldn't happen. (Quarmby 2011: 110)

This points to the need to be alert to the possibility that crime or antisocial behaviour is motivated by hatred of disability (EHRC 2011). Shakespeare (2014) also highlights the need for better support from voluntary organizations involved in victim support, not all of which are fully accessible to disabled people. The implication for social workers is the need to develop contacts and working relationships with voluntary sector and disabled people's organizations.

Conclusion

Disabled people are affected by multiple forms of disablist oppression, ranging from unintentional slights to extremes of physical violence. Drawing on Perry (2003), these types of oppression appear to be linked, with marginalization and cultural imperialism making harassment and victimization more likely.

Implications for social work of these types of oppression have been identified throughout the chapter. An overarching issue has been the need to adopt an approach based on social relational conceptions of disability and the barriers that sustain the marginalization and subordinate position of disabled people. Engagement with organizations of disabled people and a willingness to work towards outcomes that disabled people want is key (PCF 5.12, SoP 9.4, 9.8). It is important that social workers provide effective protection, but wherever possible alternatives should be sought to restricting the freedom of the victim. Collaborative work should include the police at an early stage. There is also potential for creative approaches drawing on support from organizations of disabled people and the development of protective social networks. Oliver et al. (2012) argue for an approach based on citizenship, which acknowledges the economic and political participation of disabled people and their human rights. Therefore social workers should look beyond the provision of care for disabled people and facilitate their contribution to the community.

None of this is easy within the budgetary and organizational constraints in which social work operates. However, in face-to-face encounters with individual disabled people and families, there is considerable potential for anti-oppressive social work practice. For example, in the case study about Gail, a different approach to the social worker's initial visit would have cost nothing.

Recent social care policy provides support for choice and control for disabled people; however, there is some way to go before this becomes a reality for all. Social workers need to take a broader approach to their professional role, which involves more than processing assessments and support plans. The *Code of Ethics* of the British Association of Social Workers (2012) is grounded in social justice and human rights, and its practice principles include empowering people and challenging discrimination and the abuse of human rights. Social workers should be prepared to promote these principles within their own organizations, but they should also acknowledge the expertise of disabled people and their organizations and be prepared to work with them to promote social justice.

Key messages

- The social relational approach to disability/disablism is a useful tool for identifying oppression, as it highlights both barriers to activity and the psycho-emotional effects of disablism.
- Disabled people are particularly affected by marginalization in key areas of social participation, and this limits their contribution. They are also affected by powerlessness, 'cultural imperialism' and violence, all of which are types of oppression.
- Social work has been seen as part of the problem in spite of its anti-oppressive rhetoric. Professional expertise has been regarded as a barrier to user control and choice.
- However, there is a role for social work in challenging oppression. This will require a willingness to work with disabled people, both individually and collectively, to address the barriers that threaten their social participation and human rights.

Activities

- How has social work been complicit in the oppression of disabled people? Drawing on your experience at work or on placement, can you think of any examples of professional assessment of need taking precedence over individual choice? Do you think this was justified?
- How can social workers intervene to prevent low-level harassment of disabled people from escalating? How can they protect people who have already been victims of violence?

Suggested further reading

Hansbro, J., Shah, P., Uren, Z., Lone, J., Cuciureanu, F., Gifford, G., and Sotiropoulou, N. (2013) *Fulfilling Potential: Building a Deeper Understanding of Disability in the UK Today.* London: Department for Work and Pensions.

Reeve, D. (2014) Psycho-emotional disablism and internalised oppression, in Swain, J., French, S., Barnes, C., and Thomas, C., eds, *Disabling Barriers – Enabling Environments.* 3rd edn, London: Sage.

Roulstone, A., and Mason-Bish, H. (2013) *Disability, Hate Crime and Violence.* Abingdon: Routledge.

6 Disability and Diversity

Issues considered in this chapter:

- The differing experiences among diverse groups of disabled people
- Understanding disability as a category of human diversity
- Disability, diversity and implications for social work practice

Introduction

A defining feature of humanity and human experience is difference, and users of social work services specifically are 'characterised by immense diversity' (Thompson 2006: 170). Consider the people you know, the people you have worked with, or those you may have met on your social work placements, and identify the ways in which they are different. You may have considered factors such as age, gender, social class, race, ethnicity, sexual orientation, language, religion or culture. Such categories of difference, or dimensions of diversity, are many, and therefore the diversity of the population is considered to be multidimensional. Being able to recognize such diversity and consider its impact on the life experiences of service users is a feature of professional social work capability (PCF 3), and professional social work standards in England, Wales and Scotland all refer to the necessity of respecting diversity and understanding its impact on practice (HCPC SoP, 5; Scottish Social Services Council Code of Practice, §1.6; Care Council for Wales Code of Practice, §1.6). Indeed, respect for human diversity is central to the profession, as stated in the global definition of social work approved by the International Federation of Social Work in July 2014. Thompson (2011b) maintains that respecting diversity is a key element of anti-discriminatory practice; referring to the 'diversity approach', he argues that discrimination is challenged by framing human differences as beneficial to society, enriching the communities in which we live, rather than as problems in need of solutions. Valuing diversity is therefore one way, albeit not the only way, to reduce discrimination.

Morris (2011a) suggests that valuing diversity is a key element of any system that seeks to enable disabled people to achieve access to full citizenship. While disability is itself a dimension of diversity, disabled people, just like the rest of the population, are highly diverse. However, this diversity is not always recognized. Physically impaired people have been portrayed as a homogeneous group, reflected in the ubiquitous use of images of the young male wheelchair user as representative of disabled people (Marks 2008). This assumption of homogeneity can be linked to a sole focus on an 'impairment label' (Martin 2011: 17), such as 'wheelchair user' or 'visually impaired', and may result in the denial of a person's individuality. Burton

(2012) argues that such focus results in oppressive practice, as it denies the complexity of people's lives and the impact of multidimensional oppression. Consider the dimensions of diversity and their potential impact on life experiences as you read the following case profile.

Case profile: Claudette

Claudette is a 58-year-old woman who lives in South London. Her parents were originally from St Kitts but came to the UK in the late 1940s. Claudette married when she was twenty-four and had one daughter, Valma. Throughout life, she has experienced periods of moderate to severe pain in her legs and chest as a result of sickle cell disease. More recently, the pain has been exacerbated by the development of arthritis, which has impacted on her mobility, as has some sight impairment linked to her health conditions. Claudette divorced after twenty-three years of marriage and was single for two years before starting a relationship with a man she met through her local Anglican church.

Claudette's impairment characteristics are only one element of who she is. Her gender, race, sexuality, marital status and faith are all key features of her identity. Claudette may consider these characteristics as very important to her sense of identity and not see herself as a 'disabled person'. Indeed, Peters (2000: 583) observes that, for some disabled people, 'disability is not necessarily central to their self-concept'. Diversity in all these dimensions is evident throughout the current UK disabled population. For example, at least 1 million of the UK's 11 million disabled people are from black and minority ethnic (BME) communities (Trotter 2012), and there is a significantly higher incidence of physical impairment among older BME people than among older white people in the same age bracket (Purdam et al. 2008) and higher incidence among those of lower economic status (Miller et al. 2014). Lesbian, gay and bisexual (LGB) people are represented in the disabled population (Debenham 2012; Formby 2012), as are both intersex and transgendered people (Mitchell and Howarth 2009), with some localized studies suggesting that disability among these minority groups reflects the national average (SCIE et al. 2011).

Many disabled people describe having a sense of multiple identity (Purdam et al. 2008; Peters 2000). While Claudette may experience disability throughout her life, her sense of identity is not restricted to that of a 'disabled person'; as a heterosexual, black, Christian woman, her identity is multidimensional. The coexistence of these facets and their impact on life experiences has been termed 'intersectionality' (Barnartt and Mandell 2013) – a concept that is of particular importance to social workers working with disabled people, as they need to understand the ways in which disability intersects with other aspects of people's lives. However, little is known about such intersectionality, as it has not received the same level of research attention as race and gender. Indeed, Harris and Roulstone (2011) observe that the diversity of disabled people generally has lacked examination, even within disability studies. While some studies do exist, issues of gender, sexism and disability, ethnicity, culture and disability, and socio-economic status and disability remain limited in the literature (Thompson 2006; Purdam et al. 2008; Harris and Roulstone 2011; Trotter

2012; Moriarty 2014). Furthermore, Rembis (2010) argues that much disability research has tended to reflect heteronormative notions of sexuality, thus rendering the voices of LGB disabled people absent; Mitchell and Howarth (2009) found that research on the intersection of disability with trans status was almost non-existent.

In order to develop appropriate services, to meet needs effectively, and practise in an anti-discriminatory and anti-oppressive manner, social workers must identify, recognize and value diversity among disabled people. Regrettably, there is limited research exploring the health and social care experiences of diverse groups of disabled people, despite various calls for such studies from, *inter alia*, the Department of Health and local authorities (Orme 2002; DoH 2007a; Mitchell and Howarth 2009; Diversity Trust et al. 2012).

Diverse people, diverse experiences

Unacknowledged and unrecognized diversity

Vernon (1999) and Harris and Roulstone (2011) highlight the fact that the multiple dimensions of diversity impact on people's experience of disability. For example, the impact of the life course on the experience of disability has already been outlined in chapter 3. Therefore, best practice demands that social workers avoid an approach to working with disabled people that focuses solely on impairment characteristics and instead explore what Orme (2002: 10) terms the 'multiplicity of experiences' of those using their services. However, as noted in the introduction to this chapter, the diversity of disabled people can often go unrecognized or unacknowledged. For example, Priestley (2014) observes that, for many disabled children and young people, their impairment characteristics take precedence in terms of their attributed identity over their gender, ethnicity, sexual orientation and class. The gender identity of disabled adults can also be overlooked or marginalized. Morris (1993a) describes the construction of disabled women needing care as 'non-women' by feminists challenging the 'burden of care' placed on female members of the family, while Abbott et al. (2014), in their study of the experiences of disabled men, identified that social care services did little to acknowledge the impact of gender in planning, assessment or the delivery of care and support. They describe disabled men as being 'de-gendered' by social care services, which 'seem to be completely gender-less – it's not even gender neutral, because gender's not even in there.... I think the actual impact of social care can be incredibly emasculating' (disabled man, quoted in Abbott et al., 2014: 3).

Sexuality and sexual orientation are also dimensions of diversity that can be overshadowed. An assumption of asexuality has been ascribed to both disabled men and women (Rembis 2010; Higgins et al. 2012; Abbott et al. 2014) – an assumption that is made not only in the context of sexual identity but also in the expression of that identity, as captured candidly in the following observation of one disabled mother: 'It's even shown up by how disabled loos don't have condom machines – as though disabled people won't have sex!' (cited in CSCI 2009: 25).

When a disabled person's sexual self is acknowledged, research suggests that there is often an assumption of heterosexuality (Rembis 2010; Debenham 2012) and the Department of Health (2007a) acknowledges that disabled people's desire for or involvement in same-sex relationships goes largely unrecognized and unsupported.

As a result, disabled LGB people can experience poor access to sexual health services, support and information.

Multiple minorities, multiple oppression

Understanding the experiences of diverse groups of disabled people is complex. Concepts such as 'multiple minority group status' and 'intersectionality' have been used to describe the relationship between different dimensions of identity (Harris and Roulstone 2011; Barnartt and Mandell 2013), yet it can prove difficult to determine whether experiences are linked to one particular dimension or the interaction of such statuses (Mitchell et al. 2013). In relation to discriminatory experiences, some disabled people describe an 'amplification' effect where one '-ism' amplifies the adverse effects of another (Thompson 2006) – for example, racism exacerbating the impact of disabilism. A reciprocal relationship between disability and migration status is noted by Trotter (2012: 30), who observes that 'being a migrant affects the experience of being disabled … [and] being disabled … alters the experience of migration.' Other disabled people describe being marginalized or discriminated against on the basis of more than one characteristic, an experience disabled people from BME communities have called a 'double bind' (Trotter 2012) and LGB disabled people have labelled a 'double coming out' (Debenham 2012; DoH 2007a). While such experiences can be conceptualized as 'double' or 'simultaneous' oppression, Dupré (2012) argues that it is important to recognize that oppressed people are rarely oppressed on the basis of one dimension; seeking to separate out such experiences may oversimplify the effect they have on disabled people's lives. Social workers should be aware of the current legal framework for equality, which acknowledges this intersectionality by bringing all protected characteristics within a single piece of legislation (the Equality Act 2010) and enabling people to bring discrimination cases on multiple grounds.

Diverse groups of disabled people experience simultaneous oppression and discrimination in a number of ways. While significant numbers live in poverty, financial hardship is a particular challenge for disabled people from BME communities (Trotter 2012), and, in their study of the effects of austerity on LGB people, Mitchell et al. (2013) observe that *disabled* LGB people are particularly adversely affected. This group has also been identified as more at risk of homelessness (Debenham 2012) and more likely to have experienced hostility, victimization and hate crime than non-disabled LGB people (Guasp et al. 2013). Disabled women have particular challenges in the world of paid employment compared to non-disabled women (Harris and Roulstone 2011), and there is evidence that disabled people from BME communities are less likely to be employed than white disabled people (Purdam et al. 2008). Disabled women and BME people also experience greater levels of hostility (Rembis 2010). These issues of inequality and discrimination, explored further in chapter 5, reflect a diverse experience of disability and disabilism.

Some disabled people occupying multiple minority statuses report feeling isolated from their own communities. The isolation can be twofold. For example, some disabled LGBT people have described feeling excluded by the LGBT community owing to impairment and by the disability community owing to being LGBT (Formby 2012). In addition to a lack of acceptance, isolation may be a result of discrimination or limited access to peer support and community spaces. For instance, Asian disabled people, particularly women, have highlighted low levels of available peer support and inaccessible community and religious spaces (Vernon 2002), and LGBT disabled people describe difficulty in meeting each other and accessing the 'gay scene' (DoH 2007a; Formby 2012). Disabled women have also been marginalized from broader women's movements (Hague et al. 2007). However, intersectional analysis of their experience has identified the disproportionate impact of disability on women in comparison to men. Some of these experiences have been noted above; Milner and O'Byrne (2009) add that disabled women are more likely than disabled men to have lower self-esteem and poor self-image and are less likely than disabled men to enter rewarding intimate relationships. There is also evidence that disabled women are more likely to be victims of domestic violence than non-disabled women (see chapter 10). Social workers must be alert to such individual experiences to ensure they identify the *particular* barriers faced by individual disabled people.

In addition to isolation from their own communities, diverse groups of disabled people may face barriers accessing mainstream 'disability services' and services aimed at particular groups. For example, Trotter (2012) highlights both a shortage of culturally appropriate disability services and a range of BME community-specific services that are inaccessible to disabled people. This reflects the experiences of some adults ageing with disability, who report that disability services fail to meet their needs as older people, while older person's services present as inaccessible (Göransson 2008) (see chapter 3). In such situations there is a clear risk that people from marginalized groups will fall between the gaps in service provision (Harris and Roulstone 2011), resulting in high levels of unmet need among such groups (Manthorpe 2013). This situation should be of concern to social workers, as it is evident in health and social care provision; disabled people's experiences of such services are now considered.

Diversity and the experience of health and social care services

There is limited research literature exploring the health and social care experiences of diverse groups of disabled people. However, some studies have explored the experiences of LGBT and BME disabled people and disabled women. This research tends to reveal a picture of dissatisfaction with services.

Case profile: Anesh

Anesh is a 32-year-old man who lives in a two-bedroomed bungalow with his uncle and aunt. Anesh has arthrogryposis multiplex congenita, a rare condition resulting in physical impairment. He needs some support with personal care, which is usually provided by his uncle. Anesh uses a wheelchair to mobilize both indoors and outdoors. While he finds that inaccessible public transport impacts on his ability to meet up with his small circle of close friends, he prefers to make use of public transport, finding taxis too expensive and preferring not to ask 'too much of his uncle'. Anesh describes himself as a Hindu; although he rarely engages in organized religious activity, his faith is of cultural and spiritual importance to him. He came out as gay to his friends five years ago but has decided not to disclose his sexuality to his uncle and aunt.

Difficulties accessing health and social care services have been reported by disabled people in both BME (Trotter 2012) and LGB communities (Debenham 2012). In part, this may be the result of a lack of information. Anesh does not like asking 'too much of his uncle'; services from, or organized by, his local authority adult social care team could resolve this situation, yet Anesh may lack information on those to which he may be entitled. In her study of the social care experiences of twenty-eight Asian disabled young adults, Vernon (2002) observed that many lacked information about their potential entitlement to services and how to access them. This lack of information was not related to poor or absent translation of material into minority languages, as most of the participants were English speakers, but it did result in low awareness and limited use of services such as direct payments (see chapter 9). Low uptake of direct payments among BME disabled people has been observed in later studies (Purdam et al. 2008; Moriarty 2014). There is also evidence that LGB disabled people lack adequate information on sexual health services and safer sex (DoH 2007a). This may impact on Anesh's expression of sexual identity and his general well-being, particularly when combined with poor access to 'gay social spaces' and limited availability of peer support.

BME and LGBT disabled people who are accessing health and social care services have expressed dissatisfaction (Debenham 2012; Brawn et al. 2013); for some in the transgender community, this has been described as 'severe dissatisfaction' (Hines 2007: 466). The research suggests various reasons for such discontent. BME disabled people, including children, have reported the experience of discrimination when using social care services (Marchant and Page 2003), as have LGBT disabled people (SCIE et al. 2011). Such discrimination may be direct or the result of assumptions being made on the basis of cultural stereotypes. For example, assumptions about Asian families preferring and being able to 'look after their own' may have contributed to Anesh's dependence on his uncle and aunt for support. Such assumptions appear commonplace, yet are not supported by research findings (Katbamna et al. 2004; Trotter 2012). In the words of one BME disabled adult, 'when we go and ask for extra support they say no, you can do it yourself, and it's because you're from an Asian background so they think you've got close family, an extended family who can look after them' (cited in Trotter 2012: 29).

Alternatively, Anesh may have actively rejected any social care services offered, finding them inappropriate for his particular needs. While to some extent BME and LGBT disabled adults' social care needs are no different from those of the wider disabled population, concerns have been raised regarding cultural sensitivity in social care provision that has tended to focus on impairment category (Harris and Roulstone 2011; Trotter 2012). Issues such as religious obligations, dietary requirements and lifestyle experiences are at risk of being neglected or overshadowed where a 'one size fits all' model of social care is adopted (Vernon 2002; Brother 2003; Hines 2007; Mitchell and Howarth 2009; Harris and Roulstone 2011).

Negative experiences of, and suboptimal support from, health and social care services have led not only to higher levels of unmet need among those occupying multiple minority statuses (Marchant and Page 2003; Diversity Trust et al. 2012; Miller et al. 2014) but also to a lack of confidence and trust in service provision. Anesh may be concerned about service providers' response to his sexual orientation, particularly as he has made the decision not to be 'out' to his uncle and aunt.

Indeed, Guasp (2012) observed that disabled LGB people were more likely than non-disabled LGB people to fear poor treatment in hospitals, in care homes and by domiciliary care workers: 'Would I be comfortable in a nursing home as an openly gay man? Who knows!' (37-year-old disabled gay man, cited in Diversity Trust et al. 2012: 2).

The social workers' role is therefore not limited to addressing the particular barriers faced by diverse groups of disabled people but includes rebuilding trust and confidence in those who have had poor experiences when using such services. Trotter (2012) suggests that one way to restore confidence and trust is to increase the visibility of both services and diverse groups of disabled people in particular communities. This can be achieved through the dissemination of accessible information about services (translated into community languages), outreach activity and the inclusion of images of diverse disabled people in service leaflets, publications and posters (Guasp 2012; Trotter 2012).

Disability as a category of human diversity

Olkin (2002: 136) argues that 'disability will have to board the diversity train' if the oppression of disabled people is to be challenged – in other words, that disability itself needs to be recognized as a category of human diversity. The classification of disability as such is acknowledged in legislation (for example, the Equality Act 2010) and in the work of the Equality and Human Rights Commission, which is tasked with addressing the seven 'strands' of equality: gender, gender identity, race, sexual orientation, religion or belief, age *and* disability. The UN Convention on the Rights of Persons with Disabilities also acknowledges disability as a part of human diversity in the statement of general principles (Article 3(d)). While those occupying minority statuses may share the experience of prejudice and discrimination (Orme 2002), recognition of disability as a category of diversity suggests a particular commonality among disabled people (Olkin 2002). Such a feeling of commonality and common identity is highlighted by Peters (2000) in her examination of disability culture. However, unlike other dimensions of diversity, such as race and gender, disability is arguably universal in nature. Sapey (2002) observes that anyone can experience disability at some point in their lives; indeed, McRuer (2006) argues that the experience of being disabled is inevitable for all who live long enough, a point captured by the disability campaigner, author and comedian Francesca Martinez (2104) in her description of non-disabled people as the 'not yet disabled'. The conceptualization of disability as a universal human experience is also evident in the principles of the World Health Organization's International Classification of Functioning, Disability and Health. In the words of the deafblind essayist, poet and braille instructor John Lee Clark (2014: 81): 'Disability is everywhere. It is, in fact, universal, for to be human is to be disabled.'

Conceptualizing disability as a universal human experience mirrors the affirmative model (see chapter 2) and is arguably a positive perspective for social workers to adopt. Acknowledging the power of 'othering attitudes' in creating social exclusion, often realized through segregated disability services, Martin (2011) observes that this 'universal experience' perspective challenges the notion of disabled people as 'the other'. Furthermore, Zola (2005: 20) suggests that it serves to 'demystify the specialness of disability': disabled people are no longer seen as a group of 'different' people with 'special' needs but, rather, as people with the same rights as the rest of the population. The UK Supreme Court has recently confirmed the universal nature of these rights in the context of determining what amounts to a deprivation of liberty for a disabled person (*Cheshire West and Chester Council* v. *P 2014 UKSC 19*).

Recognition of 'disability' as a normal and, indeed, positive feature of human diversity, a move away from segregated services, and a focus on universal rights can certainly be considered features of positive social work practice. However, Thompson (2011b) and Roulstone (2012) add an important caveat to concentrating solely on this 'diversity approach', noting that the significant structural oppression and power imbalances faced by many disabled people may be overshadowed or downplayed. Furthermore, disability as a dimension of diversity is dissimilar to other dimensions in various ways, and the nature of disablist oppression is different to that experienced by other minority groups (Dupré 2012). For example, Olkin (2002) observes that, unlike people from BME communities, disabled people are often living within a 'non-disabled family'; this experience of being 'the only one' may increase feelings of 'otherness' and isolation but also renders the family less able to support the disabled person to address the particular challenges of that multiple minority status. Indeed, Olkin argues that, for some disabled people, the understanding, attitudes and behaviours of family members may be part of the challenge. Although they share his ethnic, cultural and religious status, Anesh's aunt and uncle do not share his experience of disability and may adopt dominant medical or individual models in their response to his situation, or even perpetuate a sense of stigma in relation to his physical impairments and disability experience. While it is not unique to BME communities, stigma was identified by BME disabled participants in Trotter's (2012) focus groups as particularly problematic. Social workers must identify and sensitively challenge such attitudes in Anesh's situation, as they function as barriers to his social inclusion just as much as the inaccessible public transport.

Though disability can be considered a universal human experience, diversity in this experience is further evident when one acknowledges that disability is also culturally constructed and defined (Ingstad and Whyte 1995). Indeed, Trotter (2012: 16) observes that, for some cultural and ethnic groups, 'disability is an alien concept'. Not all embodied difference is perceived as disabling by all peoples; Marks (2008) offers the example of foot-binding in pre-Revolutionary China, an act that resulted in walking difficulties, but one seen as aesthetically desired, not disabling. Moving beyond specific cultural definitions of disability and observing cross-cultural similarity, Peters (2000: 3) argues that there is clear evidence of a 'thriving disability culture'. While it has been suggested that 'disability culture' and the 'disability community' is centred on political activism and campaigning (Davidson-Pain and Corbett 1995), Peters (2000) refers to disabled sports clubs, the disability press, disability studies scholastic communities, and the disability arts and film movement to highlight that political activities are not the sole endeavour of the disability community. Social workers can value diversity when working with disabled people by acknowledging and supporting this disability culture, as it offers a powerful counter-narrative to more dominant portrayals of disability that reflect deficit-based models (Dupré 2012).

Diversity, disability and social work practice

The Health and Care Professions Council (HCPC) recently revised their guidance for disabled applicants seeking to register as health and social care professionals. They note that having a physical impairment will not prevent registration and should not be a barrier to professional practice. However, disabled practitioners are under-represented in the social work profession; barriers in accessing and gaining professional social work qualifications and inaccessible social work agency environments are undoubtedly causal factors (Sapey et al. 2004; Marks 2008). Furthermore, Olkin (2002) observes that language is powerful in constructing disabled people as *them* (service users) and not *us* (professionals). Reflect on your own thoughts when choosing to read this text, entitled *Social Work and Disability*. Did you consider disabled social workers, disabled social work students or disabled social care workers? Or did you picture disabled people only as service users? While disabled people are under-represented in the profession, many 'informal' carers are themselves disabled, despite use of the simplistic categorization of people as either 'carer' or 'cared for'. Milne et al. (2014) note that, in relation to older disabled people, such basic distinctions rarely reflect the reality of people's lives. Studies of the experiences of disabled social work students exist, yet less is known about the experiences of disabled qualified social workers (Sapey et al. 2004; Stanley et al. 2007; Sin and Fong 2009). Disabled social workers may experience greater pressure to conform to non-disabled norms of performance in the statutory sector, where standardization and intensification of work can increase the feelings of vulnerability of anyone perceived to be less productive. This is particularly the case for social workers with invisible impairments, who can experience challenges both to their status as disabled people and to the validity of any adjustments made for them (Castle 2007). For those entering the profession, one of the most challenging barriers can be the attitude of non-disabled social workers; for some social workers with invisible impairments, hostility from colleagues can lead to social isolation and distressing psycho-emotional effects, while some whose impairments are visible have complained of the overprotective attitudes of colleagues (ibid.). This suggests not only a failure to value diversity in the workforce but also a lack of recognition of the strengths and attributes disabled practitioners can bring to social work services, including direct experience of the impact of disabling barriers.

Valuing diversity and difference

In order to recognize, respect and value diversity in practice, social workers need to adopt a person-centred approach; every disabled service user is different and each situation is different. Indeed, in the words of disabled lawyer Prue Hawkins (2014), 'when you are dealing with something as diverse as the issue of disability, a blanket rule is simply not appropriate. One size indeed does not fit all.'

For each individual service user, social workers must pay careful attention not only to disabling barriers and the impact of impairment but also to other dimensions of diversity and the ways in which these intersect with disability. This necessitates a good understanding of the 'dynamics of difference' (Dupré 2012: 170). There is some evidence that the particular needs of some groups of disabled people, such as those who identify as transgender, remain largely unknown among practitioners

(Hines 2007), and therefore social workers have a responsibility to develop their knowledge of the particular needs of specific groups. However, while such knowledge offers a broad understanding of the experiences of diverse groups of disabled people, Thompson (2006) warns against applying it to practice in an inflexible or rigid way. Making assumptions about the needs of disabled people on the basis of broad knowledge about issues related to their race, gender, sexual orientation, or any other dimension of diversity can result in a failure to acknowledge their uniqueness as individuals. Social workers need a nuanced understanding of diversity and must acknowledge that the needs and preferences of particular groups are rarely universal. For example, while assumptions may be made about Muslim women preferring female support workers, in Trotter's (2012) study, one disabled Muslim woman describes how, for her, the personality of the support workers is more important than their gender. Avoiding assumptions and cultural stereotypes is therefore essential, as they too can act as a barrier to desired services (Vernon 2002).

A nuanced understanding of diversity is not in itself sufficient for best practice. Social workers need to acknowledge the different dimensions of disabled people's lives in practical ways. Vernon (2002) observes that acknowledging disabled people's cultural and religious identities by organizing the provision of appropriate meals (for example, vegetarian, Halal or Kosher food) or facilitating access to space for prayer/worship can go a long way in restoring their confidence in social care services. Disabled people's sexual identities can also be acknowledged by ensuring issues relating to sexuality are discussed during social work assessments. Bywater and Jones (2007) highlight that it is important for such discussions to go beyond consideration of the impact of impairment on sexual technique; they suggest that social workers also explore the psychological, relationship and emotional dimensions of sex. A study by Abbott and his colleagues identified that disabled men would value such discussions: 'it would be good in general, in the care industry, if they thought about these things more. Things about sex ... Relationship things. It might be just me, and if I did talk about it, it would be fine' (disabled man, cited in Abbott et al. 2014: 3). In discussing sexuality in assessments, social workers must also acknowledge that some disabled people are LGB. Debenham (2012) suggests that such recognition is an essential first step in supporting LGB disabled service users; it rejects the perception of disabled people as asexual and affirms diversity in their sexual orientation and expression.

Cultural, religious and sexual identities can be sensitive albeit important elements of assessment, and such discussions and practical interventions are therefore best facilitated in the context of supportive professional relationships. Indeed, Manthorpe (2013: 1) refers to research identifying such relationships as 'key'. Furthermore, Trotter (2012) observes that diverse groups of disabled people do not differ in their preference for positive, trusting relationships, and that cultural and religious needs are more likely to be met in this context. In seeking to assess and meet diverse needs, social workers should be mindful not to overlook the more uniform need for supportive relationships and essential care and support.

Seeing the whole person

While it is important to acknowledge and explore the different dimensions of disabled service users' identities, social workers should not fragment or 'unpick' their identities into discrete units. As Thompson (2006) observes, dimensions of diversity are part of the dimensions of lived experience *as a whole* rather than a series of unconnected aspects of life, and therefore they need to be understood as such. Indeed, 'unraveling people's identities is rarely a fruitful way to proceed' (Harris and Roulstone 2011: 98). Social workers therefore need to consider the whole person, and the whole of their lives, in their own specific context (Marks 2008). Failure to do so results not only in the risk that areas of need will be overlooked or misunderstood but also that a hierarchy of oppression will be perpetuated (Coulshed and Orme 2012). However, Coulshed and Orme observe that maintaining a focus on the 'whole person' can be challenging owing to the very way in which social care services are organized by 'service-user category', requiring people to identify their 'dominant area of need'; this area of need is based solely on service-user 'group' (old age, disability, mental health problems, looked after child, and so on) rather than on holistic lived experience.

The think tank brap (2011) suggests that adopting a human rights approach can be beneficial in professional practice centred on the *whole person*, with its emphasis on universal rights rather than the identification of need based on a single aspect of identity. Such an approach also dismantles any hierarchy of oppression and enables equality disputes, perhaps between service user and carer or service user and directly employed personal assistant, to be resolved. Focus on the *shared* experience of marginalization and minority status among different groups of people can also serve to deconstruct a hierarchy of oppression; the coming together of those occupying minority status has been observed to better challenge oppression (Peters 2000). As such, there have been calls for disabled people to form allegiances and collaborative partnerships with groups of BME people and sexual minorities (Rembis 2010). Social workers can act as allies to these partnerships and use their professional power constructively to support them.

Valuing diversity through increased choice and control

The provision of segregated disability-specific services can result in a process of 'othering' disabled people, and therefore social workers should work in partnership with disabled people to remove the barriers that prevent access to mainstream services. Increasing the accessibility of universal services is considered a key element of the personalization of social care systems (DoH 2007b). Furthermore, when undertaking needs assessments, social workers must explore the extent to which such existing community services can contribute to meeting needs and desired outcomes as part of the wider duty on local authorities under the Care Act 2014 to prevent, reduce or delay needs. However, Moriarty (2014) observes that access to mainstream services may not be a desired outcome for, *inter alia*, people from LGBT or BME communities, who may feel disadvantaged by them. Indeed, some LGBT people fear discrimination and prejudice within mainstream provision and therefore prefer LGBT-specific services (SCIE et al. 2011; Mitchell et al. 2013); Hines (2007) observes that, for trans disabled people, care was almost always provided from within an individual's own social circle. Social workers must therefore identify and challenge barriers to accessing specialist but non-disability services in addition to those affecting mainstream services.

Diverse groups of disabled people may also prefer to make use of services aimed at promoting choice and control, such as personal budgets and direct payments (see chapter 9). For example, Asian disabled people participating in Vernon's (2002) study valued direct payments as a means of increasing their choice and control over service provision, as they were enabled to employ personal assistants who shared their cultural and religious identities. LGBT disabled people may also use direct payments to employ personal assistants from the LGBT community or to fund 'gay friendly' care and support services (DoH2007a; SCIE et al. 2011). However, in order for such choices to be realized, services that can meet the particular needs of diverse groups of disabled people need to be available. There have certainly been calls for greater collaboration between social care providers and LGBT support groups (Debenham 2012) and groups of Asian disabled people (Vernon 2002) to develop such assistance. Collaboration with black-led user groups has facilitated culturally sensitive support planning and better outcomes for disabled people from BME communities (Harris and Roulstone 2011; Trotter 2012). Moriarty (2014) observes that such organizations are key to enabling such people to benefit from personalized services. Social workers can play an active role in working with disabled people and community organizations to co-design and co-produce such services and can act as coordinators and facilitators of such collaborations.

Being able to employ staff with shared characteristics is not the only benefit of services such as direct payments and personal budgets. The increased sense of control that they can offer disabled people (Hatton and Waters 2013; Waters and Hatton 2014) can be positive in its own right. Such increased control can be particularly important for disabled women, who may experience a lack of control over their lives owing to societal expectations that they should play a dependent role (Thompson 2006). Disabled men have also described how an increased sense of control over care and support services validates their gender identity or sense of 'feeling like a man' (Abbott et al. 2014: 3).

Conclusion

Human experience is characterized by multidimensional diversity, and recognizing, respecting and valuing this diversity is core to best social work practice. Disabled people are undoubtedly a highly diverse population; however, their diversity is not always acknowledged and, as such, they can be portrayed as a homogeneous group: 'the disabled'. Research identifies that disability is experienced differently by diverse groups of people, characterized by the way in which dimensions such as gender, race and sexual orientation intersect with 'disability'. Many disabled people occupying multiple minority statuses describe the experience of simultaneous oppression and also report dissatisfaction with health and social care services. Such dissatisfaction is related both to a lack of information about and poor access to services and to the experience of discrimination when using services. Disabled people have also reported that health and social care services have not met their needs appropriately, as they have focused on their 'impairment category' rather than responding to needs related to other aspects of their identity.

Social workers can value diversity in the context of work with disabled people by developing a nuanced understanding of difference; this involves acknowledging the different needs of diverse groups, such as LGBT and BME disabled people, while simultaneously acknowledging that the preferences of such groups are rarely universal. Social workers should explore the various dimensions of service users' identities in assessments and not concentrate solely on the impact of impairment, but they must do so in a way that sees the person as a 'whole'; adopting a human rights approach can support such practice. Social workers should also explore the opportunities that services such as personal budgets and direct payments can offer – for example, the prospect of employing personal assistants with shared characteristics and having a sense of increased control.

Key messages

- Disabled people are not a homogeneous group but, rather, a highly diverse population; this diversity can go unrecognized and unacknowledged, resulting in service delivery that fails to meet needs appropriately.
- Diverse groups of people experience disability differently and therefore may present with different needs. Social workers must not focus solely on impairment characteristics but should explore the impact of intersectionality.
- Disabled people occupying multiple minority statuses can encounter simultaneous oppression. Social workers can act as allies to partnerships of those with a shared experience of marginalization to challenge this oppression.
- Conceptualizing disability as a universal characteristic and feature of human diversity can challenge the process of the 'othering' of disabled people. However, social workers must remain mindful of the significant structural oppression and power imbalances faced by many disabled people.

Activities

- Revisit chapter 1 and identify the different dimensions of Helen's identity. How do these characteristics impact on her experiences and how would they inform your interventions?
- How could the approaches considered in this chapter inform best practice with Claudette and Anesh?
- Develop your knowledge of disability culture by exploring the work of disabled artists, filmmakers, poets, writers and comedians. Contact your local user-led disability organization for more details.

Suggested further reading

Barnartt, S. N., and Mandell, B. (2013) *Disability and Intersecting Statuses*. Bingley: Emerald.

Dupré, M. (2012) Disability culture and cultural competency in social work, *Social Work Education: The International Journal*, 31(2): 168–83.

Thompson, N. (2011) *Promoting Equality: Working with Diversity and Difference*. 3rd edn, Basingstoke: Palgrave Macmillan.

PART III

DISABILITY AND SOCIAL WORK PRACTICE

7 Communication and Engagement

Issues considered in this chapter:

- The importance of communication skills in social work
- Psycho-social issues arising from language and communication needs, their relationship with social exclusion, and their implications for social work practice
- How communication needs can be met, including use of assistive technology and multidisciplinary work with other professionals

Introduction

Communication is a fundamental component of human existence. As Morris (2014a) suggests, it is 'at the heart of being human'. Most activities in our everyday lives involve language and communication, whether enacted linguistically or otherwise, intentional or not. We are used to thinking of communication as being achieved primarily through language. Although language is the most complex communicative tool at our disposal, communication also relies on other means. Among these are body language, the way we dress, and physical contact. It is often the case that these work alongside language to achieve meaning and establish communication. Communication goes beyond the mere transmission of information between people and enables us to express our feelings, needs and desires, to develop our identity, to form and sustain relationships with others, and to maintain quality of life (Luna et al. 2002; Hodge 2007; Goldbart and Caton 2010; Communication Trust 2011). In this sense, communication is connected to the enjoyment of core human rights.

Good communication skills are central to positive social work practice. The necessity of effective communication is evident across all domains of the Professional Capabilities Framework but is specifically mentioned in 'intervention and skills' (Domain 7). Being able to communicate successfully is also noted as key in the HCPC Standards of Proficiency (SoP 8), the Scottish Code of Practice for Social Service Workers and Employers (Section 2.2) and the Welsh Code of Practice for Social Care Workers (Section 2.2). Strong communication skills enable social workers to engage and form positive working relationships with service users, carers, families and colleagues (Egan 2010; Baxter and Glendinning 2011), address sensitive issues and respond to conflict and distress (Thompson 2011a), disseminate knowledge about the social care system and options such as direct payments (Baxter and Glendinning 2011), and promote dignity in social care settings (Manthorpe et al. 2012). Supportive communication also supports safeguarding; Morris (2014a) observes that Serious Case Reviews and reports concerning poor and abusive practices in health and social care settings often highlight that service users were denied their right of communication.

A person's communication may be affected by illness or impairment, which can present a particular challenge to social workers in this field. For example, Parkinson's disease, stroke and head injury can impact on both verbal expression and a person's understanding of written and spoken communication; cerebral palsy may affect speech; and conditions such as motor neurone disease can affect speech and facial expression as a result of weakening in the mouth, throat and chest muscles and vocal cords. Sensory impairments, particularly deafblindness and dual sensory loss, also impact on communication. According to the Communication Trust (2011), as many as 10 per cent of all children have long-term speech, language and communication needs, some of which are linked to physical impairment. However, it would be wrong to assume that the challenges to communication are solely the result of impairment. Disabling barriers to effective communication include a failure to meet communication needs, a lack of skill, knowledge or communicative ability on the part of the practitioner, or a failure to make reasonable adjustments, including the provision of interpreters. As Thompson (2011a) highlights, where communication is challenging, practitioners must reflect on the question of whose difficulty it is. He goes on to argue that negative assumptions about the value of what disabled people have to say and consequent propensity to speak on their behalf are the most significant barriers to effective communication. Morris (2014a) challenges us to consider how we would feel if we were consistently ignored when we spoke or communicated for ourselves and reminds practitioners of their responsibility to recognize what is being communicated.

Various textbooks offer more detailed guidance on effective communication and analysis of the theoretical underpinning of communication skills (see, for example, Egan 2010; Thompson 2011a; Koprowska 2014). This chapter does not seek to offer comprehensive coverage of such issues; instead, it considers the impact that language use and communication needs have on disabled people and outlines a positive social work response. Acknowledging that communication is more than the transfer of information in written and spoken forms, the chapter starts by considering the power of language in the context of social work with disabled people.

Language, disability and social work

As a means by which we understand ourselves, our experiences and the world we live in, language is inherently powerful. It is a tool that has been successfully used to further the work of social groups (Kelly 2011), and Peters (2000) observes that disabled people globally have kept a careful eye on the use of language in the media, academic publications and political speech. While constructive use of language is key to the development of positive working relationships, Thompson (2011a: 63) highlights that it can also 'be used to attack and destroy, to belittle, undermine ... [and] incite hatred'; he adds that poor communication can result in discriminatory and oppressive practice. A survey conducted in 2014 by the Anti-Bullying Trust identified that one in ten adults has used discriminatory language in everyday conversation and aimed abusive language at disabled people (National Children's Bureau 2014). The survey found that linguistic terms such as 'spaz', 'spastic' and 'mong' were used by

44 per cent of adults in informal everyday conversation and considered by some as mere 'banter'. Regular use of such terms has normalized this language, and Lauren Seager-Smith (national coordinator of the Anti-Bullying Alliance) argues that this has perpetuated the bullying of disabled people, particularly disabled children. Disablism in language is similarly evident in comedy, where disabled people are often portrayed as 'less than' the non-disabled population in ways that go without public challenge or critique (Martin 2011).

Language has also been used, whether intentionally or not, in ways that dehumanize disabled people. In what he describes as a 'downgrading of human life', Monbiot (2014) gives the example of the term 'stock' being used during parliamentary debates about welfare reform by Lord Freud and the Department of Work and Pensions to describe disabled people. Terms such as 'wheelchair bound' and 'special needs' are also frequently used, yet understandably viewed as degrading, patronizing and dehumanizing (Peters 2000; Olkin 2002). What impact do you consider use of such language has on disabled people's emotional and psychological well-being? While it certainly reflects a lack of respect (Thompson 2011a), it also undoubtedly contributes to the experience of psycho-emotional disablism (Reeve 2008) explored in chapters 2 and 9, and in some cases it may be indicative of hate crime (see chapters 5 and 9).

However, it is not just explicitly discriminatory or oppressive language that can impact on positive practice. The language used to define and describe social work is itself an aspect of practice; social workers should be aware that the language they use reflects their assumptions, the model of disability informing their practice, and the nature of the practitioner–service user relationship being developed and sustained (Hawkins et al. 2001; Olkin 2002; Thompson 2011a). The language we use indicates the view of the world we adopt and informs the way we establish and maintain identities (Hawkins et al. 2001). Any attempt for practice to be informed by the social model of disability is compromised when social workers use language that reflects individual or medical models, such as 'suffering with' or 'people with disabilities'. This latter term is rejected by the UK disability movement (and, more recently, the US disability movement) as it locates the disability with the person rather than as the result of externally imposed barriers (Olkin 2002). However, a study of language use among experienced social workers identified high levels of 'medical model' language in their discourse with and about disabled people (Hawkins et al. 2001). Such language not only locates the 'problem' with the person rather than with society (impacting on the quality of the assessment, the nature of intervention and, potentially, the self-esteem of the service user) but also perpetuates notions of deviance and undesired difference. These notions are central to the construction of disabled people as 'them' and professionals as 'us', a key feature of 'othering' (Martin 2011; Olkin 2002). This is further exacerbated by the frequent use of professional jargon, which distances the practitioner from the service user (Hawkins et al. 2001). Both approaches lead to discriminatory and oppressive practice.

A further example is the uncritical use of the terms 'care' or 'caring for'. Kelly (2011) maintains that such terms have oppressive legacies, which stem from their association with lives that were controlled and institutionalized. The terms 'personal assistance' or 'support' are preferred, as they acknowledge the control and agency of disabled people and are therefore more empowering. Such terms are evident in personalized models of social care, explored in chapter 9.

While language change in practice is immediately possible, it is clearly important for social workers to reflect critically on their own use of language and to ensure that it 'supports the ideals' espoused by the profession (Hawkins et al. 2001: 1) (PCF Domain 6). This can be a complex task. For example, Kelly (2011) refers to the proliferation of terms used to describe social care support, including 'support work', 'personal assistance' and 'attendant care', and the challenge the practitioner has in determining appropriate terminology. Furthermore, Trotter (2012) highlights the challenge of selecting apposite linguistic terminology in the context of social work practice with those who have different cultural understandings of disability. For example, Mandarin speakers have no word that translates directly as 'disability' but, rather, a variety of impairment-specific terminology (Partridge 2013); this poses a challenge to social workers seeking to reflect a distinction between impairment and disability, as adopted in the social model, and highlights the importance of sensitivity to both linguistic *and* cultural diversity (PCF 3).

A useful and empowering starting point is being sensitive to the terms disabled people use themselves and ensuring that they have the 'final word' on preferred terminology (Kelly 2011; Martin 2011), even where this does not reflect the world view of the worker. In doing so, social workers must be mindful of 'insider' and 'outsider' terms. For example, while the disability movement has reclaimed for itself formerly derogatory terms, such as 'crip', their use among 'outsiders' could be perceived as highly offensive (Olkin 2002; Peters 2000).

Psycho-social issues, communication and disability

Thompson (2011a) argues that acquiring a set of practical skills is not in itself sufficient to establish successful communication; social workers need to reflect on the wider psycho-social and political concerns relating to communication-based needs. As you read the following two case profiles, consider how wider issues relating to communication may be impacting on the lives of Kate and Joel.

Case profile: Kate

Kate is twenty-two years old and lives with her parents and younger sister, Eliza. Kate has cerebral palsy, which affects all of her limbs and her speech. She is a wheelchair user and has an electronic communication aid which she finds difficult and tiring to use; her sister often talks over her or completes her sentences. Seeking to gain increased independence from her parents, Kate has directly employed her own personal assistant, Maya, who is from Poland and has come to the UK only recently. She has also joined a community group concerned with environmental issues but finds the meetings difficult to join in with owing to the pace of the discussions.

Case profile: Joel

Joel is an eleven-year-old boy who lives with his foster carers, Shonitta and Dalton. Joel is visually impaired and has other communication and language difficulties. Shonitta is also visually impaired. Joel attends mainstream school and has additional support from a teacher for the visually impaired. He also attends a group for 'looked after' children organized by a local children's charity but does not appear to enjoy this. Shonitta and Dalton have regular meetings with their social worker but have recently felt excluded from the decisions that are being made about Joel's situation.

Social isolation and limited participation

Communication is key to establishing, developing and maintaining personal relationships, a quality social life, and engagement in civic participation (Parrott and Madoc-Jones 2008; Mackenzie et al. 2011). As such, communication and social inclusion are intrinsically linked. However, research suggests that those with communication impairments experience high levels of marginalization from social life and lack opportunities to develop positive personal relationships. For example, Koprowska (2014) observes that those with hearing impairments are often excluded from group activities owing to the difficulties in following group conversation, while Göransson (2008), Butler (2009) and Bodsworth et al. (2011) all highlight high levels of social isolation among deafblind people. Mackenzie et al. (2011) found that those with communication impairments such as aphasia had particularly reduced levels of engagement not only in social and leisure activities but also in education and civic participation. Furthermore, despite legal rights under the Children Act 1989, the Children Act 2004 and Article 13 of the Convention on the Rights of the Child, as well as clear policy intentions (see, for example, DoH and DfES 2004: 29), there is evidence that disabled children are excluded from participation in decision-making forums concerned with their care and support. In their study of the processes and outcomes of social care participation activity, Franklin and Sloper (2009) found limited numbers of disabled children having active involvement in their reviews. Similarly, limited levels of participation were observed by the VIPER project, which also explored disabled children's participation in decision-making forums concerned with social care services (VIPER Project Team 2012). Both studies, and indeed others (see, for example, Clarke et al. 2006), identify those with communication impairments as being at particular risk of exclusion from participatory activity, especially for those children from BAME communities. Both Kate and Joel may be experiencing similar levels of social isolation in their lives and limited engagement in their group activities.

Disablist attitudes and communicative norms contribute significantly to this experience of exclusion and social isolation. Marks (2008: 44) highlights that the 'ordinary rules of interaction offer ... limited time for each speech turn', impacting on both those with speech impairment and those using communication aids which involve spending time. People are afforded insufficient time to contribute to the conversation and consequently are spoken over or have their sentences finished for them (Hodge 2007; Mackenzie et al. 2011); this is clearly something Kate experiences, and it inevitably acts as a barrier to her achieving increased self-determination and autonomy. Failure to make reasonable adjustments, such as ensuring additional time, the provision of communication facilitators, and/or communication aids, can also impact on meaningful participation and active engagement in social and civic life. A number of participants in the study of civic participation by Mackenzie et al. (2011) reported that their communication needs were not accommodated in civic meetings. Disabled children participating in the VIPER project (VIPER Project Team 2012) and Franklin and Sloper's (2009) study identified lack of a staff skill and effort, a lack of resources to assist with communication, limited availability of communication aids, and a lack of time to facilitate communication as key barriers to their participation. Both the environmental group that Kate attends and Joel's 'looked after children' group may be failing to accommodate their communication needs, resulting in their limited meaningful participation.

Attachment and communication needs

Impairment per se is not associated with insecure attachment; however, research findings suggest that higher numbers of disabled children than non-disabled children are insecurely attached (Howe 2006). In his examination of interaction between disabled children and their caregivers, Howe highlights that communication difficulties may impact on parental stress levels and caregiving quality, and therefore attachment security. Woodcock and Tregaskis (2008) observe that parents of disabled children often prioritize the development of effective communication methods in meeting their children's care needs. However, where parents have difficulties interpreting and understanding their child's communication, their stress levels may increase and the child may become distressed. Consequently, parents may become less emotionally available and offer less responsive caregiving; these factors are associated with increased risk of insecure attachments (Howe 2006). Howe draws on the example of visually impaired babies, who have been found to show less facial expression and to smile more transiently. Parents may interpret this communication as unresponsiveness, which can adversely affect the parent–child relationship. Such miscommunication may have impacted on Joel's early attachment experiences, adding further complexity to his current situation as a looked after child. The fact that one of his caregivers now shares his impairment may support effective communication (Harris and Mohay 1997; cited in Howe 2006).

Communication with families and social care staff

Studies of the relationships between social workers and families of disabled children have identified poor communication as a barrier to inclusive practice (Woodcock and Tregaskis 2008). Use of professional jargon and communication strategies that privilege professional agendas over the concerns of caregivers may have resulted in Shonitta's and Dalton's recent feelings of exclusion. Shonitta's lived experience of visual impairment is a source of expertise that could be harnessed to ensure Joel's meaningful inclusion in social work processes. This can only be achieved through 'open and equitable channels of communication' (ibid.: 65).

Social workers should also be alert both to the effectiveness of communication between social care staff, such as personal assistants, and service users and to the need for communication knowledge and skills training (Goldbart and Caton 2010), particularly in the context of increased personalization (see chapters 4 and 9). As Bondi (2008) argues, good care necessitates good communication. While Maya, Kate's personal assistant, may have numerous qualities, her level of English may impact on the quality of support offered. Participants in Manthorpe et al.'s (2012) study of the experiences of disabled service users receiving care and support from migrant care workers all identified competence in spoken English as necessary. Many reported experiences of communication breakdown when difficulties arose in both understanding and being understood: 'I have had an experience where one [care worker] that came to me from [agency] – she was a lovely lady – but her English was awful and communication was really, really difficult' (disabled adult, cited ibid.: 304). Manthorpe and her colleagues observe that these difficulties raise particular challenges for those with severe communication impairments. Noting that 'disability networks ... have commented on ... care and migration' (ibid.: 300), they identify a need for further research in relation to directly employed migrant personal assistants (such as Maya) and recommend that social workers be alert to the need for care worker training, risk management and meticulous support planning (PCF 7).

It is clear that failure to acknowledge, meet and address communication needs may lead to social isolation, social exclusion, limited participation in civic life, and poor experiences of social care and support. This has implications in relation to disabled people's right under Article 8 of the ECHR to respect for private and family life (Human Rights Act 1998) and rights under the UNCRDP (see, for example, Article 19 and Article 29). Social workers must therefore consider these wider psycho-social issues related to communication-based needs when undertaking assessments and planning intervention and support. This chapter now turns to consider some strategies for addressing such needs.

Social work practice: meeting communication needs

Core communication skills

Social workers have legal and professional duties to involve disabled service users fully when they carry out social care functions, such as assessment and care and support planning. This necessitates both strong communication skills and an ability to support those with communication impairments that impact on the articulation of needs, wishes and feelings (Foster et al. 2006). Egan (2010) argues that certain core communication skills are useful irrespective of the setting and specifically highlights empathy and active listening. Thompson (2011a) and Koprowska (2014) note the importance of paraphrasing and summarizing, attention to paralanguage (for example, gesture, facial expression and pitch) and the use of varying question types. Such skills are vital not only in establishing communication but also in facilitating conversations which may be highly emotive, personal, embarrassing or otherwise difficult. Woodcock and Tregaskis (2008) offer the example of work with parents of disabled children, who may wish to discuss strong emotions arising from daily encounters with disabling barriers.

Social workers should also allow adequate time to establish communication and recognize that additional time or repeat visits might be needed when working with those with communication impairments. This may prove particularly positive when working with Kate; the Communication Trust (2011) recommend reassuring people that you will wait, so that they do not feel pressured or rushed. Spoken language can also be supported with visual communication, such as facial expression, gestures, written material, diagrams and pictures (Mackenzie et al. 2011). While heavy case-loads and work pressures can impact on the time social workers have available, Woodcock and Tregaskis (2008) observe that those who take the time to establish effective communication are often considered to be the most helpful.

Developing specialist communication skills

Communication impairments do not result in the experience of disability if communication partners develop their own skills and understanding (Communication Trust 2011). It was noted earlier in this chapter that care workers might need training in developing their communication knowledge and skills (PCF 5 and 7). However, social workers themselves need to consider their own training and professional development needs in relation to effective and, where necessary, specialist communication skills. Indeed, 'putting the social model into interpersonal practice means addressing our own "special communication needs", in order to meet those of service users' (Koprowska 2014: 166).

However, a lack of specialist communication skills among social workers has been observed by disabled people, parents of disabled children, researchers and social workers themselves, and there have been various calls for more training and skill development (Woodcock and Tregaskis 2008; Franklin and Sloper 2009; Mackenzie et al. 2011). Expanding one's skills base does not necessitate becoming an expert in all communication systems. Rather, it requires the development of communication knowledge; recognition of, validation of and respect for the many methods of communication other than spoken language; time spent getting to know individual service users and their communication preferences; and liaison with other professionals (Communication Trust 2011). Lack of visual impairment specialism does not preclude engagement with Joel, showing an interest in his communication methods, and learning from him and those around him. In the words of one children's social worker: 'I've said it time and time again, it's about being individual, children are individuals, they all have their communication needs, so it's about finding out what system that child uses ... I don't use British Sign Language, I can't read Braille, but I will access someone who can' (cited in Franklin and Sloper 2009: 6).

Augmentative and alternative communication (AAC) and assistive technologies

Augmentative and alternative communication (AAC) describes a range of techniques, systems, aids and equipment used with or instead of spoken communication to support those with oral communication impairments. Goldbart and Caton (2010) identify two broad categories of AAC: unaided communication and aided communication. Unaided communication refers to features that do not involve spoken language, such as body language, facial expression, gesture and signing. Aided communication makes use of aids or equipment, from simple tools such as pens and paper, writing boards, wipe boards and communication charts to electronic equipment and high-tech devices such as voice-output communication aids (VOCAs). Major technological advances in the field of AAC have seen the development of increasingly powerful and sophisticated equipment for disabled people (Hodge 2007;

Lopez et al. 2014). The range now includes multi-message devices, voice amplification systems, synthetic voice aids, real-time communication systems controlled by eye gaze and eye movement, and a 'Mobile Lorm Glove' that makes use of pressure sensors to enable deafblind tactile alphabet users to send and receive text messages (Luna et al. 2002; Hodge 2007; Anon 2012; Lopez et al. 2014).

Hodge (2007) argues that AAC has the potential to increase participation, promote interpersonal interaction and reduce the marginalization of those with communication impairments. She adds that such systems may also prevent 'communicative dependency' on others. Research certainly highlights the ways in which AAC has been transformative in the lives of those with communication impairments or communication needs. For example, one participant in Hodge's study describes receiving a voice-output communication aid as a 'turning point', as it enabled him to 'gain his independence' and freed him from 'forced ... relationships of [communicative] dependency' (ibid.: 462). Harris (2010) and Pilling and Barrett (2008) highlight the positive impact that communication technologies (including mainstream technology) have had on the D/deaf community. Power et al. (2007: 291) suggest that Deaf people have 'had their communication options transformed' by emerging technologies; similarly, Emerson and Bishop (2012) observed increased interpersonal communication, independence and social inclusion in their study of videophone use among deafblind younger people offered such equipment. The 'voices' of the participants capture their experiences:

> Having access to textphone, fax, mobile phone (SMS) and e-mail has made me completely independent. (Deaf adult, cited in Pilling and Barrett 2008: 101)

> I like to communicate with my friends ... But then when we were apart, I could not communicate with him. Now with the videophone, I can connect with him and we have fun talking. (Deafblind young person, cited in Emerson and Bishop 2012: 628)

> Before I had my videophone, I was always bored ... Now I can videophone my friends every day. (Deafblind young person, cited ibid.)

Exploring the potential of both specialist AAC systems and mainstream technology may offer Joel the potential of fuller participation in the 'looked after children' group and facilitate communication with his friends and peers, particularly when he is not at school. Kate already has an electronic communication aid but finds this difficult and tiring to use, suggesting it has not been transformative in her experience. Hodge (2007) notes that limited numbers of people benefit from AAC; indeed, Harris (2010) highlights research that suggests a third of assistive equipment issued is abandoned and unused. It is therefore important that social workers understand and seek to dismantle the barriers to effective use of AAC: limited state provision and cost; design and operation limitations; lack of training in use; and self-consciousness.

Despite UK policy initiatives aimed at improving accessibility and state provision of AAC, such as the Communication Aids Project (CAP) and the Integrated Community Equipment Service (ICES), Clarke et al. (2006) and Hodge (2007) observe that state provision remains limited and inequitable. While home adaptations and equipment are listed in the Chronically Sick and Disabled Persons Act 1970, they are not specifically listed in the Care Act 2014 as something that local authorities must offer in order to meet needs (Clements 2015). AAC equipment may be funded privately, through charitable organizations or Access to Work monies, but, with prices of up to several thousand pounds, cost remains highly prohibitive for many disabled people (Harris 2010). Such financial barriers may reduce opportunities for Joel in securing AAC and prevent Kate from sourcing more high-tech communication aids suited to her needs.

Equipment design and operational limitations may also prove to be barriers to effective AAC use. Disabled people have highlighted, *inter alia*, limited vocabulary, poor tone and slowness in voice-output communication aids, errors in voice recognition software, and limited interactivity owing to an inability to interrupt in conversation as particularly problematic (Hodge 2007; Power et al. 2007; Harris 2010). Wheelchair users have described difficulties in securing communication aids to their wheelchairs, and those with conditions causing involuntary and uncontrolled movements describe having difficulty operating certain devices (Hodge 2007; Harris 2010; Cockerill et al. 2014). Such issues may be linked to Kate's difficulties in using her communication aid. The development of smaller devices and the use of wireless and Bluetooth technology has gone some way to addressing these design and operation problems. However, lack of training in the operation of these newer technologies may also act as a barrier to effective use. Referring to what has been termed the 'digital divide', Power et al. (2007) note that not all people have the necessary skills to benefit from such technologies. Participants in both Hodge's (2007) and Harris's (2010) studies experienced a lack of training or poor quality training, difficulties in learning how to use new equipment, and an absence of ongoing human support.

A final barrier relates to the self-consciousness of the user. Söderström and Ytterhus (2010) observe that technologies have a secondary role as symbols of identity and belonging. Drawing on interviews with visually impaired younger people, they observed that mainstream technologies were embraced where they symbolized youth identity, while devices that marked them out as different, such as assistive communication aids, were rejected. Where the assistive technology was necessary in order to function, willing use of such devices was dependent on the younger person's determination of 'normality'. Hodge (2007) also observed that a sense of being marked out as different and self-consciousness impacted on some adults' use of voice amplification devices, particularly in public.

AAC technologies are not therefore a panacea to communication difficulties. However, when used alongside other systems, they do have considerable potential. Despite the limited employment of such technologies in practice (Parrott and Madoc-Jones 2008), social workers should seek to dismantle the barriers to their effective use. This can entail advocating for greater state provision and the creative use of personal budget monies to fund equipment; providing information and referring service users to communication aids centres to try equipment before making private purchases; facilitating learning and training (social workers were identified as key facilitators in Harris's (2010) study); including ongoing support with communication aids in care and support plans; maximizing the potential of mainstream technologies and promoting accessible mainstream design; and normalizing the use of communication aids in order to reduce stigma. It is also important to acknowledge and validate people's choice not to make use of technologies: 'Electronic aids are not for me – at this stage a notepad and pen are much easier' (adult with motor neurone disease, cited in MNDA 2013: 48).

Working with others

Disabled people have worked closely with specialist organizations to produce a range of materials to support good communication; social workers will undoubtedly find these useful. For example, individuals from the Essex Coalition of Disabled People authored *The Good Practice Guide*, aimed at support workers and personal assistants working with disabled people with communication impairments and published by Scope in 2002, and Communication Forum Scotland, an alliance of specialist organizations in Scotland, produced a very useful online resource: *Talk For Scotland: A Practical Toolkit for Engaging with People with Communication Support Needs.*

Morris (2014a: 2) suggests that effective communication can be established when one draws upon the 'skills and experience of those who know the person best and understand how and what they communicate'. In her book *Don't Leave Us Out: Involving Disabled Children and Young People with Communication Impairments*, Morris (1998b) identifies children's friends as excellent sources of information on how to communicate with them, often in creative and innovative ways. Parents, relatives and primary caregivers also have expertise in establishing communication. Luna et al. (2002) observe that many disabled children and adults establish effective, even if idiosyncratic, systems for communication within their families, and Goldbart and Caton (2010) highlight the positive input parents have had in communication training for social workers.

While family and informal networks are clearly important, Koprowska (2014) emphasizes the need for independent communication support. This is particularly pertinent in safeguarding situations but also reflects best practice in promoting self-determination, autonomy and, indeed, privacy for service users, who may wish to discuss matters of a very personal nature (PCF Domains 2 and 4). For example, it is unlikely that Kate would wish to discuss her personal life in the presence of her parents and younger sibling. To facilitate this, social workers should work closely with other professionals who may be more familiar with the service users' communication systems or have the necessary expertise and skill (Franklin and Sloper 2009). This includes not just speech and language therapists (SALT) but also teachers and ancillary school staff, interpreters, relay interpreters (for Deaf people with additional learning difficulties or mental health needs), communicator-guides (for deafblind people) and intervenors (for congenitally deafblind people with complex needs).

Conclusion

Communication is a central component of our human existence. It enables us to share information, express our feelings, needs and desires, develop our identity, form and sustain relationships with others, and maintain quality of life. As social work is a 'people profession', it is unsurprising that good communication skills are fundamental to practice, something recognized in professional codes of practice. Social workers working in disability settings will encounter service users with a range of communication impairments and communication needs who are also inevitably facing numerous disabling barriers. As such, they must pay particular attention to their language use and communication skills, developing specialist skill and liaising closely with disabled people, their families and friends, and other professionals.

Furthermore, social workers must be alert to the wider psycho-social impact of communication need. This includes social isolation; reduced opportunity for participation; potential impact on attachment; and the effect on relationships with family and both formal and informal caregivers. Such issues must be explored in assessment and be carefully addressed in care and support planning and in direct intervention.

Key messages

- Physical impairment may impact on communication, and disabling barriers can present a range of communicative challenges.
- Language acts as the most complex communicative tool at our disposal. Social workers must pay careful attention to their use of language, ensuring it reflects social work values and the preferences of the disabled people with whom they are working. Particular attention must be paid to cultural and linguistic differences.
- Social workers must be alert to the wider psycho-social impact of communication impairment and communication needs.
- Strategies for good practice include the effective use of core communication skills; the development of specialist communication skills; maximizing the potential and use of AAC and assistive technologies; and collaborative practice with disabled people's organizations, families and friends, and communication and language professionals.

Activities

- Reflect on your own use of language and observe the language of others in everyday discourse relating to impairment and disability. What impact does this have on disabled people?
- Complete your own 'communication skills analysis'. What are your strengths and where is there scope for development? Seek feedback on your communication skills from colleagues and service users.
- Visit the website www.talkingpoint.org.uk. Here you will find a range of information about speech, language and communication development and ways in which you can support children and young people with communication needs.

Suggested further reading

Hodge, S. (2007) Why is the potential of augmentative and alternative communication not being realized? Exploring the experiences of people who use communication aids, *Disability & Society*, 22(5): 457–71.

Morris, J. (2002) *A Lot to Say: A Guide for Social Workers, Personal Advisers and Others Working with Disabled Children and Young People with Communication Impairments*. London: Scope.

Thompson, N. (2011) *Effective Communication: A Guide for the People Professions*. 2nd edn, Basingstoke: Palgrave Macmillan.

8 Working with Disabled Children

Issues considered in this chapter:

- Key issues in assessing the needs of disabled children and their families
- Social work intervention with disabled children and with parents
- Overview of interprofessional approaches required by legislation
- Disabled children who are 'looked after' and permanency

Introduction

'If you have worked with more than 20 children over time, you should have worked with at least one who is disabled' (Marchant 2001). Despite this assertion, it is still unclear exactly how many disabled children there are in Britain. This is in large part due to the differing definitions of disability used by various data sources. Blackburn et al. (2010), in their reanalysis of the Family Resources Survey 2004–5, report that 7.3 per cent of children were experiencing disability as defined by the Disability Discrimination Act. However, this was an estimate based on the results of a national sample survey. Another figure is the estimate of 770,000 disabled children under sixteen in Britain that appeared in *Improving the Life Chances of Disabled People* (PMSU 2005).

Drawing on information obtained from local authorities and the NHS, it has been estimated that between 3.0 and 5.4 per cent of all children under eighteen are disabled (Mooney et al. 2008). However, data from local authorities and the NHS are often linked to eligibility for services, which can be different in health, education and social care. Disabled children who do not meet local thresholds for services from disabled children's teams may be eligible for services from other social work teams – for example, safeguarding or 'children in need' teams. But there is not always a formal mechanism for recording disability in these circumstances, and it appears that 'the number of children in contact with social care disability teams is only a small proportion of those who might be considered disabled' (ibid.: 31).

Recent trends have seen an increase in the numbers of children with severe and complex impairments (O'Loughlin and O'Loughlin 2012), some of whom have complex care needs requiring multi-agency support (HM Treasury and DfES 2007). There has also been an increase in the diagnosis of neurodevelopmental impairments, including learning disability, autistic spectrum conditions and attention deficit hyperactivity disorder (ADHD) (Bonell et al. 2011). Blackburn et al. (2012) state that children with neurodevelopmental conditions form the largest impairment-based group among disabled children, a number of whom are also affected by physical impairments, leading to complex support needs.

The key legislation for social work with disabled children, the 1989 Children Act, requires local authorities 'to minimise the effect on disabled children within their area of their disabilities, and to give such children the opportunity to lead lives which are as normal as possible' (Schedule 2, Part 1, §6). The Act emphasizes that disabled children are 'children first' (Marchant and Jones 2000) and that they should be brought up and cared for within their own families wherever possible. Disabled children are regarded as 'children in need' under Section 17 of the Act, and partnership with parents is stressed. The emphasis is now on the inclusion of disabled children within mainstream policy, services and communities, although Marchant (2001) and Middleton (1996) have commented on their segregation from mainstream children's services. Disabled children are still entitled to services under the Chronically Sick and Disabled Persons Act 1970, and there have been further attempts to strengthen services since the 1989 Children Act. The most recent initiative is the Children and Families Act 2014, discussed later in the chapter; this will have a significant impact on social work practice.

The National Service Framework for Children, standard 8, states: 'Children and young people who are disabled or who have complex health needs receive co-ordinated high-quality child and family-centred services which are based on assessed needs, which promote social inclusion and, where possible, which enable them and their families to live ordinary lives.' Morris (1998a: 9–10) summarizes the rights of disabled children under the UN Convention on the Rights of the Child (UNCRC) and focuses particularly on their right to inclusion in the community and 'to do the kinds of things that non-disabled children do'. This includes access to play and leisure activities, the right to have their views taken into account, and the right to be protected from abuse and neglect. Of particular importance for social care professionals is their right to live with their parents, unless this is not in their best interests, the right to receive any support necessary to enable their parents to look after them, and the right to regular reviews of placements if they have to live away from home.

However, this does not mean that disabled children should be treated in exactly the same way as non-disabled children. Marchant and Jones (2000) stress that both impairments and the disabling barriers that inhibit inclusion may create additional needs. This indicates that the social relational model of disability (Thomas 1999, 2004) is a useful tool for assessment and intervention with disabled children and their families (Connors and Stalker 2007). Medicalized approaches to childhood disability may have paid insufficient attention to strengths, achievements, individuality and environmental barriers, but paradoxically there has also been a tendency to ignore particular barriers arising from impairment, particularly communication needs (Morris 1998b). This is despite the fact that local authorities have a statutory duty under the Children Act 1989 to take the wishes and feelings of children into account when making decisions.

Although there has been a history of institutional provision for disabled children, reanalysis of disability surveys carried out in the 1980s indicated that 91 per cent were living with their own families (DoH 1998a). However, they are still more likely than non-disabled children to be living away from home. Cousins (2006) states that disabled children are nine times more likely to become 'looked after' by local authorities than non-disabled children. However, the reasons for many of these children being 'looked after' are not always a direct result of care needs associated with their disability: 62 per cent of all looked after children entered the care system for reasons of abuse or neglect and only 4 per cent for reasons directly related to disability; however, as many as a quarter of all 'looked after' children are disabled (ibid.). It has been noted that disabled children are disproportionately at risk of abuse and neglect (Sullivan and Knutson 2000) (see chapter 10). This chapter will therefore consider the issues involved in working with disabled children living away from home as well as with their families.

For children who are born with an impairment, or who develop one very early in life, it is health professionals who may be the first to offer advice to families. This may involve disclosing a diagnosis to parents. The way this news is imparted is crucial, as some parents regard the behaviour of professionals at this time as 'deeply insensitive' (Connors and Stalker 2003: 128). There is now accessible advice for professionals involved in disclosing a diagnosis based on respect for the child and parents (Scope 2003). This may lead to a referral to children's social care services. Historically, some disabled children have had little contact with social workers until health and education professionals begin to anticipate the end of their school days and the transition to adult social care services. However, there is now greater clarity about the need for social care assessment of children placed in residential schools or in regular short break (or 'respite') care, leading to greater social work involvement.

There is still a long way to go before disabled children and their families have access to ordinary lives and social inclusion, and there remain significant unmet needs and poor outcomes (Every Disabled Child Matters 2015). Cousins (2006: 4) has referred to 'families under considerable stress, with limited supports'.

Social work assessment and disabled children

By the time a social work assessment takes place, many children and families will already have been assessed by other professionals. While this should provide useful information, social workers should also be aware of how these previous encounters have been experienced and perceived. Marchant and Jones (2000) highlight that assessments may have been based on a deficit model of disability and without any active involvement of the child. Parents have also reported that dealing with professionals has been the most difficult aspect of caring for a disabled child (DoH 1998a). Research has consistently identified common shortcomings in service provision:

> substantial numbers of families report a 'constant battle' to find out about what services are available and about the role of different agencies and different professionals; to get professionals to understand their situation and their needs; to obtain recognition of their own knowledge of their child; to negotiate delays and bureaucracy. A major reason for the problems families face with services is the multiplicity of agencies and professionals involved. (Sloper et al. 1999)

The Early Support Programme was introduced to tackle some of these issues. It aimed to promote multi-agency assessment, coordinated support and the timely provision of information needed by families and to ensure that assessment leads to prompt provision of practical help. Key working arrangements aim to provide continuity and a single point of contact for families. The programme was originally developed in 2002 for children up to the age of three but was later extended to include disabled children and young people up to adulthood.

The system of assessment for children changed as a result of the Munro review (Munro 2011) and is set out in *Working Together to Safeguard Children* (HM Government 2013, 2015). However, social workers are still expected to collect and analyse information in respect of the three domains set out in the triangle of the Assessment Framework (DoH 2000a). These are the child's developmental needs, parenting capacity, and family and environmental factors.

Case profile: Max

Max is eleven years old and lives with his parents and sister. With full-time assistance from a support worker, he attends the nearest mainstream high school, some miles from his home. Max was born prematurely and has both a significant visual impairment and a learning disability. He also has a mobility impairment and is waiting for 'corrective surgery' on his legs. More recently he has found it difficult to hear the teacher in class and has attended the audiology clinic. He travels on the school bus but has not yet learned to use a service bus on his own. Max has missed a lot of school days on account of outpatients' appointments and illness. It takes him a lot longer to do his homework than others in his class, and helping with homework has become a major commitment for his parents. They also need to help Max with the regular exercises that the physiotherapist has prescribed. His father works, but his mother has found it impossible to take paid employment because of the need constantly to be available for hospital appointments and looking after Max when he is ill. She also cares for her uncle, who has Parkinson's disease. Initially things were going well at school, and Max had a particular close schoolfriend who lived nearby. Since this friend moved away, Max has had difficulty making new friends, and on several occasions he has arrived home upset after other young people have been unpleasant to him on the bus. At his latest review, the school staff suggested that Max would benefit from attending a residential special school rather than remaining at their school. They thought he would be more able to make friends and would have easy access to the equipment and support related to his visual impairment. Max and his parents were upset about this prospect.

In assessing Max's needs, school staff have focused on two issues: needs related to his visual impairment and the need for friendship. Both of these, they suggest, could be better addressed in a specialist residential setting. However, equipment and support can be provided in mainstream settings, and it is unlikely that residential provision would have been suggested for a non-disabled child who was having difficulty making friends. The reason for this, aside from the expense, would include the attachment of children to their parents and siblings and their right to inclusion within their local communities. Article 9 of the UNCRC states that children have the right to live with their parents, and Article 23 states that services should be provided so as to facilitate children's social integration and participation in the community. Marchant and Jones (2000) stress that the starting point in assessment should be the assumption that disabled children have the same needs and rights as other children, otherwise there is a danger that poor care could be tolerated.

Assessment and outcomes

The outcomes which government in England want children to achieve are specified in the *Every Child Matters* (ECM) framework (DfES 2003): to be healthy, stay safe, enjoy and achieve, make a positive contribution and realize economic well-being. These apply to *all* children. Similar 'well-being indicators' have been developed in Scotland: safe, healthy, achieving, nurtured, active, respected, responsible and included. The Scottish well-being indicators have been developed under the aegis of *Getting it Right for Every Child* (GIRFEC) and the National Practice Model (Scottish Government 2012). This will be enshrined in law when the relevant sections of the Children and Young People (Scotland) Act 2014 are implemented in August 2016. The Scottish government has been explicit as to how social workers should integrate the well-being indicators into assessment. The indicators should be used to identify needs and concerns. The National Practice Model states that these should be used in conjunction with the 'My World Triangle', which involves 'How I grow and develop', 'What I need from people who look after me' and 'My wider world'. This is similar to the English 'assessment triangle' and allows practitioners to consider the child's progress in meeting the well-being indicators, or outcomes, in the context of the strengths and pressures of her family and wider environment.

While the outcomes in ECM and GIRFEC are the same for all children, some have been perceived as difficult for all disabled children to meet. Sloper et al. (2007) researched the views of children and parents in England where children had complex healthcare needs, did not communicate using speech, or experienced autistic spectrum conditions and degenerative conditions. Overall, the ECM outcomes were found to be appropriate for disabled children: 'Like other children, many of the disabled children we interviewed wanted to have friends and interests, be part of the local community, acquire social and self-care skills and future independence, feel confident and respected by others, and experience success and achievement' (ibid.: 20). However, the researchers found that communication was a significant omission from the ECM outcomes. There is a similar issue with the Scottish GIRFEC framework: 'the importance of seeking children's views is a recurring theme ... but the fact that some disabled children ... may need support to communicate is not highlighted' (Stalker and Moscardini 2012: 15).

In their research in England, Sloper et al. (2007) found that some outcomes were seen as 'fundamental', meaning that they had to be achieved before it was possible to achieve other 'higher-level' outcomes. These fundamental outcomes were being healthy, being able to communicate, and staying safe. However, the meaning of these outcomes could be very different for some disabled children. The nature of both children's and parents' concerns about health have varied on the basis of the child's impairment and situation: 'What does "healthy" mean for a child with a life limiting medical condition and how would he be supported to achieve it?' (Stalker and Moscardini 2012: 15). Sloper et al. (2007) found that children with complex healthcare needs and those with degenerative conditions focused on being comfortable and free from pain, which was a prerequisite for the achievement of any other outcomes. For some children, a balance had to be struck between potential gains from therapies and quality of life. For children with autistic spectrum conditions and those who did not communicate through speech, difficulties in using health services were seen as impediments to maintaining good health. Emotional well-being was also regarded as an important aspect of 'being healthy'. This could range from the issues arising for children with autistic spectrum conditions to the need for emotional support for those with degenerative conditions. For some children this included support at the end of life.

The way that 'higher-level' outcomes were interpreted by children and parents in the study by Sloper et al. (2007) depended on the child's impairment and circumstances. 'Enjoying and achieving' was a desired outcome for all groups of disabled children, but the components of this carried different meanings for different groups of children. These included identity, self-esteem and friendship for many, although there were exceptions to this for some with autistic spectrum conditions. Lack of contact with other children outside of school was often seen as a barrier to achieving friendship. Many children wanted to be involved in more experiences and activities in the mainstream community, but some did not participate because local facilities were inaccessible. Similarly, education and self-care skills were interpreted differently by parents on the basis of what was possible for their child. There were also differences in the type of 'positive contribution' to which children and parents aspired. While children with good cognitive abilities aspired to paid employment as adults, parents had more limited ambitions for children with learning disabilities. However, all children and parents valued being able to make choices and being involved in decision-making about their own lives, and feeling loved and respected was considered important by all.

While Sloper et al.'s (2007) research supports the assertion in the practice guidance that the needs of disabled children are the same as those of other children, social workers should guard against applying normative developmental models (see chapter 3). The views and experience of disabled children and their parents, and also the abilities of particular disabled children, are important in interpreting the ECM or GIRFEC outcomes and the domains of the 'assessment triangle'. Social workers should pay attention to fundamental outcomes, such as being healthy, emotional well-being, safety and being able to communicate, on which the 'higher-level' outcomes depend. The nature of these outcomes will often call for multidisciplinary assessment and support. However, Marchant (2001) has warned against assuming that a child's impairment is responsible for all limitations, as children's abilities can also be affected by environmental and social barriers.

Engaging with disabled children

There is a history of communication with parents rather than with disabled children during assessment (Social Services Inspectorate 1998), and the recent focus on children's rights under the UNCRC and the Children Act 1989 has presented a challenge to this practice. Article 12 of the UNCRC states that the views of children should be taken into account when adults are making decisions. The contribution of disabled children, who sometimes express views different from those of their parents (Stalker and Connors 2003), is vital to assessment.

> That is one of the things that really annoys me … being spoken to through my parents. If they want to speak to me, speak to me, not anybody else but me, I won't accept anybody talking to me through anybody else but me … People tend to think that I am a lot less intelligent than I am. (Disabled teenager, cited in Audit Commission 2003: 41)

To engage children in the assessment process, social workers need to develop specific communication skills. For some D/deaf and disabled children, this may involve non-verbal communication or assistance from people who know the child and her or his means of communication best (Morris 1998). Stalker and Connors have discussed the reasons that some workers do not attempt to communicate with disabled children:

> because they think it will be too time-consuming and too difficult, because they think some children will not understand what is happening to them nor have a particular view about it, or because they see themselves as lacking the necessary skills or confidence. On most of those counts, they will probably be wrong. (2003: 33)

They argue that many of the skills are the same as those needed to communicate with any child, and the basics of some non-verbal methods of communication are not hard to learn. However, it is apparent from the work of Stalker and Connors that prior experience, forethought and consultation with parents are needed and that additional time may be required for preparation (see chapter 7).

Parents and siblings

The Children Act 1989 stresses partnership with parents, and the policy document *Aiming High for Disabled Children* (HM Treasury and DfES 2007) is subtitled 'Better Support for Families'. Parents have expressed concerns about other children in their families, whether they have the time and energy to focus on their needs, the ways that non-disabled children's lives could be restricted by the needs of a disabled sibling, and sometimes the way that friendships are affected (Beresford et al. 2007b). Some siblings have a significant involvement in providing support for the disabled child: 'Sometimes I sleep on the couch in my sister's room to give mum and dad a break. It's hard to sleep because I'm afraid she'll stop breathing. It's hard to cope with school the next day 'cause I'm shattered' (Scottish Government 2010: 37).

The Assessment Framework addresses parenting capacity, and the assessment of parent-carers has rightly focused on this. As a result, most support services for parents have been delivered in the form of services to the child, including short break provision. Research indicates that parents of disabled children provide significantly more care than other parents (Roberts and Lawton 2001), and the stresses and poor outcomes for parents and families are well documented (Audit Commission 2003). These pressures often result from families not receiving the services they need (McLaughlin et al. 2008). A recent survey revealed that nearly half of the sample of parents had consulted their GP because of stress, with a significant proportion of those being prescribed anti-depressants (Scope 2014b).

Until recently there has been little knowledge of the outcomes that parents wish to achieve for themselves, as opposed to the support they need in order to continue caring for their disabled children. Beresford et al. (2007a) found that parents wished to reclaim aspects of their personal identity that they felt had been lost due to the pervasive demands of being a parent-carer. Paid work, interests and personal relationships were seen as key to maintaining personal identity. Parents also considered it important to maintain physical and emotional health, both of which could be undermined by the physical and emotional demands of caring. They reported a need both to feel skilled and informed about their child's condition and needs and to maintain a balance between the 'hands-on' caring tasks and spending quality time with their child as a parent. This is consistent with the findings of other survey research: 'I would like to be a parent to my disabled child and my other children rather than a doctor, nurse, social worker, fighter and carer' (Contact a Family 2011: 10).

Maintaining a family life was a desired outcome for respondents in Beresford et al.'s (2007a) research, as it could be difficult to do things as a whole family on account of the needs of both the disabled child and other siblings. Having additional help on family outings was cited as necessary, as well as disability-aware staff in the venues the family visited. Outings that would appear routine for other families could be impossible to manage. As a respondent to another recent survey said: 'I'd like to be able to take all my children to the park and end with having a meal in a restaurant' (Contact a Family 2011: 14). It could also be difficult for parents to maintain their relationship with each other as they would wish without help with caring and domestic tasks, short breaks and assistance with the disabled child's sleep problems. Parents wanted siblings to have a positive adjustment to having a disabled brother or sister, some quality parental time without the disabled child, and positive experiences for the whole family together.

Parents have a right to request an assessment of their own needs under the Carers and Disabled Children Act 2000, and these rights have been strengthened with the implementation of the Children and Families Act 2014, which requires the local authority to offer a separate assessment on the appearance of need; it is no longer necessary for the parent to be providing a 'substantial' amount of care. For the first time, the assessment must consider the well-being of the parent, not only the support needed for her to continue to provide care. The assessment must also consider the safety and welfare of the disabled child and any other children for whom the parent has responsibility. Under the Care Act 2014, parents of disabled children can ask for an assessment of their own needs in advance of the child reaching eighteen. The local authority has the power to provide support under this legislation even though care is being provided for a child rather than an adult. Siblings who are 'young carers' have acquired similar rights under the Children and Families Act 2014 and may also be considered 'children in need' under Section 17 of the Children Act 1989.

Family and environmental issues

In terms of the 'family and environmental' issues considered in the English assessment triangle, or 'My wider world' in the Scottish triangle, assessors need to be aware that disabled children are more likely than others to live in a household where there is poverty (Beresford 1995; Emerson and Hatton 2005). Gordon et al. (2000) found that the parents of disabled children were less likely to be in paid work than other parents, and Dobson and Middleton (1998) have reported on the additional costs involved in caring for a disabled child. Children have a right to an adequate standard of living under Article 26 of the UNCRC. Some of the adults in Beresford et al.'s (2007) research found they did not have the financial resources to fund the things that would have made it easier to cope with the additional demands of parenting a disabled child. Having sufficient resources to provide suitable housing, equipment and domestic help was an important desired outcome.

Housing is a major problem for many families with disabled children. Some families have experienced limited space and lack of access to some parts of the house for the disabled child. A lack of equipment and housing adaptations makes some parents' care of the disabled children more physically arduous than it needs to be. There is also limited personal space and privacy in many cases.

> The psychological and material impacts of poor housing and income will reduce all family members' resources for increasing activity within the home, and engaging in desired activities outside the home ... [S]trategies for inclusion cannot be limited to activities in public spaces ... if the housing and financial difficulties faced more privately by families on a daily basis are not addressed. (Clarke 2006: 20)

The inaccessibility of local services and leisure facilities is also an important part of the wider environment (Beresford et al. 2007). This means that many disabled children are not able to access their right to leisure and play as specified in Article 31 of the UNCRC: 'My son is desperate to go to the local park and play with the other children but he can't because there are no disabled swings there. I hate walking past the park as he just cries, because he wants to go there more than anything' (Contact a Family 2011: 13).

Bennett (2009: 24) found that the difficulties of many families came from 'a lack of support services, attitudes towards disability and a lack of support from professionals'. This suggests that the needs of disabled children and their families arise as much from disabling barriers as from impairment. Many of these barriers are located in wider communities or at local and national policy level and have persisted despite equalities legislation. Therefore, in addition to developmental and parenting issues, social work assessment needs to give sufficient emphasis to issues in the wider social environment which restrict the lives of disabled children and their families. This will include consideration of the family's contacts and support networks within the community, as families with disabled children can become isolated (Contact a Family 2011) and excluded from the informal ways in which parents of non-disabled children share childcare and give each other a break.

Transformation and resilience – 'Welcome to Holland'

Professional understandings of responses to the birth of a disabled child have often been grounded in the assumption that parents will experience grief. This is often believed to follow the process that Kübler-Ross (1969) identified with respect to people with a diagnosis of terminal illness, involving stages of denial, anger, bargaining, depression and acceptance. This has since been extrapolated to cover responses to bereavement and other types of loss. An alternative approach has been Olshansky's identification of 'chronic sorrow' as the most prevalent parental reaction. Olshanky (1962) argued that 'stage models' tended to label parents who failed to reach the acceptance or resolution stage as abnormal or neurotic, whereas in his experience it was quite 'normal' to continue to feel sadness. The negative assumptions conveyed by both these models about disability have led to their rejection by advocates of the social model of disability (Oliver 1990). The normalizing ideology that underpins the 'tragedy' approach to childhood disability is described in chapter 3.

While sweeping statements such as 'a child born with a disability is always a tragedy for the family' (Kandel and Merrick 2003: 741) are incompatible with the equal valuing of all children, some parents of disabled children certainly experience painful emotions. Kandel and Merrick make the point that '[t]he child is unable to fulfil the hopes and ambitions he/she was expected to' (ibid.: 743). Parents may experience tension between the expectation that they should love and protect their child and the dominant social values they may have internalized about disability. This may be exacerbated by the practical difficulties that families experience, the negative responses of others and the shortcomings of available support services.

Emily Perl Kingsley, in her essay 'Welcome to Holland' ([1987] 2001), has likened the experience of having a disabled child to a planned flight to Italy on which the plane is unexpectedly diverted to Holland. The moral of the story is that, by focusing on Italy – or the non-disabled child they expected to have – parents are missing the opportunity to appreciate what is positive about Holland, and the child they actually have. However, this is not to say that this will be easy for parents. Kingsley herself acknowledges that 'the loss of that dream is a very very significant loss.' Similarly, Barnett et al. (2003) entitle their article about parents' adaptation to the birth of a child with 'special needs' 'Building New Dreams'.

There have been numerous challenges to Kübler-Ross's 'stage' model. Blacher (1984) found little empirical evidence to support it, and there has since been a stream of research into the positive aspects of having a disabled child in the family (Scorgie et al. 2004; Allred and Hancock 2012). Attention has focused on the power of 'cognitive adaptation', or changed parental perception, to influence both the experience and the resilience of families (Scorgie and Sobsey 2000; Bayat 2007): 'My son is, as I have come to realize, my teacher. He is teaching me patience, acceptance, and how to see how much I have, instead of what I am missing' (Bayat 2007: 710). This has been regarded as part of a process of *transformation*, including personal growth (for example, becoming stronger and more compassionate) and changes in perspective. McConnell et al. (2015) conclude that the benefits reported by parents of disabled children are not merely imagined benefits which have been constructed to protect parents from stress. They are 'real' and are 'outcomes of a transformational life-learning process' (ibid.: 29).

Scorgie et al. (2004) suggest that the process of transformation involves constructing new self-identities and assumptions and that, in order to achieve this, parents have to address three different but overlapping questions, which they summarize as image-making, meaning-making and choice-making. *Image-making* is to do with identity and life trajectory. This is the question that concerns itself with the loss of dreams – the image parents hold of themselves and their family and how they imagine the future, their own future as well as that of their child. For non-disabled parents, this may be the first time that they have been associated with a stigmatized social category. There may also be implications for them and their child which will be lifelong. The information that parents are given at the time of diagnosis, and the way it is given, will play a part in shaping their images of the future.

Meaning-making involves the existential questions parents ask: *Why* do they have a disabled child, and how does this fit with their existing belief system? This is complicated by the interpretations that others will offer, which sometimes imply parental guilt as the answer to the question 'Why did this happen to *us*?' Although parents draw on different beliefs and philosophies to reinterpret their situation, it is important for them 'to believe that good can emerge, not so much from, but in the midst of the difficulties of life' (Scorgie et al. 2004: 98).

Thirdly, parents have to deal with *choice-making* and how they are going to manage on a day-to-day basis. Here the major issue that affects transformation is the parents' control over decision-making. While control is important in itself, Scorgie et al. (2004) argue that it also has an effect on processes of image-making and meaning-making. For example, if the goals of parents are constantly described by professionals as 'unrealistic', and decisions are taken out of their hands, this is likely to limit the images and meanings that they can construct. This suggests that professionals should not always assume that parents will be devastated by the birth of a disabled child (Carpenter and Egerton 2007). Kearney and Griffin (2001) found that parents gained a great deal of 'joy' from their disabled children but experienced 'sorrow' in connection with their dealings with other people, including professionals who interpreted their optimism and hope as signs of being 'in denial'.

Allred and Hancock (2012: 13) acknowledge evidence that the birth or diagnosis of a disabled child is 'typically a profound, life-altering experience', and that '[p]art of the durability of the grief model is that it resonates with certain parents.' However, evidence of the transformative effects of having a disabled child, along with research evidence of the factors associated with family resilience (Bayat 2007), suggests that optimism and self-efficacy have an impact on how a family responds. Professionals influenced primarily by models based on grief may convey an overly pessimistic view of the future, and this may serve as a self-fulfilling prophecy.

McConnell et al. (2015) report that most parents in their study described real benefits, such as the strengthening of emotional bonds between family members, personal growth, and transformation in their perspectives. There is now a stream of literature suggesting that professionals should focus on helping families to achieve these benefits rather than focusing solely on alleviating stress. Scorgie et al. (2004) argue that professional intervention should facilitate hopeful images, meanings and parental choice, while McConnell et al. (2015) also suggest creating opportunities for families to learn from more experienced parent-carers who can speak of the positive impact their disabled child has had. Bayat (2007) argues for a strengths-based approach in which professionals are prepared to share control with parents and which capitalizes on the factors associated with family resilience. Among the factors he identifies are the ability of families to pull resources together and to be connected; meaning-making in the face of adversity (including changes in world view and personal growth); and becoming an advocate for the disabled child: 'We are stronger knowing that no matter how hard the struggle to have our child accepted ... we all pull together to make things happen. And we know our child is the best thing that has happened to the family and is loved and cherished just like our other children' (Bennett 2009: 15). This may seem inconsistent with the considerable challenges that families face. While Scorgie et al. (2004) maintain that transformation does not require the absence of stress, parenting a disabled child often involves 'a fight for the support, consideration and respect that their child and family is entitled to' (McConnell et al. 2015: 42). Some parents are under extreme stress:

> My own health has deteriorated. I have suffered with depression for over two and a half years. I don't feel I can ever get off tablets. I have anxiety attacks that feel like I am having a real heart attack. (Mencap 2003: 5)

> My position is unsustainable and because I am not receiving enough support I feel like I can't go on and am considering giving up my son into care. Being with my son is intensive and I can't go on doing 17 hours a day with only 3 hours a week help and no holiday. (Bennett 2009: 23)

There is evidence of unmet needs of a fundamental nature – for example, some parents experience sleep deprivation and have expressed concern about the effect on siblings: 'It not only affects me and my son (who has a disability) it affects his two sisters, their lives and education. Going to school tired each day because they've been woken up several times overnight' (Family Fund 2014: 6).

Social workers therefore need to be open to a range of family responses to childhood disability. Transformative experiences should be acknowledged as strengths rather than dismissed as 'unrealistic', but at the same time families whose experiences have brought them to 'breaking point' (Mencap 2003) should not be pathologized and held responsible for problems arising from lack of support. Certainly some families have become closer and more resourceful as a result of having a disabled child, but equally there are others for whom the demands have contributed to family breakdown and social isolation (Contact a Family 2011; Mencap 2003). There is evidence that couples with a disabled child are at an increased risk of separation (Glenn 2007) and that this is particularly marked during the first two years of the child's life (Clarke and McKay 2008). Disabled children are more likely than their non-disabled peers to live in lone-parent families (Lyon et al. 2006).

If social work practice is to foster strengths and resilience in families, it is worth attending to parents' views about what will make families stronger. Some families have been strong and resilient with relatively little support from formal services:

> We are stronger because we know that we have to get on with it – we try to respect each other, learn from each other, laugh at one another and love one another. Oh, and on the odd occasion that we get a good night's sleep we do all the above, with value added. (Bennett 2009: 16)

However, parents have identified a number of things outside their own family resources which would make their family stronger, such as more opportunities for accessible play and leisure, the opportunity for their child to reach her or his full potential, a support package to meet their child's needs, and flexible and regular short breaks. The major barriers to families living ordinary lives were said to be lack of services, negative attitudes towards disability, and lack of support from professionals.

The issue of short breaks was obviously important to parents, as were flexible and responsive services; these are considered in the next section of this chapter.

Short breaks

Local authorities have a legal duty to provide breaks from caring for parents of disabled children as a result of amendments made to the 1989 Children Act by the 2008 Children and Young Persons Act. The Breaks for Carers of Disabled Children Regulations 2011 set out the requirements in England. In Wales, the regulations are the Breaks for Carers of Disabled Children (Wales) Regulations 2012, which are explicitly linked to Article 23 of the UNCRC, relating to the rights of disabled children to enjoy a full and decent life in conditions that promote dignity and self-reliance and an ability to participate in the community. Local authorities have a duty to provide daytime care in the child's home or elsewhere, overnight care at home or elsewhere, educational or leisure activities outside the home, and services to assist carers in the evenings, at weekends and during school holidays. Some of these services, particularly leisure activities, can be provided under Section 2 of the Chronically Sick and Disabled Persons Act 1970. However, the Children Act 1989 is the key legislation if the child is to be cared for overnight outside the home. Chapter 4 explains when this service can be provided under Section 17 of the Act and when it is appropriate for the child to be regarded as 'looked after'. This is also explained in the statutory guidance.

Parents value short breaks but have experienced difficulties in accessing these in sufficient quantity (Mencap 2013). This is disappointing, as in 2007 the government committed substantial funding to short breaks, and further funding has been committed since 2010. However, this was not ring-fenced and, in view of the difficulties still experienced by parents and carers, Mencap has questioned whether it has all been used for short breaks as intended.

The purpose of short breaks was originally restricted to giving family carers 'respite' so that they could continue to provide care. While this is still an important rationale, the term 'respite' constructed the recipients of support as burdens and pays insufficient attention to the impact of periods away from family carers on disabled children. There is evidence that parents benefit more from a break if they know that their child is happy (Platts et al. 1996). Although much short break provision is of good quality, it is sometimes incompatible with the needs of the child: 'The staff at the respite centre are not always fully trained to meet my son's needs, so often he plays up because he is not being understood and then plays up because he is frustrated' (Mencap 2013: 5). Increasingly, short breaks are treated as a service for both parents and disabled children, who may benefit from taking part in new activities, broadening their social contacts, and, for older children, beginning to develop more independence from their families. Siblings also benefit, as parents can devote more time to them and they are able to engage in activities that might otherwise have been impossible (Robertson et al. 2009).

There are now a variety of short breaks, not all of which involve the disabled child being away from the family home overnight. They can be day, evening or weekend activities, and can be based in the child's own home, a community setting, the home of an approved carer, or a residential setting. Leisure activities and sitting services can be considered as short breaks.

Collins et al. (2014) found that short breaks helped parents with disabled children to continue to provide care, but some parents felt that their need for a break had not been met and that social workers had limited understanding of what the carer role means. Parents wished to use short breaks to reduce their own social isolation and to care for non-disabled siblings, whereas local authority conceptions of a break appear to be linked to the focus on parenting capacity for the disabled child. However, Robertson et al. (2009) found evidence that many parents used short breaks in order to relax and catch up on sleep. They conclude that there is evidence for the potential of short breaks to improve the well-being of disabled children, parents and families. Other research evidence suggests that short breaks, when used flexibly as part of an approach based on prevention rather than response to crisis, are able to prevent disabled children entering the 'looked after' system (Harrison et al. 2011). Robertson et al. (2009), however, warn against assuming that short breaks can solve all the problems and suggest that they may need to be combined with other services in order to increase their impact on well-being.

Short breaks are a valued service which parents regard as a lifeline and which most disabled children appreciate. Parents are aware of the impact of short breaks on their child: 'The breaks have developed Douglas's social skills and interactions, his communication skills have vastly improved and most importantly his confidence and independence have reached new heights' (Welch et al. 2010: 119). Comments from children themselves often focused on the activities they were involved in during their short breaks. Things that they enjoyed included

> 'Being with my friends.'
> 'Stay up late! Time away from mum and dad.'
> 'We play and we counted how many times I went down the slide.'

> (Ibid.: 95)

This indicates that short breaks not only allow parents to 'recharge their batteries' but also have a positive impact on disabled children and their siblings. Those parents who receive direct payments to fund their short breaks report greater flexibility and control over their timing and suitability (Welch et al. 2010). Such flexibility and service user control are attributes of the broader principle of personalization.

Personalization and disabled children

Research evidence of the shortcomings of traditional services for disabled children and their families suggest that personalization may have a great deal to offer. For example, there have been problems with the provision of information about available services (Beresford 1995), with coordination of the services provided by different agencies (Audit Commission 2003: 3), with the flexibility of services, and indeed with access to sufficient services:

> Service provision is rarely based on the priorities and needs of individual families. What is provided is often too little and too late to make the best possible improvement to their everyday lives. For example, many families still miss out on their full entitlements to benefits because services don't pass on key information ...

Among key principles of personalization are prioritizing the needs and aspirations of the service user, involving people in the design of their own support packages (otherwise known as 'co-production'), and service-user control. Through access to direct payments, the Carers and Disabled Children Act 2000 extended self-directed support both to the parents of disabled children and to disabled young people themselves from the age of sixteen upwards. More recently, direct payments have been only one way that *personal budgets* for social care are delivered. A personal budget is a ring-fenced sum of money that has been deemed sufficient to meet needs identified in a social care assessment. *Putting People First* (DoH 2007b) supported the further extension of self-directed support through *individual budgets*. An individual budget works on the same principles as a personal budget but includes funding from a number of different streams – for example, social care and education.

The last Labour government commissioned an evaluation of pilot programmes for individual budgets for disabled children and their families. These drew in funding for social care, education and health provision. It was found that the majority of parents and young people who had individual budgets reported feeling they had greater control over the help they received, and over half rated the support received through the pilot more highly than the support they had formerly received (Johnson et al. 2011). There was also an improvement in access to social care, in particular the use of personal assistants and short breaks. The quality of young people's social lives showed a significant improvement, and this was often the result of the flexible use of personal assistants and mainstream or community provision. There was also an improvement in the social life of some parents. The overall levels of stress experienced by families had not greatly reduced as a result of the pilots, although lone-parent families reported a greater than average improvement.

Following publication of the Green Paper *Support and Aspiration: A New Approach to Special Educational Needs and Disability* (DfE 2011), the coalition government funded the SEND Pathfinder programme, a set of pilot studies to test the proposals in the Green Paper, among which were the introduction of integrated Education, Health and Care Plans, to replace the existing Statements of Special Educational Needs, and individual budgets for children, young people and their families. Interim findings from the evaluation (Craston et al. 2014) were that families on the Pathfinder programme were more positive about some aspects of the assessment and planning system than families on the existing system. For example, they were significantly more satisfied both with the way their opinions and suggestions were listened to and with the effectiveness of information sharing between professionals. Feedback on the delivery of support was significantly more positive among Pathfinder families than among the comparison group, in particular regarding the amount of choice of provider they had, the support being sufficient to meet their child's needs, and the suitability of both the education and social care services that they had received. It was concluded that there had been a positive impact on children's confidence and aspirations. However, there was no evidence at this interim stage that the Pathfinder programme led to improved health or quality of life of children, young people or parents.

The legislation that resulted from the Green Paper and pilot studies was the Children and Families Act 2014, which was fully implemented in April 2015. Previous social care legislation remains in place, and the Children and Families Act does not introduce any new duties to deliver social care services. The Code of Practice states that, if a need is established for social care services that can be provided under the Chronically Sick and Disabled Persons Act 1970, those services must be provided under that Act rather than under Section 17 of the Children Act 1989. However, additional services can be provided under the Children Act. The Education, Health and Care Plans introduced by the Act are designed to last until a young person is twenty-five years old. This will therefore require the involvement of social workers from adults' as well as children's services.

This new legislation includes a duty for local authorities to have regard to the child or young person's wishes and a duty to promote the participation of children and parents in any decisions made under the Act. Local authorities and other agencies should engage directly with young people rather than their parents when they reach the end of the school year in which they reach the age of sixteen. Children, young people and their parents should be provided with the information, support and independent advice they need in order to participate in assessment and planning. In particular, local authorities must publish a 'local offer' of services available to support children with special educational needs and disabilities; they must also involve disabled children and their parents in the development of the local offer.

The focus of the Children and Families Act is on outcomes, aspirations and preparation for adulthood. Local authorities should be supporting the child or young person and their parents to help them achieve the best possible educational and other outcomes, preparing them effectively for independent living and employment. Early identification of needs and early intervention are emphasized, as is collaboration between education, health and social care services.

Reflecting the principles of personalization, the Act asserts service-user control over the support provided. This is to be achieved through individual budgets for Education, Health and Care Plans. These new plans will follow Education, Health and Care Assessments and will replace the old Statements of Special Educational Needs. They will include health and social care provision as well as education. However, eligibility for an EHC Plan will be the same as for the previous Statement of Special Educational Needs and therefore emphasizes educational need in the first instance. Children with health or social care needs will be eligible for an EHC Plan only if they also have special educational needs.

Section 20 of the new Act states that a child or young person has a special educational need if they have a learning difficulty or a disability which calls for special educational provision to be made for them. However, not all children with special educational needs will need an EHC Plan. As under previous legislation, many needs should be met through additional support provided within schools. In deciding whether to carry out an EHC assessment, local authorities should follow guidance in the Code of Practice. This sets out the issues that should be taken into account, including the degree of difficulty a child is experiencing, whether help already offered by the school has brought about an improvement, and the child's physical, emotional, social development and health needs. Local authorities can develop their own criteria for access to an EHC Assessment and Plan but must be prepared to depart from these where it is warranted by individual circumstances. Their criteria should not exclude particular groups of children or types of need.

These reforms have several implications for social work practice. Given the emphasis on their aspirations and wishes, communication with children will be central (PCF 7). Social workers will require skills in carrying out person-centred assessments and in encouraging children to express the outcomes they wish to achieve. Partnership working with children and parents will be crucial given the requirement to facilitate their fullest possible participation in the assessment and planning process.

The Code of Practice also emphasizes collaboration with other professionals in assessment and planning. If families are to be spared from repeating their story to many different professionals, assessment will have to be coordinated and information shared with the consent of children and parents. (Where there are safeguarding concerns, consent to share information is desirable but not essential.) It may be a challenge to develop integrated multi-professional assessments and plans when historically professions and services may have developed different priorities. The Council for Disabled Children (2014) has developed an EHC 'Outcomes Pyramid' which offers a useful way of overcoming this problem by linking the aspirations of young people, the outcomes, steps towards the outcomes, and service provision. Professionals are advised to start at the top of the pyramid, with aspirations. It is then possible to work downwards to the outcomes that will facilitate the child's aspirations, next to steps towards meeting the outcomes, then to the needs that make it difficult to take those steps, and only lastly to the health, education and social care provision that will meet the needs. In many cases, outcomes can be applicable across health, education and social care (ibid.:2014). The same child may be the subject of various social care assessments in addition to the EHC Assessment. Where possible, repetition should be avoided by using information gained from one assessment to inform others.

Case profile: Carol

Carol is sixteen years old and lives with her parents. Her ambition is to work with animals, earn her own living, and to go on holiday with friends her own age like her older brother does. Carol has cerebral palsy and epilepsy. Her epilepsy is poorly controlled, and this has made her parents anxious about her going out on her own. This frustrates Carol, as she wants to be more independent. Her parents support her if she has a seizure at home, and staff have been trained to assist her if this happens at school. Although she can speak, people who don't know her well have difficulty understanding her. Carol feels that some of her classmates are too impatient to take the time to try and have a conversation with her, and she has been the victim of some 'jokes' about the way she speaks. Carol uses a walking aid to help her get around. She receives some additional support at school and has had a Statement of Special Educational Needs for some years. However, there have been difficulties in providing speech therapy, and she has been on the waiting list for a long time. Carol spends most of her spare time at home. She has become very anxious about her forthcoming GCSE exams, is not sleeping well and finds it difficult to concentrate on revision. She has had several seizures during the night. Her parents, who are tired owing to disturbed sleep, are worried about Carol's future.

As Carol has had a Statement of Special Educational Needs, she will from now on have an Education, Health and Care (EHC) Plan. Any health and social care services that she requires can be added to the educational provisions. This will provide an opportunity to develop an integrated approach to meeting her needs. Following the format of the Outcomes Pyramid, professionals could begin with Carol's aspirations. She has stated her desire for more independence, a holiday with friends of her own age, and to have a job. Friendship and financial independence are key elements in this, reflecting participation in the community and the desire to make a positive contribution. The task of assessment using the Outcomes Pyramid is to identify what is needed in order to make this happen. Carol needs to develop more friendships with her peers, gain suitable qualifications and be able to go out alone safely. These are the *outcomes* that are required. *Steps* towards these outcomes might involve increased interaction with other young people, both in school and outside, progress with her school work, and greater parental confidence in her safety when she goes out on her own. It is at that stage that assessors should be considering the *needs* that are preventing Carol and her family from taking those steps. It may be decided that Carol needs support in order to access community activities with other young people; she may need help in dealing with anxiety and with developing her verbal communication to her full potential. She also needs to achieve better control of her epilepsy. Further support with study strategies may be needed, as well as intervention with the attitudes and behaviour of some young people in her school class. By this stage, the services that Carol needs from social care, health and education in order to achieve her aspirations become much clearer.

When Carol is transferred to an EHC Plan, she will be entitled to an individual budget to fund her support. This could be paid to her directly, as she is sixteen years old, and this would give her the responsibility of purchasing services herself. She might do this with support from an independent organization commissioned to help recipients of direct payments. Alternatively, the local authority might administer the budget on her behalf or arrange for a third-party organization to do this. Social workers would need to develop confidence in setting up direct payments, be able to advise Carol themselves where appropriate, and also be knowledgeable about sources of independent support and advice.

Transition

Bryony Beresford focuses on both transition between children's and adults' services and achieving transition to adulthood more generally: '... for young disabled people, the process of transition from children's services to adult services, and from childhood to adulthood, is more complex, extremely problematic and, in many cases, highly unsatisfactory' (2004: 582). On reaching adulthood, young disabled people are less likely than their non-disabled peers to achieve employment or to have moved out of the family home (Hirst and Baldwin 1994). Both employment and independence are important to Carol, as are friendships, social life and leisure. These are issues that are sometimes neglected in transition planning (Morris 1999).

Beresford (2004) argues that transition planning is not only about moving to adult services but about helping disabled young people to move to a new stage of life in a way that takes their preferences and aspirations into account. This often calls for a multi-agency approach. Morris (1999) found that, for young people who require healthcare as well as social support, transition meant the loss of specialist services and a shortage of suitable services and housing in the community. Morris describes their situation as being 'warehoused', with little meaningful activity or social life.

In some cases, she found that transition to adulthood had meant losing touch with people who understood how a young person communicates.

As Carol is now sixteen, she should already have had a transition assessment. Recent legislation has strengthened arrangements for transition assessment and planning. The local authority must carry out a transition assessment under the Care Act 2014 when a young person is likely to have needs for care or support after the age of eighteen. For young people with an EHC Plan, the transition assessment can be combined with an annual review of the EHC Plan. The Care Act and the Children and Families Act share an emphasis on personalization, outcomes and integration of services. After Carol turns eighteen, the social care elements of the EHC Plan can be provided under the Care Act by adult social care.

Other people entitled to a transition assessment are young carers under eighteen and adult carers of a young person who is preparing for adulthood. The provisions in the Care Act for transition assessment do not apply only to young people receiving services from children's social care; they can apply to any disabled young person. Where someone has been supported by children's services, the local authority *must* continue to provide services until steps have been taken to put adult social care services in place.

Disabled children who are 'looked after'

Disabled children are more likely to be 'looked after' than their non-disabled peers. Although many enter the care system for similar reasons to other children, there are two additional routes particular to disabled children. One of these routes is through the use of short breaks, discussed earlier. Short breaks can be provided in certain circumstances under Section 17 of the Children Act 1989, and in these cases the child is not 'looked after'. However, Section 20(4) of the Children Act 1989 must be used if the child has a substantial package of short breaks, sometimes in more than one place, and if the family is less able to monitor the quality of care a child is receiving while away from home (see chapter 4).

The other route into the 'looked after' system particular to disabled children is through placement in residential schools. Although the number of children in such schools appears to have declined as a proportion of all children and young people aged up to nineteen (Morris 2005), two-fifths of disabled children in residential care are in boarding schools (Pinney 2005). Abbott et al. (2001) found that educational reasons for placement included the inability of local schools to meet particular needs, particularly those of children with autistic spectrum conditions and Deaf children using British Sign Language. In some cases, a factor was a lack of appropriate support for parents to enable them to continue caring for their child at home. Although many of the children had been unhappy at their previous schools, they experienced homesickness while at boarding school. Aspects of school life that were viewed positively included the friends they had made there. There were a number of different interpretations of the Children Act 1989 in terms of the responsibility of local authority social care services towards children placed in residential schools, and in many cases local authorities were not complying with their duty to carry out regular reviews, produce a care plan and ascertain the views of the child (ibid.). Morris (2005) argues that, given current knowledge about the vulnerability to abuse of children spending prolonged periods away from their families, there is a need for local authorities to ensure their safety. Cognitive or communication impairments can make the disclosure of abuse difficult.

A Department of Health circular issued in 2003 stated that children should not be maintained in residential schools by local authority children's social care services unless they were 'looked after'. This provides for regular reviews, care planning and ascertaining the child's wishes. Assistance should also be given to parents in maintaining contact with their child. Residential special schools that accommodate any child for more than 295 days a year are now required to register as children's homes and to be inspected on that basis. Children whose school place is funded entirely by education are still not 'looked after'. However, Section 85 of the Children Act 1989 requires health and education authorities to inform the director of children's services in the child's home area if they intend to accommodate a child for three months or more. Once informed, children's social care should ascertain whether the child's welfare is being adequately safeguarded and whether they need to exercise any of their functions under the Children Act 1989.

Disabled children who are looked after and permanence

Stability is thought to lead to better outcomes for children, and this premise has been put into action through striving for permanence (Baker 2007). The aim of this is 'to provide the child with stability, roots, attachments and the opportunity to trust a select group of intimate others. This will develop the child's positive sense of identity and self-esteem, which is of particular importance to disabled young people' (Cousins 2006: 37). In practice, it has meant a preference for returning children to their own families or, alternatively, to a permanent substitute family through adoption. However, disabled children are more likely than other looked after children to be placed in residential care. The exception to this is children with severe and multiple impairments, only 7 per cent of whom are in residential placements (Gordon et al. 2000).

There is evidence that disabled children wait longer than other looked after children for a permanent placement; those with learning disabilities wait the longest (Ivaldi 2000; Cousins 2006). Fewer prospective adopters come forward for children with learning disabilities than for children with physical impairments.

The assessment of disabled children who are, or are to become, looked after is complex. There is a danger of attributing behaviours to the child's impairment when in fact it may derive from trauma or grief (Cousins 2006). However, these factors can be difficult to disentangle, and Cousins identifies the ways in which a child's impairment can interact with the processes through which attachments are formed. As with other children who are leaving their family of origin, disabled children may be experiencing feelings of loss and insecurity. This is likely to be exacerbated by communication impairments and, in the case of very young children and those with learning disabilities, difficulties in understanding what is happening.

For children in residential settings which fall outside the looked after system, there can be barriers to developing permanence with a family. Some of these children are in residential schools during term time and healthcare settings for part or all of the school holidays, which militates against stability and a sense of belonging. Of those who are looked after, some are accommodated rather than the subject of care orders; as parents retain responsibility in these cases, it can be difficult to plan for permanency. Baker (2007: 1177) suggested that disabled children are at risk of experiencing a 'reverse ladder of permanence', citing that they are less likely to be adopted, are more likely to be placed in residential care, see their family less often, and are looked after for longer periods. After conducting research that compared the experience of disabled and non-disabled children over a three-year period, she concluded that the picture was more complicated than she had originally anticipated. Her study confirmed other research indicating that children with learning disabilities were less likely to be adopted. Those disabled children who were adopted were adopted later and tended to be adopted by their foster carers. Disabled children were less likely to achieve permanence by returning home, and those who did so waited longer than other children. Children whose impairments were clear and obvious were more likely to achieve permanence with their foster carers than those whose impairments were less clear or those who were non-disabled.

Given the difficulties in matching some disabled children with prospective adopters and the length of time that some children have to wait, Cousins (2006) has identified foster care as an alternative route to permanence. She also recognized that some foster carers go on to adopt disabled children and points out that disabled children are more likely than non-disabled children to remain with foster carers after the age of eighteen. While long-term fostering can provide stability, it can also allow a disabled child to maintain contact with her own family. Special guardianship under the Adoption and Children Act 2002 can be used to give the foster carer parental responsibility, which is shared with the birth parents. This lasts only until the child is eighteen, but under the Children and Families Act 2014 children will be able to choose to stay with their foster carers until they are twenty-one. This appears to be a positive development given the difficulties identified for disabled young people leaving care (Rabiee et al. 2001). A further provision of the Children and Families Act is the placement of looked after children with foster carers who are also approved adopters, with the aim of speeding up the adoption process. In this instance, it appears that the primary objective of the foster carer would be to adopt. This potential scenario may therefore be quite different from one that involves a foster carer deciding to adopt a particular child with whom they have already formed a bond over a period of time.

For those disabled children who are adopted, post-adoption support is important. It should be recognized that parenting a disabled child will involve a lot of the same difficulties faced by birth families. Following adoption, disabled children are once again 'children in need', and their adopters are eligible for an assessment of their own needs as parent-carers. In terms of legal status, the disabled child has come full circle.

Conclusion

Disabled children are 'children first' and have the same rights as other children, though it is apparent that, for various reasons, disabled children often experience greater difficulties. Some of these arise from impairment, but many others derive from social, environmental and attitudinal barriers that have persisted despite equalities legislation. While services should have promoted social inclusion, they have sometimes been a source of frustration to disabled children and their families.

However, there is potential for this to change as a result of recent policy and through the practice of committed professionals. Social work requires a particular commitment to engage with disabled children, who have historically been excluded from consultation about their own futures. The emphasis on the aspirations of disabled children in recent legislation, and the focus on planning for adulthood, on outcomes and on personalization, provides professionals with a promising starting point. This needs to be balanced with the needs and aspirations of parents and siblings. As disabled children have a right to a stable family life, it is also in their interests to support families as a whole. Parent-carers and siblings, particularly if they are 'young carers', should also be supported to maintain well-being. Social workers need to be flexible in the way they interpret both outcomes for disabled children and the responses of parents to their children's disability.

Recent policy has stressed the importance of collaboration between health, education and social care services, and the Children and Families Act 2014 has formalized this in a novel way through the introduction of a single plan covering all three services. At the time of writing it is too early to evaluate the effectiveness of this beyond the pilot stage. However, it is apparent that interprofessional work will become more crucial in delivering outcomes for disabled children and that children's services will follow the lead of adult social care as regards personalization and self-directed support.

Key messages

- Disabled children have the same rights to family life and participation in the community as other children. They also have the same need for permanency and belonging. However, they face additional barriers in meeting needs and accessing rights.
- They should be able to aspire to the same outcomes as non-disabled children, although these may have to be interpreted flexibly according to individual circumstances.
- Engagement and communication with disabled children is crucial if they are to participate in the decisions that affect their lives.
- Social workers should respect the knowledge that parents have about their disabled child and recognize that parents respond to childhood disability in a range of ways, some of which can support the resilience of families.
- Personalization and interprofessional collaboration are key features of current policy and practice.

Suggested further reading

Bennett, E. (2009) *What Makes my Family Stronger: A Report into What Makes Families with Disabled Children Stronger – Socially, Emotionally and Practically*. London: Contact a Family.

Council for Disabled Children (2015) *The Role of Social Care in Implementing the Children and Families Act 2014*. London: Council for Disabled Children.

Cousins, J. (2006) *Every Child is Special: Placing Disabled Children for Permanence*. London: British Association for Adoption and Fostering.

9 Working with Disabled Adults

Introduction

While Harris and Roulstone (2011: 35) describe it as 'challenging and rewarding', particularly at a time of increased personalization, social work with disabled adults has received limited practice attention; indeed, social work with and social care for disabled adults are often seen as underfunded, Cinderella services (Roulstone 2012; Brawn et al. 2013). Disabled adults have been highly critical of adult social care provision, seeing it as a system that contains numerous barriers to independent living (Morris 2004; Duffy and Gillespie 2009) and one which does little to realize disabled people's rights. Furthermore, disabled people, disability organizations and disability studies academics have been critical of the social work role (Leece and Leece 2010). As a result of negative experiences, social workers have been seen as 'part of the problem' in relation to the fight for independent living and, accordingly, dismissed by the disability movement (Harris and Roulstone 2011; Evans 2012). The failure of social workers to adopt the social model of disability (see chapter 2) and respond to self-assessed need and increasing personalization within adult social care led Oliver to 'announce the death of social work at least in relation to its involvement in the lives of disabled people' (2009: 51). Although this criticism appears to overlook the legal and policy constraints and organizational contexts in which they work (Harris and Roulstone 2011), it is not only disabled people who have questioned the need for social workers in contemporary adult social care systems. Increased use of self-directed support has arguably left their role with adults unclear. Leece and Leece (2010) observe that the role of social work has been queried both by government and by various commentators in the literature.

This introduction may lead you to query the necessity of this chapter, and indeed of this book. However, the Department of Health and numerous social work bodies, such as the Social Care Institute for Excellence, the British Association of Social Work, the College of Social Work and Skills for Care, have all asserted the key role social work should continue to play in contemporary adult social care systems. Roulstone (2012) argues that, owing to demographic changes, social work practice with disabled people warrants more, not less, attention; indeed, it is estimated that, by 2020, the number of disabled people requiring social care will have increased to 1.3 million (Brawn et al. 2013). Social care is a feature of daily life for many disabled adults, and they will therefore inevitably come into contact with social workers. Clare Evans (2012), a disabled woman and the director of a user-led network, highlights that, in her experience, disabled adults have not only needed but have also valued social work intervention, particularly at times of crisis. There is undoubtedly anecdotal evidence of positive practice in frontline social work; indeed, some participants in Leece and Leece's (2010) study expressed a desire to have more time with social workers in order to facilitate the development of positive working relationships.

The British disability movement continues to advocate for the realization of the right to independent living enshrined in Article 19 of the UN Convention on the Rights of People with Disabilities. As social care can play an essential role in securing this right (Just Fair 2014), the disability movement continues to shape the system, bringing about service options, such as direct payments, through campaigning and lobbying. Leece and Leece (2010) suggest that such changes in the system will require a 'radically altered' social care workforce. While professional social work has a key place in this workforce, social workers need to reflect critically upon the criticisms of the disability movement and reconsider their role (PCF Domain 6; SoP 11.1). Oliver et al. (2012) support this critical reflection by detailing the weaknesses in social work practice. However, as Harris and Roulstone (2011) observe, they offer limited consideration of *positive* practice. This chapter explores how social workers can engage in positive practice with disabled adults. Considering assessment, use of direct payments and personal budgets, work with disabled parents, and direct therapeutic work, it highlights that positive practice is underpinned by a commitment to human rights (PCF Domain 4; SoP 2.7, 9.4), a clear understanding of the concepts of choice and control (PCF Domain 2; SoP 9.2, 9.3, 9.4), and a willingness to 'hand over' control (PCF Domain 7; SoP 2.9, 9.8). As highlighted by disabled service users at a series of seminars on personalization organized by the Social Care Institute for Excellence, there is a 'need to move back to the ethos of independent living' (SCIE 2012: 13).

Assessment and self-assessment

Assessment is a key function of social work with adults. This includes care and support needs assessments, carers' assessments, mental health and mental capacity assessments, and risk assessment. Social workers need a clear understanding of assessment practice and process, as this is the means by which disabled adults gain access to care and support services.

The 1990s saw a move away from service-led assessments (which focused on assessing disabled people for a particular existing social care service) to needs-led assessment (which concentrates on the identification of individual need). While this shift appeared more person-centred, the focus on 'assessed needs' rather than 'individual rights' was criticized by disabled adults (Drewett 2010). Assessment was considered a disabling and disempowering experience through which disabled adults were represented as 'needy and dependent' (Ellis 2005: 693). Furthermore, 'need' was defined by the social worker, not the disabled adult, which led to what Morris (2013) calls a 'social worker knows best type of attitude'. In practice, the identification of 'needs' rather than 'rights' resulted in an emphasis on deficits, and therefore assessments reflected a medical model rather than a social model of disability (Morris 2004; Lymbery and Morley 2012). Assessment also centred increasingly on the determination of whether adults met local authority eligibility criteria for publicly funded social care services. Eligibility criteria largely address 'risk' rather than 'need', and, as such, assessment concerned professional judgements on the consequences of not providing a service. Such focus has resulted in less than positive experiences for disabled adults, as captured in the words of Ruth Picardie:

> Alerted by the local social services that my 'care needs' were to be assessed by a member of the disability team, I became, well, perhaps not incandescent, but certainly breathless and headachey with rage. How *dare* they! How dare some stranger come barging into my house, snooping around and passing judgement – after only the most superficial of acquaintances – on whether I was sick enough to merit a subsidized cleaner. (1998: 42)

Social work assessment has therefore been considered problematic for disabled adults seeking to realize their right to independent living. Picardie's reference to 'the most superficial of acquaintances' is telling, as Ellis (2011) identified that, in adult services, some assessments were conducted over the telephone, with very little, if indeed any, participation of the disabled adults themselves.

These weaknesses in assessment practice, and the fact that disabled people are in the best position to understand their own needs, have led disabled adults to argue for the increased use of self-assessment – the option of assessing their own needs for social care purposes (Renshaw 2008). Self-assessment has also gained increased attention from policy-makers and has come to be seen as a key component of the personalization agenda (Abendstern et al. 2014). While the Scottish and Welsh governments refer to supported self-assessment (Scottish Government 2010b) and the right to full participation in assessment (Welsh Government 2014), self-assessment is particularly promoted in England (Abendstern et al. 2014). *Improving the Life Chances of Disabled People* (PMSU 2005) and the later cross-sector concordat *Putting People First* (DoH 2007b) place clear emphasis on self-assessment as key to facilitating independent living. Milner and O'Byrne (2009) point out that the use of self-assessment to maximize choice, control and independence for disabled adults is steadily increasing. However, it is interesting to note that the notion of self-assessment was supported at a much earlier date by the Central Council for Education and Training in Social Work (Renshaw 2008).

Self-assessment is defined in a number of ways across policy documents and statutory guidance, as well as in practice (Abendstern et al. 2014). Various terms, such as 'self-directed assessment', 'supported self-assessment' and 'user-centred assessment', are used. Essentially, disabled adults take the lead in identifying their own needs and desired outcomes and also their preferred way of meeting and achieving these. This can be facilitated by the completion of self-assessment questionnaires. Some local authorities – for example, Hampshire County Council, Bedford Borough Council and Darlington Borough Council – facilitate self-assessment through the use of online assessment tools. Take a look at these online forms and search other local authority websites for similar assessment tools. What are your thoughts on these tools and this approach to assessment? Does it make you query the role of social work? Does it make you question the nature of assessment? For many disabled adults, self-assessment is a positive move towards an empowering system of adult social care. It recognizes the expertise of disabled adults in identifying and defining their own needs (Marini et al. 2012) and ensures that any subsequent support plan starts with outcomes that are congruent with service users' wishes (Lymbery and Morley 2012). However, more importantly, it maximizes control in a concrete way by shifting the power from the social worker to the service user (Harris and Roulstone 2011).

Some social workers have seen this shift as a challenge to their own professional expertise (Ellis 2011) and therefore as a threat to any continued role. You may have felt this way when reviewing the online assessment tools. The increased use of self-assessment will ostensibly reduce the role of social workers (Leece and Leece 2010), something that is clearly recognized by government (DoH 2007b, 2008) and which may account for the reduction in qualified social work posts in some local authority adult social care departments (Lymbery and Morley 2012). However, in practice, the use of self-assessment has been limited, and there is some research evidence that uptake of online self-assessment in particular has been low (Abendstern et al. 2014). The Scottish, English and Welsh adult social care legislation (Social Care (Self-Directed Support) (Scotland) Act 2013, the Care Act 2014 and the Social Services and Well-Being (Wales) Act 2014), and accompanying guidance, suggests an ongoing role for social work in assessment, tempering the language of 'self-assessment' with the term 'supported self-assessment'. If social workers are to have a continued role here, it is essential for positive practice that they reflect on both the criticisms of previous assessment practices highlighted by disabled adults and the potential limitations of self-assessment. This requires attention to the power dynamics within the assessment process. As you read the following case profile, identify the potential limitations of self-assessment in this situation and consider how social work involvement could secure positive outcomes.

Case profile: Giorgio and Nicole

Giorgio is a 38-year-old man who lives in a four-bedroomed council property. He has three children, aged eight, five and three, and a range of health problems, including diabetes, sleep apnoea, asthma, depression and generalized anxiety. He is morbidly obese, and his GP has advised that this is adversely impacting his physical health. He also has mobility problems and is unable to walk even short distances without significant pain in his back and knees. Giorgio was supported by his partner, Nicole, with personal care, shopping, meal preparation and parenting; she also managed the household bills. However, following ongoing difficulties in their relationship, Nicole has left Giorgio, taking the children with her, stating she 'wanted to be a partner, not a carer'. Giorgio contacts adult social care in a state of distress; he has never approached the local authority before but does not know how he is going to cope with his physical, financial and emotional needs. He is concerned that the council will require him to move out of his property if he is living there alone and advises that he is reluctant even to go out alone on his old mobility scooter, as he has faced verbal abuse from local people about his weight.

Coulshed and Orme (2012: 47) observe that self-assessment processes 'assume a high level of knowledge by the service-user'. While Giorgio may have expertise on his health conditions, physical impairment and associated needs, his knowledge of social care systems and services may be limited, as he has not used them before. Indeed, if they have no prior knowledge of services, particularly when appropriate information is lacking, disabled adults can experience disadvantage when first contacting adult social care departments (Baxter and Glendinning 2011). Furthermore, the damaging effect of previous verbal abuse on self-esteem (Reeve 2008), his state of distress and the crisis he now faces may all impact on Giorgio's ability to self-articulate his presenting needs with confidence (Foster et al. 2006: Coulshed and Orme 2012: Abendstern et al. 2014). His needs are not all associated with impairment. Indeed, a range of factors contribute to a need for support: low income, health needs, discrimination, family conflict and safety needs. Lymbery and Morley (2012) suggest that such issues may go unidentified and therefore unaddressed when self-assessment is used. Where disabled adults have complex conditions and high support needs, self-assessment can prove particularly challenging.

Giorgio may therefore welcome and benefit from social work support in assessing his needs. In their study of five local authority projects using self-assessment for preventative services, Abendstern et al. (2014) observed that the majority of service users opted for support in completing the assessment in all five projects; this was particularly so for older disabled adults. There was also evidence in this study of self-assessment leading to an inappropriate response which failed to meet the service users' needs. The courts have certainly been critical of local authorities for relying solely on self-assessment where this has led to inadequate service provision (*R(B)* v. *Cornwall CC [2009] EWHC 491*).

It is also important to recognize assessment not only as a means of accessing support but also as a service in its own right; this is indicated by the low legislative threshold for care and support needs assessment, which is the appearance to the local authority that an adult may have needs (Care Act 2014, Section 9; Social Work (Scotland) Act 1968, Section 12A; Social Services and Well-Being (Wales) Act 2014, Section 19). Consider difficult times in your own life when you have shared your problems in conversation with family and friends. Giorgio may find it helpful to have the opportunity to discuss, explore and reflect upon his situation and problems with someone trained to listen actively and empathically; self-assessment may preclude such intervention.

Social workers committed to the principles of independent living and anti-oppressive practice should undoubtedly promote the use of self-assessment by disabled adults (Milner and O'Byrne 2009). However, in some circumstances, such as those considered above, the use of *supported* self-assessment can be considered best practice. Such an approach is not without its challenges. Leece and Leece (2010) note that, despite their training in advocacy and assessing need, local authority social workers retain a gatekeeping and rationing function. In a time of austerity, the possibility that funding issues will influence the assessment is evident. Coulshed and Orme (2012) highlight this as a reminder of the power held by social workers in the process of assessment. However, the following can contribute to positive social work practice in supported self-assessment:

- *a constructive use of professional power.*   Foster et al. (2006) note that professional power can be used positively and proactively to support disabled adults to challenge the rationing of support. Knowledge of the European Convention on Human Rights and the Human Rights Act 1998 is essential here (Cemlyn 2008); recent case law has clearly indicated that these can be used to challenge limited social care provision for disabled adults (see, for example, *McDonald* v. *the United Kingdom ECHR 141* (2014) and the out of court settlement for Jan Sutton (Sutton 2012))
- *a clear focus on the outcomes associated with independent living.*   Concentrating on user-led outcomes associated with independent living, such as those developed by disabled adults in the Outcomes for Disabled Service Users project (Harris et al. 2005) may provide a framework for holistic supported self-assessment. In this project, social workers were trained to focus on the service users' desired outcomes across twenty-six domains, including safety and security, parenting and relationships, communication, and independence, as a result of their intervention. Foster et al. (2006), in their research project aimed at implementing outcome-focused assessment in local authority disability teams, found that such an approach could move assessment practice beyond the mere identification of professionally defined 'needs'.
- *adoption of the social model and/or affirmative model of disability within assessment and assessment dialogue.*   Milner and O'Byrne (2009) suggest that social workers can ensure that assessment is an empowering experience by exploring political perspectives and social and affirmative models of disability within the process. This does not just entail a focus on rights and the identification of disabling barriers but also requires careful use of language. For example, Milner and O'Byrne suggest that posing questions such as 'In what ways has disability made you a stronger person?' and 'What is good about your body?' is a useful way to avoid a deficit model of disability in assessment. The location of the assessment should also be considered. Evans (2012) observes that undertaking assessments in a disabled people's organization, a venue associated with the empowerment of disabled people, can serve to reduce power imbalances.

Undertaking care and support assessments in adult services often involves collaboration with other professionals (see chapter 11). However, working in partnership with disabled adults themselves in the assessment process is key to maximizing choice and control. This means engaging in assessment *dialogue*, moving beyond the exchange model, to share not just knowledge, but skills, personal strengths and expertise (Coulshed and Orme 2012; Gaylard 2009; Oliver et al. 2012; Renshaw 2008). Indeed, as observed by a disabled woman with experience of assessment processes:

> The biggest thing is about asking and not telling. [Social workers] need to get into the habit of asking what would be helpful. They don't seem to enter into a dialogue .... I would expect a [professional] to be trained to the task and have an excellent knowledge base, and I would expect to have an exchange of knowledge – theirs would be knowledge from their training and mine would be about my own body, and my lifestyle. (Cited in French 2004b: 104)

Maximizing choice and control for disabled adults

The Social Care Institute for Excellence (SCIE 2010b: 4) identifies the distinctive role of social work in services for adults as 'mak[ing] sure that services are personalised and that human rights are safeguarded'. To achieve this, social workers must practise in a way that contributes to the maximization of choice and control. The previous section of this chapter explored how social workers can do this in the context of assessment. Following assessment, and once eligible needs and outcomes have been identified and agreed, a support plan is developed; in this plan, adults explore and outline how their needs and outcomes will be met. The support plan can be developed by disabled adults themselves or with support from family and friends, a broker, service providers or a social worker. Helen Sanderson Associates, working with the social enterprise In Control, have published guides to developing support plans and support plan examples on their website; you may wish to explore these (Helen Sanderson Associates 2012). Social workers are no longer always directly involved in the support planning process, as increasing numbers of disabled adults are developing their own. However, where social workers are involved, best practice necessitates an ongoing focus on choice and control. At the support planning stage, French and Swain (2008: 406) observe that this requires social workers to 'encourag[e] disabled people to exercise choice of services appropriate to their desired lifestyles'. Direct payments and personal budgets are seen as key ways in which disabled adults can exercise and realize such choice, although it is important to note that they are not the same thing.

Direct payments

Described by Leece (2003: 1) as 'probably the most radical and exciting change to the delivery of social care since the implementation of the NHS and Community Care Act', direct payments are cash payments made directly by local authorities to service users in place of directly provided or commissioned services. Service users can use these monies to purchase private personal assistance, agency care and support, and equipment. As outlined in chapter 4, the disability movement had a pivotal role in campaigning for the introduction of direct payments, and they have been available to disabled adults of working age in England, Wales and Scotland since April 1997, when the Community Care (Direct Payments) Act 1996 was implemented. They became available in Northern Ireland the following year. Since that time, legislation and policy guidance has developed further, widening the groups of people who are entitled to direct payments to include older people, parents of disabled children and carers. Legislation in the early 2000s made it mandatory in England and Scotland for local authorities to make direct payments to eligible adults. More recently, the Care Act 2014, the Social Care (Self-Directed Support) (Scotland) Act 2013 and the Social Services and Well-Being (Wales) Act 2014 (and associated guidance and regulations) have reflected government desire to improve and increase the use of direct payments.

Beresford (2014) observes that there is a large body of research highlighting the positive impact of direct payments, which have been shown to maximize choice and control for disabled adults and to improve their overall health and well-being. In addition, those making use of direct payments have reported having greater quality of life, enhanced social lives, and improved emotional and psychological well-being. Furthermore, Prideaux et al. (2009) note how their use has enabled disabled adults, as they take on the role of an employer, to acquire and develop a range of skills, including interviewing and recruitment skills, accounting and management. There is a clear legal duty for local authorities to make direct payments; the greater choice and transfer of control that they can offer suggests that social workers should be promoting their use. Such increased sense of control is candidly captured in the words of one disabled adult in Leece and Leece's study of personalization in adult social care: 'Give us the money and we will sort the problem out' (2010: 215).

Re-read the case profile of Giorgio above. How might direct payments restore a sense of control in his life? What would be the benefits of this approach to meeting his needs and desired outcomes? Being able to employ someone already known and trusted to provide support would certainly be an advantage, particularly at a time of emotional distress. Use of direct payments may also provide consistency in support by enabling Giorgio to employ regular personal assistants rather than relying on agency social care, which could mean a number of support staff coming to his home.

Personal budgets

Informed by the experiences of direct payments, personal budgets are a relatively more recent development in adult social care. They have received a significant amount of attention from policy-makers, researchers, academic commentators and practitioners and have been the subject of ongoing debate (Glasby 2014). Seen by many, including government, as central to a personalized system of adult social care (Wood 2011), personal budgets are clear, upfront statements of how much money from local authority social care is available to meet an individual's assessed eligible needs and desired outcomes. A personal budget can be received as a direct cash payment, be managed by the local authority, be paid to and managed by a social care provider (in which case it is known as an Individual Service Fund) or be taken as a mixture of these methods. Individuals can use the funds in their personal budget to purchase care and support services from the local authority or third-sector social care providers, to purchase equipment, or to employ personal assistants directly. Furthermore, personal budgets can be used to purchase 'non-traditional' services and support, provided these meet outcomes that have been agreed in the assessment. Examples of such 'services', often noted in the literature, research and media, include football season tickets, air conditioning units, garden sheds, gym membership and pets. You may wish to watch the short Social Care Institute for Excellence film *Personalization for Someone with a Physical Disability* (SCIE 2011) to see how personal budgets are used in practice.

Unlike direct payments, personal budgets (and individual budgets: see discussion later in this chapter) were not introduced through legislation but, rather, trialled in pilot programmes (such as the In Control pilot sites (2006–8) and the individual budgets pilots, involving thirteen local authorities (2005–7)) and promoted in policy documents and cross-sector agreements. Various commentators have been critical of such a lack of legislative underpinning. For example, Mandelstam (2010) observes that personal budget implementation lacked the scrutiny and debate that the passing of legislation would have entailed, and Clements (2011) notes the uncertainty for local authorities that a lack of legal framework produced. In England, implementation of the Care Act 2014 remedies this situation, as personal budgets are now on a statutory footing; however, the language of personal budgets is not included in the latest Scottish and Welsh legislation. While the governments in Wales and Scotland have embraced increased personalization in adult social care, as evidenced by explicit commitment to greater use of direct payments and self-directed support, they have put less emphasis on personal budgets (Scottish Government 2010; Welsh Government 2014).

The evidence base for personal budgets has been described as both 'patchy and incomplete' yet 'small but growing' (Glasby 2014), and findings from the research have been mixed, highlighting a number of positive outcomes but also various negative outcomes and barriers. For disabled adults, research suggests that the experience of personal budgets has been largely positive, with individuals reporting such outcomes as improved choice and control over their support, better quality care, greater satisfaction with the support received, and improved social life (Glendinning et al. 2008; Hatton and Waters 2011, 2013). In her report reviewing progress against the aims of the Independent Living Strategy, Morris (2014b) observes not only an increase in personal budget use but also improved outcomes where these have been well delivered. However, the research also suggests that personal budgets work particularly well when taken as a direct payment, and commentators have emphasized that choice and control have been restricted for those using local authority-managed budgets (Beresford 2014; Morris 2014b). While Hatton and Waters (2013) note, in the Second National Personal Budget Survey, that younger disabled adults were the largest group receiving personal budgets as a direct payment, older adults may experience less positive outcomes if using local authority-managed funds.

Evidence that use of personal budgets, particularly when received as a direct payment, can result in positive outcomes such as increased choice and control suggests that social workers should promote their use. However, they have been subject to what Glasby (2014: 260) has called 'fervent criticism'. Some of this criticism has focused on the political underpinnings of personal budgets (see chapter 4), and, in April 2014, a number of social work academics, practitioners and activists wrote an open letter to all directors of adult social services drawing attention to research evidence that supported their concerns (Slasberg 2014). However, it is not just on a political level that personal budgets have been critiqued. Concerns have also been raised about how they are being operationalized by local authorities, in particular the use of resource allocation systems (RAS) to determine personal budget amounts. It was the In Control programme which first persuaded government to use an RAS for personal budgets, and since then points-based systems have been developed, including the one developed by the Association of Directors of Adult Social Services (2009) in collaboration with eighteen local authorities. However, it has been suggested that the use of such systems lacks transparency. Indeed, Clements (2011: 1) is explicit in his criticism, noting that, where RAS systems are used, 'any science in the process is jettisoned in favour of witchcraft.' The courts have also been critical of RAS systems for a lack of transparency, albeit they have not been declared unlawful (see, for example, *R (Saava)* v. *Kensington & Chelsea RLBC [2010]* and *KM* v. *Cambridge County Council [2012]*), and even a former developer and proponent of resource allocation systems, Simon Duffy (previously the chief executive of In Control), has subsequently criticized their use (Duffy 2012). While Duffy continues to believe that knowledge of the budget available in advance is a useful way of enabling service users to take control, in practice it has disempowered social workers, who would previously have been able to identify factors which might not have been revealed by the questionnaires and points systems of the RAS. Duffy maintains that local authorities have adopted the RAS without reference to human rights; that it can be used to disguise cuts and to cap budgets; and, as highlighted in the courts, that calculations are not transparent.

Individual budgets and the Right to Control Trailblazers

In her examination of the barriers to independent living inherent in the adult social care system, Morris (2004) identified the complexity caused by the existence of multiple funding sources for support. In recognition of this complexity, when budgets for social care were piloted across thirteen local authorities in England in 2005–7, they took the form of *individual budgets* rather than personal budgets. Although there is some evidence of these terms being used interchangeably, they are different in form: a personal budget draws only on adult social care monies, and individual budgets bring together multiple funding streams, including, *inter alia*, adult social care monies, Access to Work funds, and the Disabled Facilities Grant. While the evaluation of these individual budgets noted positive outcomes for disabled adults of working age, various barriers were observed in relation to the integration of funding streams, which impacted on overall outcomes (Glendinning et al. 2008).

Building on the experiences of individual budgets and the findings of the Individual Budgets Evaluation Network (IBSEN) study (Glendinning et al. 2008), government established the Right to Control Trailblazers pilot projects. Established by the Welfare Reform Act 2009 and starting in 2010, these schemes enabled disabled adults to access a personal budget that pooled resources from six funding streams: adult social care, Supporting People funds, the Independent Living Fund, the Disabled Facilities Grant, Work Choice and Access to Work. Service users were then able to exercise choice over how their budget was spent. The pilots ran until December 2013 and were evaluated in a study that compared outcomes for those in Right to Control Trailblazer areas with a comparison group of those outside the pilot schemes (Tu et al. 2013). The evaluation report authors argue that the Right to Control approach had potential for positive outcomes but was not working well in practice, with many disabled adults stating they were receiving the same service as before. In particular, there was no evidence of positive impact for disabled adults in relation to their experiences of applying for services, organizing services and their day-to-day lives. Being clear about what the funds could be used for, being able to realize choices in how the funds were spent, and having help in arranging support appeared to be key to the success of the model and resulted in some positive outcomes and increased flexibility for users. However, in July 2014, the then minister for disabled people, Mark Harper, announced that the Right to Control scheme would not be rolled out nationally.

Personalized adult social care: whither the social work role?

Despite the critique of the 'mechanisms' of personal budgets, Morris (2014c) observes that the principles of being aware of an available budget up-front and the choice and control that this can engender are positive; as such, she argues that calls to abandon personal budgets per se should be avoided. Disabled adults have long objected to professionals controlling their support, an approach reflecting what Vic Finkelstein terms an 'administrative model of disability', within which social workers 'administer' intervention (cited in Oldman 2002). Social workers should therefore promote the use of direct payments and personal budgets, taken as direct payments, as a mechanism to maximize choice and control. However, the increased use of such schemes raises questions about the role of social workers apropos disabled adults. The Department of Health and the Association of Directors of Adult Social Services have suggested that social workers' involvement in personalized adult social care is essential, but that their role will change from one of assessor and care manager to one of adviser, care navigator and broker. However, Leece and Leece (2010) found that a number of disabled adults would not choose social workers to undertake a brokerage role, seeing them as non-independent professionals who controlled access to state-funded resources. Indeed, many stated a preference for support to come from centres for independent living or disabled people's organizations; the importance of these organizations in facilitating personalized adult social care and independent living is noted in the research literature (Glasby 2011), particularly for adults from BME communities (Moriarty 2014). As such, some participants in Leece and Leece's (2010: 214) study suggest there is no longer a need for social work intervention:

> I think disabled people and their carers are perfectly capable of deciding for them-selves the services they need.

> I would not want interference from any social worker ... telling me how I should spend my money.

As noted by Roulstone (2012: 151), '[i]n the era of personalization, a preparedness to hand over forms of control is a prerequisite not an option in social work practice', and therefore social workers need to promote the use of such approaches as out-lined above, albeit the result is a reduced or non-ongoing role. However, this does not mean a complete demise of social work practice with disabled adults. Research has also highlighted that, for some, particularly older adults, personal budgets have worked best when social workers have been involved, helping them navigate social care systems and develop support plans (Glendinning et al. 2008; Newbronner et al. 2011; Hatton and Waters 2013; Just Fair 2014). Social workers may have a role in responding to situations of conflict between service users and directly employed personal assistants (Faulkner 2012), advising on matters related to direct payment use and facilitated sex (Bywater and Jones 2007) or sharing knowledge about care sys-tems and services. This recognizes that use of personal budgets is about much more than the transfer of money: 'I desperately want someone to help me at bedtime but I can't begin to start recruiting someone. This isn't just about money; it's about knowl-edge and contacts' (disabled adult of working age, cited in Brawn et al. 2013: 26).

Local authorities that have failed to provide support to disabled adults making use of direct payments have been challenged by the local government ombuds-man. For example, Thurrock Council was criticized for failing to support Ms J., a disabled woman who was struggling with her direct payment. In her report, the local government ombudsman stated that it was clear to the council that Ms J. was having difficulty managing her direct payment and therefore they should have been proactive in commissioning care and support for her (Martin 2013). Social workers in England should be particularly mindful of the 'information and advice' duty contained in the Care Act 2014 and ensure that those in receipt of care and support, however managed and funded, have access to appropriate information and advice.

Personal budgets are not a panacea to the challenge of maximizing choice and control within the adult social care system. Indeed, Morris (2004) observes that poor-quality social care services can also diminish choice and control, particularly where care and support staff have an inadequate understanding of independent living principles. Furthermore, Wood (2011) highlights the need to develop methods to afford choice and control to those deciding not to receive a personal budget as a direct payment. One such method identified in Wood's report, and of importance for social workers, is the provision of support in a personalized way (what Wood terms 'the personal touch'). Achieving a 'personal touch' requires social workers to focus on personal qualities and values over processes in their interactions with service users. Recognizing and valuing disabled adults as individuals, thus demonstrating that they are 'cared about' rather than just 'cared for', are key elements of a practice that seeks to be personalized (Reeve 2008; Beresford 2014); this approach is realized by planning services around the person and their self-defined desired outcomes.

A second method of maximizing choice and control identified by, *inter alia*, Wood (2011) and the Social Care Institute for Excellence (SCIE 2012) is co-production. While personal budgets have received considerable attention from policy-makers, practitioners, activists and academics, Needham and Carr (2012) argue that co-production is also an essential feature of personalized adult social care. Social workers should engage and join with disabled adults, their organizations and allies in co-designing and co-producing services that are more responsive to self-identified needs and outcomes. Such an approach utilizes the experience and expertise of disabled adults and places them at the centre of social care support (Joyner 2012). Although it is yet to be fully developed, this has the potential significantly to maximize choice and control (Beresford et al. 2011).

Working with disabled parents

While statistical information concerning their number lacks clarity (Morris and Wates 2006), it is estimated that there are approximately 1.7 million disabled parents in the UK. This figure is drawn largely from research commissioned by the Department of Work and Pensions and the Labour Force Survey, which since 2004 has adopted the definition of 'disability' found in the 1995 Disability Discrimination Act; it equates to 12 per cent of the 14.1 million parents in the UK (CSCI 2009). The term 'disabled parents' covers a wide and diverse group of adults, including those with learning disabilities, those who are Deaf, those with mental health needs and those with drug and alcohol problems. It also includes parents with physical impairments.

The Commission for Social Care Inspection (2009) observed that the experiences of disabled parents were largely absent from the social work literature until the mid-1990s; this perhaps reflects the pervasive perception of disabled people as receivers rather than providers of care (Marks 2008). While there have been calls for further study, particularly in relation to disabled fathers (Morris and Wates 2006), there is a developing body of literature and research on disabled parents and disabled parenting (Harris and Roulstone 2011). This includes surveys of local authorities, interviews with disabled parents, and reports on council inspections (for example, Goodinge 2000). While much of this research highlights concerns about the availability and quality of support for disabled parents, Olsen and Tyers (2004) argue that local authorities have begun to acknowledge and respond to the parenting responsibilities of disabled parents. Furthermore, Morris and Wates (2006) identify examples of good practice in both local authorities and the voluntary sector.

A particular factor adversely impacting the experience of disabled parents seeking social care support is confusion over whether this should be provided by adult social work services or children's social work teams (Olsen and Tyers 2004; Morris and Wates 2006). However, entitlement to support for disabled adults in their parenting role is clearly evident in the legislative and policy frameworks underpinning social work with *adults*. For example, the 2010 policy guidance on eligibility for adult social care required local authorities to consider the 'wider family context' when undertaking assessments, recognizing that disabled adults may need support in fulfilling their parenting responsibilities (DoH 2010c); this requirement is made more explicit in the current statutory guidance accompanying the Care Act 2014, which states that '[a]n assessment should take into account the parenting responsibilities of the person' (DoH 2014: §6.70). This guidance also requires social workers to adopt a 'whole family approach' to assessment, considering how an adult's needs impact on other family members (§6.65). *Putting People First* (DoH 2007b) states that a personalized adult social care system should seek to support all adults to sustain a family unit, and legislative and policy frameworks for direct payments in England (DoH 2003: §113), Scotland (Section 70, Regulation of Care (Scotland) Act 2001; Social Care (Self-Directed Support) (Scotland) Act 2013) and Wales (Welsh Assembly Government 2011: §1.23) have all been developed so that direct payments can assist disabled adults in their parenting role. Such law and policy reflects the principle that a child's welfare is best promoted by supporting the parents; furthermore, the *Children Act 1989 Guidance and Regulations*, Vol. 2 (DCSF 2010b) notes that children with disabled parents should not automatically be seen as 'children in need'.

Social workers in adult services therefore have clear responsibilities to support disabled adults in their parenting role. Indeed, a key element of best practice in meeting their needs is leadership by adult services (Morris and Wates 2007). However, it is not a role undertaken in isolation; social workers in adult services may need to work with colleagues from education and housing departments, and, where there are concerns about a child, despite support for parents being made available, collaboration with children's services will be required. Where concerns about a child reach safeguarding thresholds and enquiries are being made by children's social care (for example, under Section 47 of the Children Act 1989), Morris and Wates (2007) recommend ongoing involvement of adult social work services where the parents are disabled. One of the authors of this text worked closely with child protection teams when the child concerned had Deaf parents; such co-work facilitated a fuller assessment of the barriers parents were facing in accessing essential services.

While research has identified that adult social work services are increasingly recognizing disabled adults' parenting responsibilities (Olsen and Tyers 2004), Morris and Wates (2006) observe that such responsibilities are rarely considered a central issue in adult social care policy and practice; this is particularly true, they note, for disabled fathers. Think back to the case profile of Giorgio. When first reading this, did you consider the needs Giorgio may have in relation to being a father of three children? More recently, Morris (2014b), in her report measuring the progress made towards the aims identified in the Independent Living Strategy, notes that disabled adults were experiencing an increasing lack of opportunities to engage in family life. This should be of concern to social workers, not only because maintaining family relationships and carrying out caring responsibilities for a child are key outcomes in the new eligibility framework for adult social care in England (DoH 2014) but also because of proactive duties under Article 8 of the Human Rights Act 1998 (and the associated case law) to respect private and family life. Furthermore, Article 23 of the UN Convention of the Rights of Persons with Disabilities outlines signatory states' responsibilities to eliminate discrimination against disabled adults in relation to parenthood and to provide the necessary means to enable them to exercise rights related to founding a family.

Despite these legal responsibilities, a three-year study by the Centre for Research on Families and Relationships, Parenting Across Scotland and Capability Scotland found that social workers reported lacking both confidence and experience in supporting disabled parents (About Families Partnership 2012). Harris and Roulstone (2011: 105) observe that disabled parenting has made social workers 'uneasy' and likely therefore 'to adopt defensive practice'. Such defensive practice is evident in the words of the following disabled mother:

> My husband and I have Cerebral Palsy and my first pregnancy came as a bit of a surprise, though we were both ecstatic.... Sadly, the fact that a disabled couple were having a baby was met with incredulity and shock by the Disability and Maternity Services.... We were made to feel that we were the only disabled people in the country about to become parents.... Based on my experience there appears to be an automatic assumption that a disabled couple will not be capable of looking after and adequately parenting a child. (Louise Milicevic; taken from http://disabled parentsnetwork.org.uk)

What are your immediate thoughts about the potential needs of the above couple in relation to their pending role as parents? You may have considered needs related to the practical, physical tasks of having a newborn baby: carrying and handling the child, feeding, including breast-feeding, and increased levels of laundry. All adults need support in undertaking their parenting role, and a number of studies have identified that those who are disabled particularly value the services to which all parents are entitled, such as those from education and health (Olsen and Tyers 2004, CSCI 2009). However, research also highlights a number of barriers that disabled parents face in accessing and using these mainstream services, resulting in low levels of take-up (Olsen and Tyers 2004; Katz et al. 2007). Furthermore, a number of barriers are encountered by those disabled parents who need additional social care support.

Katz et al. (2007) note that barriers to parenting should not be perceived solely as a result of the inherent characteristics of either the disabled parent or support services. Indeed, these barriers can be conceptualized as one of three types: impairment/personal related barriers, social barriers, and those related to service provision. Impairment-related barriers may include difficulties carrying and handling a baby, breast-feeding, behaviour management tasks, and undertaking household tasks related to parenting (Morris and Wates 2007). Physically disabled fathers have also referred to being unable to engage in physical activities with their older children. However, it is social and service-related barriers that can be most disabling to parents with physical impairments, as highlighted in the following comments from a disabled mother: 'A lot of the problems we face are because there is a perceived contradiction between being a parent and being disabled, as if you can't actually be both. Parks can be inaccessible – many are to me and I'm a wheelchair user. Physical access to playgrounds and schools is variable' (taken from CSCI 2009: 25).

Negative attitudes towards disabled adults as parents from health and social care professionals and family members are particularly disabling. Many disabled adults report that their parenting role goes unacknowledged or that assumptions are made in relation to their capacity to parent (Morris 2004; Morris and Wates 2007; About Families Partnership 2012); indeed, some disabled adults report that they have been perceived as 'irresponsible' for choosing to have children (Harris and Roulstone 2011). Other social barriers, such as low income, social exclusion and family structure, can impact on all parents, but particularly on disabled adults. The Commission for Social Care Inspection (2009) observes that non-disabled family members are often automatically considered 'carers', thus affecting family dynamics and undermining the disabled adult in their parenting role.

As already noted, confusion often exists over which departments should be responsible, practically and financially, for supporting disabled parents. Furthermore, lack of inter-agency working and the existence of local authority policies that separate children's and adults' needs result in fragmented or non-existent support (Goodinge 2000; Morris and Wates 2007). However, these are not the only service-related barriers faced by disabled parents. Katz et al. (2007) found that only a fifth of parent support groups actively sought to include disabled parents, resulting in low take-up of such services. Lack of information, inaccessible buildings that house services, and high eligibility thresholds have also all been identified in research with disabled parents as barriers.

Acknowledging, supporting and validating disabled adults' role as parents and recognizing the barriers they face in undertaking this role are the key foundations of good social work practice (Goodinge 2000; CSCI 2009). In 2007, the Social Care Institute for Excellence developed guidelines on the principles of good practice with disabled parents (Morris and Wates 2007); these are considered a benchmark for best practice, and it is worth reading them in full. While the guidelines outline the importance of developing clear policies and protocols in relation to collaborative working across adults' and children's social services, housing, health, leisure and education departments in order to support disabled parents, they also define key principles underpinning best practice:

- *respecting and supporting the right disabled adults have to private and family life* This involves social workers recognizing disabled adults as current or potential parents, challenging assumptions that children of disabled parents are automatically children 'in need', and providing support that focuses on underpinning rather than undermining their parental responsibilities. This approach can be achieved in practice by addressing the barriers highlighted above *before* any assessment of parenting *capacity* (Morris and Wates 2006) and by building positive relationships with disabled parents in order to meet both practical and emotional needs. Katz et al. (2007) observe that such relationships are key to successful engagement, especially with disabled parents who, owing to previous negative experiences, may distrust services. Indeed, the personal, relationship-based qualities of social workers may be seen as more important than specialist knowledge or training: 'My social worker isn't trained in visual impairment but she is really approachable and I have been able to develop a really good, support-ive relationship with her' (Visually impaired mother, in Olsen and Tyers 2004: 2).

- *meeting support needs by enabling disabled parents to access universal services*   Social workers should ensure disabled parents have access to informa-tion about local services in a range of formats. Disabled parents report that having accessible information on housing support, benefits and managing finance/debt is also very helpful (Katz et al. 2007). Focusing on disabled adults' rights and enti-tlements to mainstream parenting support is essential (Olsen and Tyers 2004), and social workers should work with parents to identify and remove barriers to accessing such support.

- *supporting disabled parents to look after their children in a timely manner and addressing needs in the context of the whole family*   Disabled parents have described their need for preventative, prompt and flexible services which 'fit' in with their family life (Morris and Wates 2006; CSCI 2009). While this may neces-sitate significant packages of support, Olsen and Tyers (2004) note the potential of low cost, innovative solutions such as setting up 'walking bus' schemes with local schools. Disabled parents also report valuing support that maximizes their choice and control (ibid.). Making greater use of direct payments to fund special-ist equipment and personal assistants who can support both the children and the parents is one way to provide support that fits in with family life. However, disabled parents have highlighted that direct payments are not a panacea (CSCI 2009); social workers must therefore also work to facilitate access to the universal services to which disabled parents are entitled and provide emotional support in the context of a positive working relationships.

Most solutions to barrier removal are devised by and with disabled parents (Olsen and Tyers 2004). As such, it is unsurprising that many disabled parents report on the benefits of peer support (Morris and Wates 2006; Katz et al. 2007; About Families Partnership 2012). The value of this support is captured in the words of Louise Milicevic, the disabled mother whose words appeared earlier in this section: 'A disa-bled parent helped me put things into perspective and gave me some renewed belief in my ability. She taught me techniques to lift, change, carry and feed the baby' (taken from http://disabledparentsnetwork.org.uk). Help of this nature can be facilitated by social workers by putting disabled parents in contact with organizations such as the Disabled Parents Network or DPPI (Disability, Pregnancy and Parenthood International) or by developing more informal, local networks in partnership with local parents.

Direct work with disabled adults

As already noted, disabled adults making contact with social work services may present with a range of difficulties, some of which cannot necessarily be met by care and support packages, direct payments or personal budgets. These include, *inter alia*, relationship difficulties and family conflict, housing issues, poverty and debt, and discrimination. Milner and O'Byrne (2009) highlight that long-standing physical impairment can impact adversely on psychological and sexual well-being, in addition to daily living and social care needs. Reeve (2012) identifies that some disabling barriers affect emotional well-being, a form of oppression she terms 'psycho-emotional disablism' (see chapter 2). Negative representations of disabled people in the media, patronizing or overly protective interactions with family, professionals and the public, and being repeatedly stared at when one ventures out all have an influence on emotional well-being and can have a significant detrimental effect on an adult's self-esteem.

Roulstone (2012) argues that psycho-emotional disablism and its impact must be fully acknowledged within professional understandings of disability. While self-directed support, direct payments and personal budgets may increase choice and control – and, indeed, overall well-being – addressing psychological, sexual and emotional well-being may require social workers to engage in direct work with disabled adults, seeing themselves 'as a service' rather than just as an assessor and facilitator, navigator or broker of services. Social workers need to draw on their advocacy, communication and counselling skills to engage in this work (Leece and Leece 2010). As you read the following case profile, consider how such skills may be used in responding immediately and also in the longer term to Farkhanda's disclosure:

Case profile: Farkhanda

Farkhanda is a 46-year-old woman who lives with her husband and two daughters. She has neuromyelitis optica, which has resulted in transverse myelitis (inflammation of the spinal cord), and is currently an inpatient at a rehabilitation hospital following a relapse. During a meeting with Farkhanda in which plans are being made for her discharge, she becomes very upset. While the transverse myelitis has caused damage to the spinal cord, Farkhanda admits that she is more worried about her relationship with her husband than her social care needs. She discloses that she has financial difficulties, which have put pressure on her marriage. She becomes more upset as she expresses concerns about the impact the condition is having on her sexual relationship with her husband, and states she feels too embarrassed to discuss it either with him or with professionals.

In their examination of person-centred support, Beresford et al. (2011) observe that adult service users saw the relationship between themselves and the worker as being of key importance, rejecting a narrow focus on personal budgets alone. Leece and Leece (2010) found that some disabled adults welcomed the opportunity to build positive longer-term relationships with social workers who could offer direct support and advocacy. It is often within the context of a supportive, professional relationship that issues of psychological, emotional and sexual well-being can be explored and addressed.

Promoting Farkhanda's well-being requires the social worker to address the concerns she raises about her sexual relationship. Our sexuality is a highly significant aspect of our lives, and all adults have a basic human right to sexual expression (Bywater and Jones 2007). Many disabled adults are in fulfilling and rewarding sexual relationships. However, adults with a range of physical impairments may encounter a number of barriers to realizing this right. A number of physical conditions, including transverse myelitis, can adversely affect sexual function and cause sexual response problems (McCabe and Taleporos 2003; Esmail et al. 2007; Rembis 2010); these difficulties can result in reduced sexual activity, lower levels of self-esteem and sexual satisfaction, and higher levels of sexual depression (McCabe and Taleporos 2003; Higgins et al. 2012). A number of social barriers can also impact on disabled adults' sexual expression, such as exclusion from appropriate sex and relationship education (Bywater and Jones 2007), reduced mobility and inaccessible public transport (Rembis 2010), a lack of privacy in the context of care arrangements (McCabe and Taleporos 2003) and social isolation (Higgins et al. 2012). Furthermore, Marks (2008) observes that a sexual relationship can be placed under strain where a partner is providing intimate care.

Should her husband be providing support, Farkhanda may certainly be experiencing this last problem, and consideration should be given to reducing the need for her husband's assistance by increasing social care provision and undertaking a carer's assessment. However, she may also have internalized dominant discourses on sexuality and beauty (see chapter 6) which could lead her to believe she is no longer sexually desirable, and it is important that the social worker acknowledges the negative impact of this on her well-being and challenges such discourse. Disabled adults have been critical of the quality of information and support they have received related to expression of sexuality (Higgins et al. 2012). In her care, support and discharge planning, professionals may have neglected to discuss sexual matters with Farkhanda, thus making it harder for her to raise her concerns. Indeed, in her interviews with a hundred disabled young adults, Maddie Blackburn discovered she was the first person to discuss matters of sexuality with them (cited in Milner and O'Byrne 2009). While social workers cannot be expected to have detailed medical knowledge of the impact of various conditions on sexual functioning, it is important that they draw on their empathic communication skills, active listening and non-judgemental value base in order to create a supportive environment in which adults feel able to discuss matters of sexuality. Indeed, 'the sexual needs of disabled people are more likely to be met if things are discussed in an open and frank manner' (Bywater and Jones 2007: 86). Higgins et al. (2012) suggest that reassurances of the normality of having 'sexual concerns' and giving service users 'permission' to discuss them are key to developing a supportive environment. Finally, it is important to acknowledge that Farkhanda's concerns relate not only to her own well-being but to the context of her relationship with her husband. Esmail et al. (2007), in their study with heterosexual couples in which the female partner had multiple sclerosis, found that, just like Farkhanda, female partners found it difficult to discuss their sexual concerns with their male partners. Although consent would be needed to share information, social workers should seek to involve partners in addressing sexual concerns, facilitating and encouraging clear communication.

Using the example of sexual well-being, it can be seen that social workers have a wider, somewhat therapeutic, role when working with disabled adults which necessitates the use of strong communication and counselling skills. Leece and Leece (2010) observe that this can pose a challenge to those who have limited experience of such work or have not been exposed to education and training in approaches of this nature. Reflect on your own training and experiences on the job or while on placement. How confident do you feel engaging in this type of direct work? What personal qualities and professional values do you consider to underpin this approach? Reeve (2012) highlights the importance of self-awareness and reflexive practice, noting that a social worker's attitude towards and assumptions about disabled people impact on the way they practise. French and Swain (2008) draw attention to the use of counselling skills in interventions which seek to enable an adult with an acquired impairment to 'come to terms' with their subsequent limitations, noting that such practice does not reflect a social model of disability but, rather, an assumption of the need for individual adjustment. The use of a model of individual adjustment to explain the experience of disability has been subject to particular critique by disability activists and disability studies academics (Oliver et al. 2012; Shakespeare and Watson 2001). Oliver and his colleagues (2012) argue that such an adjustment model neglects the wider social situation; best practice certainly requires the social worker to adopt a holistic view of a service user's life and not just their impairment, psychological well-being or social environment (Marks 2008).

In addition to making use of counselling skills, social workers can support disabled adults with psycho-emotional needs by introducing them to alternative models of disability, such as the social model and the affirmative model (see chapter 2). This can be facilitated by putting them in touch with disabled people's organizations or referring them to disability awareness workshops. French and Swain (2008) observe that exposure to the social model can develop confidence, self-esteem and assertiveness, which contribute to improved well-being. In chapter 1, Helen describes how introduction to the social model impacted on her own well-being, and the authors of this text have certainly seen positive outcomes from such interventions. You may wish to watch the short film produced by the charitable organization Scope, entitled *What is the Social Model of Disability?* and available on YouTube, in which disabled adults discuss what the social model has meant for them (Scope 2014c).

Finally, the social work role with disabled adults should and can go even wider than that described above. Moving beyond individual casework, Cemlyn (2008), Marks (2008) and French and Swain (2008) all highlight how practice can be enhanced when social workers act as allies to the disabled people's movement and use their professional power to support the ongoing work towards barrier removal and independent living. This involves learning from disabled people's organizations (Evans 2012), actively challenging policy and practice, and responding critically and in partnership with disabled people to government consultation (Roulstone 2012). Dismantling disabling barriers at a national level can seem an overwhelming task, yet the disability movement has achieved notable success, not least in bringing about direct payments and persuading government to abolish the inclusion of earned income in financial assessments for adult social care. Social workers committed to anti-oppressive practice should both support and be involved in such activity.

Conclusion

The disability movement, disability activists and disability studies academics have all been critical of the social work role to the point that social work has been seen as 'part of the problem'. Furthermore, as successive policy has sought to increase personalization in adult social care, the need for and role of social work with disabled adults has been questioned. In relation to assessment and support planning, this will ostensibly diminish, as increasing numbers of adults assess their own needs and, construct their own support plans, either independently or with the support of family, friends or those working in disabled people's organizations. However, this chapter has outlined that a role does still exist for social work, albeit one that, in order to continue and ensure best practice, must reflect on the critique of the disability movement. It suggests that best practice necessitates strong partnership working, in which power is shared and the service user is recognized as the expert on their situation.

It is essential that social workers be familiar with, and promote, both approaches that enable the transfer of control and maximization of choice, such as self-assessment, direct payments and personal budgets, and those which recognize disabled adults' own expertise. However, social workers must also recognize the possible limitations of such approaches in certain situations and avoid using them to discharge their duties to support those with care and support needs. Furthermore, social work with disabled adults involves a much wider role than just assessment and support planning. Indeed, disabled adults may present with a range of needs that require direct work or approaches that transcend casework and involve activity, undertaken as an ally to the disability movement, to dismantle barriers to independent living. At a time of increased austerity, such work is undoubtedly difficult, particularly where social workers feel constrained by their own agencies' policies, procedures and finances. However, it is such work, led by the expertise of the disability movement, that can achieve significant results. This may be why, as noted in the first line of this chapter, social work with disabled adults is described not only as very challenging but also as highly rewarding.

Key messages

- In an era of increased personalization, the social work role is changing and may undoubtedly be reduced. However, social work can still make a positive contribution to the experiences of disabled adults with social care needs.
- Positive practice necessitates the transfer of control and the maximization of choice. Social workers should promote approaches that facilitate these outcomes, such as self-assessment and personal budgets taken as direct payments.
- Adult social care services should take the lead in supporting disabled adults in their parenting role.
- Social work with disabled adults involves activity outside of care management roles, including direct therapeutic interventions and activism in alliance with the disability movement.

Activities

- Visit local authority websites to find online self-assessment tools. How could these tools be used effectively to transfer control of the assessment process to the service user while still ensuring all areas of need are identified?
- If you were to develop your own support plan, what would it look like? The support planning process requires disabled adults to plan their lives out in a way that is not required of non-disabled people. Should social workers therefore challenge the need for this process?
- There is evidence to suggest that social workers lack knowledge and skills and have a fear of embarrassment when discussing sex with disabled service users (Bywater and Jones 2007). Reflect on how comfortable you would feel in discussing Farkhanda's concerns. How could you develop your skills in this sensitive area of practice?

Suggested further reading and viewing

Leece, J., and Leece, D. (2010) Personalization: perceptions of the role of social work in a world of brokers and budgets, *British Journal of Social Work*, 41(2): 204–23.

Morris, J., and Wates, M. (2007) *Working Together to Support Disabled Parents*. London: Social Care Institute for Excellence.

SCIE (Social Care Institute for Excellence) (2011) *Personalization for Someone with a Physical Disability*, www.scie.org.uk/socialcaretv/video-player. asp?guid=91834b9d-26ef-44ba-9055-c9720606edf9 [video].

10 Safeguarding, Social Work and Disability

Issues considered in this chapter:

- The scope of safeguarding practice
- An overview of the legal and policy context of safeguarding work with disabled people
- Vulnerability and risk and how an understanding of these concepts impacts on practice
- The role and function of social workers in safeguarding situations

Introduction

Awareness of adult abuse increased in the UK in the late 1980s (Fitzgerald 2008), and the protection of adults experiencing abuse developed as an area of concern among practitioners and policy-makers throughout the 1990s (Penhale and Parker 2008). While attention focused initially on the physical abuse of older people, awareness also grew of other types of adult abuse (for example, financial and sexual) and the abuse of other groups of people (including adults with learning disabilities and mental health problems). Awareness of child abuse was already better developed and child protection considered a core function of social work. However, in addition to increased concern about adult abuse, the 1990s saw the state adopt a wider view on the type of situations considered as posing a risk of harm to children (Parton 2011).

The state has remained concerned about the need to protect groups of people deemed 'vulnerable' or 'at risk'; media reporting of cases such as the death of Peter Connelly (the seventeen-month-old boy from Haringey, North London, who died in 2007 after suffering a number of injuries caused by his mother, her partner and the partner's brother) and the abusive practices at Winterbourne View (the privately owned hospital for adults with learning disabilities and autism) have also led to increased public awareness of abuse. The important role of social work in responding to abuse has been reasserted in relation to the protection of both children (Parton 2011) and adults (Pritchard 2008). The central role of social work in child protection was highlighted by central government following the report of the Social Work Reform Board (Parton 2011), and local authorities have the lead role in adult protection; the Care Act 2014 places statutory duties on local authorities to respond, reflecting recognition of adult protection work as a specialism in its own right (Mandelstam 2013). The HCPC Standards of Proficiency and the Professional Capabilities Framework make explicit reference to safeguarding as a core function of social work, highlighting the range of knowledge and skills required. These include, *inter alia*, the ability to recognize the signs of abuse and neglect (HCPC SoP 1.5; PCF 5.7), risk assessment skills (HCPC SoP 1.3; PCF 7.4) and knowledge of human rights principles (HCPC SoP 2.7; PCF 4.3).

Research on the abuse of physically impaired people appears somewhat absent in both safeguarding and disability studies literature (Calderbank 2000; Jones et al. 2012) and is arguably neglected in practice (Oosterhoorn and Kendrick 2001; Hague et al. 2011; Stalker and McArthur 2012). This chapter explores the role of social work in safeguarding disabled children and disabled adults at risk.

The scope of safeguarding

Safeguarding practice and the social work role within it is increasingly broad in scope, involving not only investigations, case conferences and the construction of individual protection plans but also preventative work, collaboration with other agencies, and involvement in situations of bullying, harassment, hate crime and domestic violence. This broadening scope is reflected in the move away from *protection*, in both children's and adults' services, to the wider notion of *safeguarding*. While the death of Peter Connelly, the Laming Report (Laming 2009) and a change in government led to renewed emphasis on the centrality of child *protection* within the broader sphere of safeguarding practice (Parton 2011), policy and practice guidance evidence the widening safeguarding agenda. For example, the 2008 *Staying Safe: Action Plan* (HM Government 2008b) highlighted bullying as a significant safeguarding issue, and the 2013 version of *Working Together to Safeguard Children* (HM Government 2013) had appendices offering guidance on bullying, child trafficking, child sexual exploitation, forced marriage, female genital mutilation, gang activity and faith/belief-based abuse. A broad scope of practice is also evident in the context of working with adults. The Department of Health (2010a: 5; emphasis added) notes that safeguarding practice includes a '*range of activity* upholding an adult's fundamental right to be safe'; in addition to investigations, this covers preventative work and after-care. Of particular interest in relation to social work with disabled people are the links between safeguarding and hate crime and safeguarding and domestic violence.

Disability hate crime

Although there are fewer adult protection reports concerning the abuse of physically impaired adults than those for other service-user groups (Penhale and Parker 2008), there is evidence of abuse within the wider community. Indeed, while police data from 2011–12 identified an overall reduction in hate crime, they also highlight an increase in disability hate crime (Home Office 2012). In addition there is evidence of a reduction in disability hate crime convictions (CPS 2014). While the Equality and Human Rights Commission (EHRC) (Sin et al. 2009) identifies those with learning disabilities and mental health needs as being most at risk, Disability Now's record of disability hate crimes notes that victims include those adults with physical impairments (Savage 2011). These data, in addition to the work of the British journalist Kathryn Quarmby (2011), support Thomas's (2011) assertion that there is increasing evidence of disability hate crime (see chapter 5).

Mandelstam (2013) highlights that, where disability discrimination is the motivator for an offence, criminal prosecution is more probable; indeed, the Crown Prosecution Service's *Policy for Prosecuting Cases of Disability Hate Crime* (CPS 2007: §4.2.3) notes that the public interest test in the majority of these cases will suggest prosecution. However, not all crime involving a disabled victim is 'disability hate crime', which is defined under Section 146 of the Criminal Justice Act 2003 as a criminal offence motivated by hostility towards disabled people, or one in which the offender, while committing the offence, or immediately before or after its commission, demonstrates such hostility. Although this statutory provision does not create any new offence, it does place a duty on the CPS to bring evidence of hostility to the attention of the court and a duty on the courts to increase the sentence.

It is the notion of hostility that is central to an offence being considered a 'hate crime'. An offender may demonstrate hostility towards disabled people generally, which then motivates an offence, or demonstrate hostility towards an individual victim because of his or her disability (Mandelstam 2013). The CPS (2007) gives examples of how hostility may manifest itself: making derogatory comments immediately before assaulting someone; using offensive terms following an offence; or assaulting a parent of a disabled child having previously made pejorative statements about disabled people. In some cases, a disabled person is targeted because he or she is perceived by the offender to be vulnerable or an 'easy target' (Mandelstam 2013). While in such cases the level of culpability of the offender is considered higher (a factor taken into account in sentencing courts), such offences are not considered 'disability hate crimes'. This distinction has been subject to critique. Thomas (2011: 109) argues that hostility is elicited by perceptions of vulnerability and that 'vulnerability simply makes it easier to carry out acts of hostility'. The separation of such cases from the legal definition of 'disability hate crime' therefore has an adverse impact on the recognition of crimes motivated by hatred towards disabled people. A review of disability hate crime (Criminal Justice Joint Inspection 2013) has called for a clearer definition to be adopted across all relevant agencies.

The impact of disability hate crime should not be underestimated. In addition to the harm caused by the offences themselves, its wider impact on disabled people's human rights and their ability to participate in society is acknowledged by the Crown Prosecution Service (CPS 2007). The report *Hidden in Plain Sight* (EHRC 2011: 11) highlighted the scale of disability-related harassment, some of which would be considered hate crime, noting that, 'for many disabled people, harassment is a commonplace experience.' While such harassment may be considered 'low level' or 'petty', the cases cited in this report indicate the damaging effect of such harassment, which in some cases escalated to the most serious of crimes, including murder. However, a range of barriers to reporting such crimes and accessing justice remain, among them fear of further harassment, failure to acknowledge disability as a motivator for hate crime, and poor inter-agency communication (CPS 2007; EHRC 2011; Criminal Justice Joint Inspection 2013).

The CPS (2007) policy on disability hate crime highlights the police, courts and the CPS as key agencies in responding to hate crimes; however, it is noted both here and in the joint review (Criminal Justice Joint Inspection 2013) that social work may also have a role. Social workers can support victims of disability hate crimes in a range of practical ways:

- liaison with police colleagues to ensure the recognition of disability hate crimes as such; investigations and prosecutions have not always acknowledged offences as 'disability hate crimes' (EHRC 2011; Thomas 2011);
- providing information to the CPS about previous incidents, which may provide evidence of hostility and therefore support prosecution;
- liaison with the police and CPS in relation to the use of 'special measures' (Youth and Criminal Evidence Act 1999) to ensure access to the criminal justice system;
- in cases where the offender has been the provider of care and support, assisting disabled victims to make alternative arrangements.

In addition to these practical steps, it can be argued that social work has a wider, and indeed more significant, role. Increasing eligibility thresholds for public funding (Association of Directors of Adult Social Services 2011; Clements 2011) may result in disabled service users focusing on their 'vulnerability' and 'dependency' (actual or perceived) in order to qualify for support; this may then be reflected in social work assessments. Thomas (2011: 108) argues that such emphasis perpetuates the view that disabled people are 'worthy of contempt and hostility'. Advocating for access to social care support as a human right, and providing such support in a way that maximizes the disabled person's choice and control (see chapter 9), mitigates against this dominant view of dependency and vulnerability, upon which hostility may be based.

Domestic violence

The abuse of physically impaired people in the form of domestic violence has received little attention in the safeguarding literature. There are few prevalence studies and only limited research concerned with disabled women experiencing domestic violence and abuse. In addition, Hague et al. (2011) note a lack of policy attention and limited services for disabled women; this should be a matter of grave concern to policy-makers and practitioners, as what research there is suggests that more than 50 per cent of disabled women in the UK may experience domestic violence and abuse during their lifetime (Thiara et al. 2011). This can take a variety of forms – physical, emotional or sexual. However, disabled women may undergo an additional form not experienced by non-disabled women: abuse that exploits the woman's impairment and/or health condition (Hague et al. 2011).

The first ever national study in the UK of disabled women's experiences of domestic violence, their needs and the services available, was published by Women's Aid in 2007 (Hague et al. 2007). Entitled *Making the Links*, it highlights how adopting the social model of disability is essential for a full understanding of the impact of such violence on disabled women. Physical, attitudinal and institutional barriers all contribute to what may be considered a situation of 'double jeopardy' for these women: an increased risk of domestic violence combined with less service provision.

The fact that disabled women are often at greater risk of domestic violence is acknowledged in the UN Convention on the Rights of Persons with Disabilities (Preamble, §Q). This increased risk has been associated with society's devaluing of disabled lives and perceptions of disabled women as asexual (see chapter 6). Women interviewed for the *Making the Links* study reported that a lack of adequate services had resulted in increased dependence on others, including partners, family and friends, for care and support. In circumstances where the care provider was also the perpetrator of domestic violence, women were left in highly difficult situations. Additionally, the dilemma of leaving behind a long awaited adapted property, the lack of care package portability, or the fear of losing a care package, particularly where needs were complex, all contributed to disabled women feeling forced to stay in abusive situations. Furthermore, domestic violence services and civil law remedies often present as less accessible to disabled women and are less able to meet their needs (Penhale and Parker 2008). Refuges and places of safety are often inaccessible to physically and sensory-impaired women. Despite investment in upgrading refuge accommodation by both government and domestic violence organizations, Hague et al. (2011) found that many parts of the country continued to lack accessible places. However, barriers do not just exist within domestic violence services. Hague and her colleagues also found that a number of disability organizations did not see domestic violence as 'their issue' (ibid.: 155). A number of outcomes for disabled women can be associated with these barriers: limited raising of domestic violence awareness in disability organizations, low rates of disclosure, and low take-up of domestic violence services.

The findings of the *Making the Links* study in relation to social work should be of particular concern to practitioners. Many women reported that the response from social care services to their experience of domestic violence was poor. Some found contact with adult social care entirely negative and rated social workers as the least helpful of the professionals involved. In some cases, social workers had failed to notice the presence of domestic abuse, largely owing to assessments focusing on the women's impairments and health needs. A failure to ask about abuse resulted in increased reluctance to disclose. A further significant factor in women's negative experiences was the offer of care home placement as an option for leaving an abusive situation. It is interesting to note that an example of good practice in the *National Framework of Standards for Good Practice and Outcomes in Adult Protection Work* (Association of Directors of Social Services 2005: 41) is the transfer of a disabled person to a care home, albeit temporarily, in response to domestic abuse. Where women, understandably, refused such placement, the case was often closed, and no alternative interventions were discussed or offered.

The authors of *Making the Links* offer a number of recommendations and suggestions for best practice across agencies, and it is worth reading the report in full. However, among the key recommendations for social workers are:

- developing a good understanding of the dynamics of domestic abuse and the needs of disabled women. This includes being alert to the potential for perpetrators to exploit a woman's impairment or health condition – for example, rendering an electric wheelchair user immobile by deliberately unplugging the wheelchair while it is being charged. Social workers should also recognize the possible power imbalance between disabled women and their personal assistants and the potential for financial and psychological forms of abuse. Facilitating training for those working in both the domestic violence and disability sectors can support the development of such awareness. Introducing disabled women to disability organizations can also serve to empower individuals, enabling them to recognize abusive practices;

- avoiding a sole focus on impairment and health needs when completing assessments. Ask about wider needs and risk, including domestic violence and abuse, and take disabled women's disclosures seriously;
- consulting with disabled women and disability organizations and providing accessible information on domestic violence services;
- avoiding offering care home placement as the only available option and instead exploring the use of floating support workers to enable disabled women to remain in their own homes; alternatively referring them to agencies for rehousing and options for care package portability across local authority boundaries.

The legal and policy context of safeguarding

Social workers can, and in some circumstances must, make use of the law to protect disabled service users from harm. It is therefore necessary to understand the range of law and policy guidance available. While the legal and policy frameworks for safeguarding children and adults have developed differently, it can be argued that both have their origins in the notion of *parens patriae*: this notion conceptualizes the state as the legal protector of those individuals who are not able to protect themselves (Maas-Lowit and Hothersall 2010). This may suggest 'weakness' or 'fault' on the part of the person needing protection. For social workers committed to anti-oppressive practice, the UN Convention on the Rights of Persons with Disabilities may prove a more useful starting point, highlighting 'freedom from exploitation, violence and abuse' (Article 16) and 'access to justice' (Article 13) as key human rights. On a national level, this link between human rights and safeguarding is echoed in the practice guidance for safeguarding disabled children (DCSF 2009) and the first policy guidance for safeguarding adults (DoH 2000b). As such, human rights and the Human Rights Act 1998 are fundamental in safeguarding work. While the state may be considered a 'legal protector', this legislation requires the state to balance such a responsibility with individuals' rights to lead autonomous, self-determined lives, free from unnecessary state interference. In practice, social workers therefore need to recognize and uphold disabled people's right to live with risk and to remember that social care services should support people, not control them.

While the Children Act 1989 signalled statutory entitlements for disabled children as 'children in need' (see chapter 4), academics and practitioners were critical of the low level of recognition of the particular vulnerability of disabled children to abuse (Miller 2003; Stalker and McArthur 2012). However, guidance concerned specifically with disabled children does now exist within the current legal framework for child protection. The 1999 version of *Working Together to Safeguard Children* (DoH et al. 1999) required disabled children to be afforded the same level of protection as non-disabled children; almost a decade later, in the *Staying Safe: Action Plan* (HM Government 2008b), the government declared a commitment to publish guidance specifically related to the protection of disabled children. Entitled *Safeguarding Disabled Children*, this was published by the Department for Children, Schools and Families in 2009. While the later editions of *Working Together to Safeguard Children* (HM Government 2013, 2015) highlight a need both for particular care when assessing disabled children and for training on how to respond early to their needs, they do not make extensive reference to disabled children; rather, they refer practitioners to the 2009 practice guidance and the earlier framework for the assessment of children and their families practice guidance (DoH 2000a), which contains a chapter on disabled children.

Safeguarding Disabled Children (DCSF 2009) emphasizes that the statutory framework for the protection of disabled children is essentially the same as that for non-disabled children; local authorities have a legal duty to investigate and respond to allegations of abuse, irrespective of disability status. However, it also provides guidance for practitioners on identifying indicators of abuse of disabled children, and the circumstances increasing their vulnerability, and includes appendices summarizing law and policy specifically relevant to disabled children, as well as useful resources and recommended training.

The Adult Support and Protection (Scotland) Act 2007 provides a statutory framework for adult safeguarding, conferring certain intervention powers on social workers and requiring other agencies to cooperate with social services when they are undertaking enquiries. Until the enactment of the Care Act 2014 and Social Services and Well-Being (Wales) Act 2014, there was no equivalent statute or practice guidance in England or Wales specifically related to the safeguarding of disabled adults. However, disabled adults were identified as potential service users in earlier statutory guidance on adult safeguarding in England: *No Secrets* (DoH 2000b) and in Wales: *In Safe Hands* (National Assembly for Wales 2000, updated in 2003). The identification in this policy guidance of disabled adults as 'vulnerable' was subject to critique. The term 'vulnerable adult' is adopted neither in the Care Act 2014 nor in the Social Services and Well-Being (Wales) Act 2014 (and accompanying statutory guidance), having been replaced with the term 'adult at risk'.

Under the Adult Support and Protection (Scotland) Act 2007, social workers in Scotland are enabled to enter premises as part of adult protection enquiries, remove adults for assessment, remove adults from a place where they are deemed at risk, and ban perpetrators of harm from a specified place. Such actions should be taken with the adults' consent, but the need for consent can be overridden if an individual is under 'undue influence' from the perpetrator. Similar power of entry provisions are found in the Social Services and Well-Being (Wales) Act 2014 but were not included in the Care Act 2014, despite requests from a range of social work and third-sector organizations. While there are no similar statutory powers in England in the Care Act 2014, there are nevertheless a wide range of laws upon which social workers and disabled adults can draw for prevention, for support, for protection and to secure justice. For example, the Care Act 2014 may be used to provide support in order to prevent a stressful situation deteriorating; legislation such as the Domestic Violence, Crime and Victims Act 2004 can be used to secure civil orders for protection; and a range of criminal legislation can be used to prosecute offences linked to financial, physical and sexual abuse. As such, it is essential for social workers working in a safeguarding context to develop knowledge of both 'social work' and 'non-social work' law.

Disability and vulnerability to abuse

Adopting the view that disabled children or adults are 'vulnerable', solely because of their impairment or their use of social care services, risks disempowering them before any social work intervention has even begun. Indeed, a causal link between disability and vulnerability to abuse is questionable. While English social care policy and law have previously drawn upon inherent characteristics (such as age and disability) as a definer of vulnerability, the experience of vulnerability or 'being vulnerable' is not unique to those with such characteristics. Indeed, vulnerability is experienced by all human beings at some point in their lives (Kottow 2003; Hoffmaster 2006). Vulnerability itself is a contested, complex and debated concept which has been explored, theorized about and researched from various perspectives and disciplines. As such, its usefulness in the context of safeguarding is subject to debate. Indeed, the Care Act 2014 has dropped the term 'vulnerable adult' and refers instead to 'adults with care and support needs experiencing or at risk of abuse'. However, as it is intrinsically linked to the notions of need, risk and the need for protection, it remains essential for social workers to understand the concept of vulnerability when involved in safeguarding work. How vulnerability is viewed impacts significantly on how safeguarding practitioners respond to allegations of abuse (Martin 2007). Social workers must consider carefully the factors that may increase service users' vulnerability to abuse, both in assessments and when planning intervention. This requires attention to the significance of situational and structural factors such as the environment, social processes, social care service provision, and the perceptions of the individual (Spiers 2000) rather than a sole emphasis on inherent characteristics, which risks locating the cause of abuse in the victim (Martin 2007) and encourages intervention driven by professional concern, with little consideration of the experience of the service user (Dunn et al. 2008). This chapter now turns to consider those factors in the context of work with disabled children and adults.

Disabled children and vulnerability

While awareness of disabled children's vulnerability to abuse has increased since the 1960s as a result of research undertaken predominantly in the USA (Miller 2003), there are limited statistical data and prevalence data, and less research, on the abuse of disabled children in the UK (OFSTED 2012). Little is known about the long-term impact of abuse on disabled children, their experience of the child protection system and their online safety (Livingstone and Palmer 2012; Sidebotham and Appleton 2012). There is a particular paucity of research in relation to physically impaired children (Jones et al. 2012; Lund and Vaughn-Jensen 2012). What research is available has been critiqued as methodologically weak, leading some to argue that there is no robust evidence base for a connection between physical impairment and heightened vulnerability to abuse (Sidebotham and Appleton 2012). However, in their review of available contemporary studies, Stalker and McArthur (2012) conclude that there is consistent and reliable evidence of an association between disability and abuse, albeit a complex one.

Research undertaken in North America by Sullivan and Knutson (2000) is often cited as the most authoritative study on the abuse of disabled children. Investigating over 40,000 children, the authors suggest that those who are disabled are 3.4 times more likely to be neglected or abused than non-disabled children. UK-based research suggests similar levels, indicating that disabled children are at greater risk of abuse and neglect than their non-disabled peers (DCSF 2009). This includes an increased risk of experiencing different types of violence, harassment and bullying. Children who live in residential settings are identified as particularly vulnerable (Paul and Cawson 2002), and, as Miller (2003) notes, disabled children are more likely to live in such settings (including educational placements).

In the UK, data on impairment type within local authority child protection cases are somewhat lacking (Cooke and Standen 2002) and, as such, the relationship between impairment type and abuse is an area needing further research (Stalker and McArthur 2012). There is some evidence of high risk where the child has multiple and complex impairments (Cooke and Standen 2002), and Sullivan and Knutson (2000) note that children with orthopaedic impairments have twice the risk for all types of abuse and neglect; furthermore, Deaf and hearing-impaired children are identified as being at four times the risk of physical abuse. However, their study found no clear association between impairment type and category of abuse. This reflects the complexity of the relationship between impairment and vulnerability; although impairment may be an indicator of risk, it is not impairment per se that necessarily increases the risk of abuse but, rather, disabling barriers in care and protection services. As you read the following case profile, consider how both her impairments and disabling barriers may contribute to Chloe's increased risk of harm.

Case profile: Chloe

Chloe is a five-year-old girl who lives with her parents, Neil and Jennifer, in a two-bedroomed house. Chloe has CHARGE syndrome and spent the first eighteen months of her life in and out of hospital for a range of surgical procedures. This was a particularly stressful time for Neil and Jennifer. As a result of CHARGE, Chloe has very little sight in her right eye and is short-sighted in her left. She has a hearing impairment and balance problems and has undergone multiple surgeries for a range of physical health problems. Neil and Jennifer have recently accessed local authority-funded short-break services for Chloe to give them a rest from providing care, particularly as Chloe does not always sleep well. Staff at the short-break facility have expressed some concern about Chloe's development; they comment that she is often very uncommunicative and has difficulties eating and walking. They also note that she has a number of cuts and bruises each time she comes to them.

The relationship between disability, impairment and vulnerability to abuse is complex. A range of factors increase vulnerability among disabled children, including the impairment, situational and structural factors, and other characteristics such as race, gender and age; furthermore, risk increases as a result of living in a society that often devalues disabled people (Calderbank 2000; Thiara et al. 2011). While working with Chloe and undertaking an assessment, the social worker may find it helpful to think about her vulnerability factors as being in three categories, as highlighted in the first report of the National Working Group on Child Protection and Disability (NWGCPD 2003):

- those connected with the impairment
- those stemming from the attitudes and assumptions of others
- those occurring as a result of inadequate service provision and systems designed for non-disabled children.

The vulnerability factors associated with a child's impairment might include reduced ability to avoid or resist abuse (DCSF 2009), an increased dependency on parents (OFSTED 2012), a range of carers being involved, often providing personal care (Oosterhoorn and Kendrick 2001; Cooke and Standen 2002), and communication difficulties (Stalker and McArthur 2012). Chloe has already had a number of professionals involved in her life and has experienced a range of invasive procedures. She may have learned from these experiences to be compliant to the actions of all adults. Disabled children may find that channels for communicating about abuse are inaccessible or that they have a limited network of people who understand their communication methods (DCSF 2009). Oosterhoorn and Kendrick (2001) note that many communication systems used by disabled children lack vocabulary concerned with abuse, sex or even body parts, resulting in great difficulty in discussing and disclosing abuse. Deaf children are identified as being at particular risk, not because British Sign Language lacks the appropriate vocabulary but because parents, educators and communication support workers lack language skills or because necessary terminology has not been developed with the children (Ridgeway 1993; Swinbourne 2012). For Chloe, as a dual sensory-impaired child, communication would be particularly challenging; indeed, as her deafblindness is congenital, she may have experienced difficulty understanding the very concept of language (Hart 2008).

It can be argued that the vulnerability arising from increased dependency on parents or carers and communication difficulties is related less to a child's impairment than to a consequence of the attitudes of others and inadequate service provision. Adopting a social model of disability in this context highlights the role society plays in creating vulnerability, not only by devaluing disabled lives but also by placing 'disabled children in situations of unacceptable risk and … [making] it more difficult for them … to be kept safe' (Sidebotham and Appleton 2012: 4). A report by the National Working Group on Child Protection and Disability (NWGCPD 2003) identifies a range of barriers in the child protection system itself, resulting in inadequate practice throughout all stages of the process. In some instances there is evidence of a failure to apply policy and procedure. The later OFSTED (2012) report, which examined the effectiveness of twelve local authorities in protecting disabled children, echoed the findings of the NWGCPD, noting a range of similar barriers in the system, which result in what Stalker and McArthur (2012: 37) call 'compromised professional responses to disabled children'.

Abuse of disabled children is under-reported, reflecting unrecognized concerns, a failure to raise concerns, and an insidious belief that disabled children are not abused (Cooke and Standen 2002; DCSF 2009; Stalker and McArthur 2012). Indicators of abuse can be inaccurately construed as features of the child's impairment (Kendall-Tackett et al. 2005), and abusive practices may be interpreted as a result of stress on parents or carers who are 'doing their best' in challenging circumstances. Neil and Jennifer have already experienced high levels of stress following Chloe's birth as a result of her diagnosis and numerous hospital visits. Professionals will undoubtedly want to empathize with their situation, but this may lead to reluctance to challenge them about any concerns being presented. The OFSTED (2012) report notes that a key feature of good practice involves alertness to the dangers of colluding with parents and carers.

Where concerns are raised and the referral leads to assessment, it is essential that this is comprehensive in nature, which may necessitate additional time being allocated for the task. While lack of knowledge about the child's impairment can adversely impact upon the quality of the assessment (Cooke and Standen 2002), social workers should explore the concerns raised and avoid focusing solely on the child's impairment or any associated health needs. Possible indicators of abuse, such as bruising, lack of communication, and certain methods of behaviour management, may be misinterpreted or missed when the child's impairment, rather than concern about abuse, is the focus (DCSF 2009). The reports by the NWGCPD (2003) and OFSTED (2012) both noted a failure to consult with disabled children as to their wishes, views and feelings about concerns raised during the assessment process. Osborne (2013) suggests that this may be linked to communication difficulties, although she highlights that this failure was evident even in cases where disabled children had no communication difficulties. In Chloe's situation, features of CHARGE syndrome may be directly related to some of the presenting issues. For example, her lack of communication may be linked to deafblindness and the cuts and bruises a result of falls owing to balance problems. Difficulties with eating have also been linked to the physical health problems associated with CHARGE. However, these presenting issues may be indicative of a lack of stimulation, an unwillingness on behalf of Neil and Jennifer to learn new means of communication, and possible physical abuse and neglect. If Chloe was not previously independently mobile, bruises in places that would not ordinarily be of concern on an ambulant child should be investigated.

In addition to referral and assessment, barriers have been identified in relation to child protection enquiries. The NWGCPD (2003) found evidence of police reluctance to investigate and noted an assumption that cases could not proceed if the child had not disclosed; as a result, few cases reached the case conference stage. A key finding of the OFSTED (2012) report was that disabled children were less likely to become the subject of a child protection plan than non-disabled children in need; child protection concerns were not being recognized even where children had been known to social care services, as children in need, for some time. As a result, appropriate protection services were not put in place.

Edwards and Richardson (2003) comment on the lack of referral to mainstream family support services for those families with a disabled child, resulting in no safeguarding action being taken unless abuse reaches levels requiring removal from the family home. In Chloe's situation, mainstream family support services may feel they lack sufficient skill and expertise in relation to her particular impairments and needs. The result is either a delay in the provision of support services, or no provision, owing to a lack of alternative suitable care. This situation is exacerbated when informal sources of support, such as that provided by grandparents or wider family, are not available; in some cases, wider family lack the confidence to provide support for a disabled child (Göransson 2008). Disabled children may therefore remain dependent on parents or carers who may be abusing them. This mirrors the experiences, discussed earlier, of disabled women who experience domestic violence at the hands of partners who also undertake a caring role: it is the lack of accessible and appropriate services that places the disabled person in a situation of increased vulnerability and risk. Where alternative services are available, OFSTED (2012) reports that many families experienced these as poorly coordinated, resulting in increased isolation; the DCSF (2009) notes this as a particular experience for disabled children from BAME communities. Such isolation is a further factor in increasing vulnerability to abuse.

Finally, as noted in relation to disability hate crime, there are barriers to accessing justice within the child protection system for the disabled child. While the Ministry of Justice guidance *Achieving Best Evidence in Criminal Proceedings* (Home Office 2007) has been positive in relation to providing instruction on meeting the needs of disabled children within the criminal justice system, barriers continue to exist which prevent cases ever reaching court, most notably the attitudinal barriers in relation to the credibility of disabled children as witnesses (Love et al. 2003).

Although there is limited research on the effectiveness of UK child protection processes for disabled children, the 2012 OFSTED report identifies a range of 'good practice' examples. The key features of good practice are informed by a human rights approach and the social model of disability: disabled children have a right to protection from abuse, and social workers should seek to remove the barriers identified above in order to make the child protection and criminal justice systems accessible. This necessitates strong communication skills, thorough assessment, outcome-focused child protection plans, and practice that remains centred on the child.

Disabled adults and vulnerability

Research on the abuse of physically impaired adults and those with long-term physical health conditions appears to be somewhat limited. While physically impaired adults may have met earlier definitions of a 'vulnerable adult', and also the more contemporary term 'adult at risk' found in the Care Act 2014 and Social Services and Well-Being (Wales) Act 2014, the perception of disabled adults as vulnerable is contentious and has been challenged by disabled people, disabled people's organizations, commentators and academics. In the 2009 review of *No Secrets* (DoH 2009), it was noted that disabled service users found the term disempowering. Labelling a disabled person as a 'vulnerable person', based solely on their impairment or need for social care services, certainly appears contrary to the social model of disability. Failure to acknowledge the significance of discrimination and societal and environmental factors in the construction of vulnerability may result in oppressive practice (Kemshall 2002; Satz 2008).

While a causal relationship between disability and vulnerability is debatable, there is evidence that some health and social work professionals equate vulnerability with disability. Consequently, disabled people are viewed as people 'in need of looking after'; practice becomes paternalistic and in some cases overprotective. For example, in a review of its adult safeguarding practices, Wirral Borough Council (2012) notes a potential overemphasis on moving disabled people to places of safety (often care homes), a situation similar to that experienced by disabled women experiencing domestic violence. Mitchell et al. (2012) add that this paternalistic approach also adversely impacts upon the take-up of personal budgets. Essentially, protection from the risk of harm and abuse eclipses work to secure and promote disabled people's rights, including the right to take risks. As disability consultant and activist Ann Macfarlane comments, 'use of the term "vulnerable" can be a good way of denying people the right to take risks' (cited in Faulkner 2012: 12).

An overemphasis on 'vulnerability' and risk and its resultant restriction of disabled people's freedoms has been challenged in Department of Health best practice guidance concerning safeguarding and the personalization of adult social care: the department acknowledges the impact that reactive and overprotective practice can have on disabled people's quality of life (DoH 2010a). Faulkner (2012) suggests that physical health and safety are often secured by social work practice and social care services at the expense of other equally important needs, such as emotional well-being, quality of life and happiness. The negative outcome of such practice is best captured in Lord Justice Munby's oft quoted rhetorical question: 'What good is it making someone safer if it merely makes them miserable?' (Re MM [2007] EWHC 2003). Munby goes on to remind practitioners that adults turn to local authorities not to have their lives controlled by them but for the support to which they are legally entitled. Therefore, when undertaking safeguarding work, social workers need to be alert to the potential for safeguarding processes themselves to be disempowering, oppressive and, ironically, in some cases, abusive.

Case profile: Michael

Michael is a 47-year-old man who lives with his partner, Clive, in a privately rented ground-floor flat. Michael worked for a small publishing company but was made redundant five years ago; Clive works at a local bank. Eight years ago, Michael was diagnosed with secondary progressive multiple sclerosis, which over time has resulted in muscle spasms, balance difficulties, fatigue and some sight loss. He has some support from agency care workers commissioned by the local authority, and Clive assists with personal care in the evenings. Michael tells his friend Julie that the care workers regularly turn up late in the mornings and that he is going to explore having a direct payment to employ his friend Greg as his PA. Julie is surprised at this, as Michael has known Greg for only a few months and she has heard negative things about his past. During their conversation, Julie also notices that Michael has bruising on his arms and face. Julie queries the injuries and finally asks outright if Clive is responsible. Michael becomes angry at this suggestion and comments sarcastically that Clive is working in the evenings now so is not around to have hurt him.

Lack of power and power imbalances are central to the experience of vulnerability and heightened risk of harm. Michael has a greater need for physical assistance than both Clive and the agency care workers. Morris (2011a) suggests that such a power imbalance within caring relationships contributes to the creation of vulnerability. Personal assistants, care workers and informal carers have all been noted as having the power to impact upon the quality of life of those they are supporting (Burton 2012; Faulkner 2012; Hague et al. 2011). However, risk of abuse is heightened not only by power imbalances between service users and carers, or between victims and perpetrators, but also as a result of restricted choice and control over one's life, limited access to financial resources and support services, and social isolation (Gill 2006; Johnson 2011). In Michael's situation, financial, social and emotional pressures have all contributed to the current situation, and inadequate social care provision has resulted in his increased dependence on Clive.

Social workers must therefore adopt a human rights approach to practice, challenging disabling barriers and maximizing the choice, control and power disabled people have over their own support and assistance. The UN Convention on the Rights of Persons with Disabilities underpins such an approach, noting that disabled people are not objects in need of protection but citizens who should be active members of society. In practice, direct payments and personal budgets (see chapter 9) have been found to offer disabled people choice and control. As such, many, including central government, have argued that self-directed support enhances safeguarding and is indeed key to reducing vulnerability and ensuring greater safety (Glasby 2011; Thomas 2011; Manthorpe et al. 2010; Duffy and Gillespie 2009). However, the relationship between safeguarding and personalized adult social care has led to much debate among policy-makers, disability activists, service users, service providers, researchers and academic commentators.

A move towards increased personalization does not mean a move to a risk-free social care landscape. Indeed, 'abuse and exploitation will still exist in an era of personalization' (Glasby 2011: 4). As service users benefit from increased levels of choice and control, social workers may need to consider with them the impact this has on the risk of abuse and neglect. The IBSEN evaluation (Glendinning et al. 2008) of the individual budgets pilot programme highlighted concerns about abuse in people's own homes, and others have raised concerns about unregulated and unchecked (via disclosure and barring systems) personal assistants being employed directly by service users (Manthorpe et al. 2008, 2010). Of particular concern is the potential for an increase in financial abuse, particularly where service users receive a personal budget as a direct payment. Situations of financial abuse, fraud and deception have all been reported in cases where service users have employed personal assistants with monies from a personal budget (Manthorpe et al. 2010). Some disabled women interviewed as part of the *Making the Links* research (Hague et al. 2007) reported abuse by personal assistants directly employed via a direct payment. These women discussed the difficult situation of having to challenge poor or abusive practice (as the personal assistant's employer) while remaining the recipient of care and support from the person challenged. Although these findings should be of concern to social workers, a study commissioned by Skills for Care of those using direct payments (IFF Research 2008) found no evidence of increased abuse and fewer occurrences of physical abuse.

Risk of abuse and neglect is highly complex in adult social care. Social workers need to reflect on the issues raised by increased use of personal budgets and direct payments. Are the risks posed by the use of directly employed personal assistants different from those present in local authority-commissioned care and support? In Michael's situation, the decision to employ Greg, a person he has not known for long, may appear to increase risk. Greg may be unreliable, not suitably trained, or dishonest. However, regulated care is not necessarily safer; Michael's current care workers present as unreliable. Disclosure and barring checks are also no guarantee of risk-free care provision. While professionals and families may express concern that disabled people are at risk when using self-directed support, social workers must consider the right of the disabled person to take such risks. As one adult protection coordinator commented in the study by Manthorpe et al. (2008), many service users feel the benefits of personal budget use outweigh the inherent risks.

Social workers must also consider carefully what they are seeking to protect disabled adults from, recognizing that any state intervention in the lives of capacitated adults can itself be abusive, breaching legally protected rights to respect for private and family life (Article 8 of the ECHR 1998). Mandelstam (2013) describes candidly how local authority failures may result in 'state perpetrated poor care'; while these are rarely interpreted as adult safeguarding concerns, social workers must explore whether commissioned services will expose service users to other forms of abuse. For example, Michael may be experiencing neglect and physical abuse at the hands of Clive. However, it would be naive to suggest that a move to a care home setting would remove further risk of harm. Indeed, Duffy and Gillespie (2009: 12) argue that such institutions are for 'disabled people ... perhaps the most dangerous places in which to live', an assertion supported by a number of reports of institutional abuse (Burton 2012; Faulkner 2012). As such, alternative solutions, including increased control for Michael, should be explored.

Considering what they are protecting disabled people from also requires social workers to examine the perspectives of the adults concerned. This is an area that has received limited research attention (Mitchell et al. 2012). However, what evidence there is suggests that, for many disabled people, the greatest concern is the risk of losing independence (Faulkner 2012), and this should therefore be the starting point for any intervention.

The social work role in safeguarding: working with disabled children

Child protection work with disabled children may occur in different settings depending on the local authority. Possible structures include work undertaken in a 'children with disabilities team', disability workers attached to the child protection team, or a child protection team with an established protocol for collaboration with the disability team. Regardless of structure, social workers have core statutory functions related to safeguarding disabled children, largely underpinned by the Children Act 1989. The duty in relation to reasonable suspicion that a child (including a disabled child) is suffering or likely to suffer significant harm (Section 47) is met by social workers undertaking enquiries (including assessments and risk assessments), contributing to strategy discussions and child protection conferences, and completing child protection plans. The 2011 Munro review of child protection called for a move towards a child-centred system in which listening to children, valuing their views, and establishing their wishes and feelings is essential. When working with disabled children, social workers may need to engage advocates to realize the child's right to be heard. Where children are isolated from their families – for example, disabled children in residential schools – facilitating access to a trusted person not only ensures that the child is heard but also provides an avenue for disclosure (Paul and Cawson 2002).

Communication with disabled children is key to safeguarding them from harm. Social workers should therefore be involved in establishing communication methods and systems and removing barriers to effective exchanges. This may require additional time, the learning of additional skills, and referral to other professionals, such as speech and language therapists (Cooke and Standen 2002; DCSF 2009). Social workers may also be involved in work to ensure disabled children have access to the vocabulary needed to discuss and disclose abuse; this will involve direct work with the child, liaison with families and support staff, and knowledge of communication equipment (Oosterhoorn and Kendrick 2001) (see chapter 7).

A central role for social workers in safeguarding work with disabled children is the completion of thorough assessments and child protection plans; child-centred practice and strong communication skills contribute to this process. Social workers should make use of the Assessment Framework (DoH 2000a) to ensure that assessments are holistic in scope; this serves to avoid a focus solely on the child's impairment and health-related needs, which may 'mask' abuse, and also enables the assessor to distinguish between impairment-related care needs and significant harm (HM Government 2013), resulting in the earlier recognition of abuse. Good observation skills and multidisciplinary collaboration are also essential to thorough assessment. OFSTED (2012) recommend that disabled children's protection plans should contain detailed and specific desired outcomes. When constructing plans, social workers should pay attention to the barriers faced by disabled children in accessing support services, protection and justice and consider strategies for the removal of these barriers, building on the strengths of the child. However, plans should also include interventions to meet the therapeutic needs of disabled children who have experienced significant harm, recognizing the obligations for promoting recovery following abuse under Article 16 of the UNCRDP. Once the protection plans are established, social workers have an equally important role in reviewing them to determine whether and to what extent outcomes are being achieved.

The social work role in safeguarding: working with disabled adults

As the personalization agenda progresses in adult social care, with increased use of self-assessment, personal budgets and self-directed support (see chapter 9), some have argued that the professional role of the social worker in statutory adult settings will be focused on safeguarding (Manthorpe et al. 2010; Wirral Borough Council 2012). Local authorities are responsible for coordinating safeguarding procedures, and social workers are involved in ensuring immediate safety needs are met, as well as in risk assessment, investigation, protection planning and liaison with other professionals, such as the police, professional regulators and health colleagues. Under Section 41 of the Care Act 2014 and Section 126 of the Social Services and Well-Being (Wales) Act 2014, local authorities have a statutory duty to make enquiries (or cause enquiries to be made) where they have reasonable cause to suspect that an adult with care and support needs is experiencing or at risk of experiencing abuse or neglect. Safeguarding in adult social work is therefore likely to continue to develop as a field of practice in its own right.

Social workers engaged in adult safeguarding work often face challenging practice dilemmas. The core functions of social work seem to conflict, particularly when working with physically impaired adults for whom a lack of mental capacity is not an issue. How does the practitioner seeking to promote choice and control, balance this with their duty to protect, when the choices being made are considered unwise or potentially harmful? How can the social worker safeguard disabled adults while supporting them to achieve independent living and accepting their right to take risks? These dilemmas mirror the complex relationship between safeguarding and personalization. Providing service users with funds to purchase their own support does not discharge social workers' statutory duties, and, while capacitated adults are free to make unwise decisions (Mental Capacity Act 2005), such situations do not mean social workers can relinquish their responsibilities to respond to safeguarding concerns. As noted by Burton (2012: 34), '[t]here is a fine line between personal care and poor care, and between personal autonomy and neglect.'

Although policy and practice guidance offer some direction for social workers in managing these dilemmas, Glasby (2011) suggests that such guidance does not always acknowledge the complexity of safeguarding situations. Safeguarding work therefore necessitates use of professional judgement and a rights-based approach. This includes capability in working with risk and involving service users in risk deci- sions and risk-taking. Disabled adults should be involved in completing their own risk assessments and constructing their own support plans, which include how risks are to be managed. Such involvement ensures that professional concerns about safety are not the only factor considered, but that those factors such as emotional well-being, quality of life, and maintenance of independence are given equal weight. In Michael's situation, concerns about abuse and neglect are not the only relevant factors. His relationships with his partner and friends, his sense of home and his desire for control of his own care and support are all important and could be under- mined by ill-considered intervention. Risk-enablement panels have emerged in adult social work services to support such shared decision-making in relation to the risks associated with self-directed support.

Adopting a rights-based approach to safeguarding acknowledges that the right of disabled adults to increased choice and control should negate neither their right to be free from exploitation, violence and abuse nor their rights (under the Human Rights Act 1998) in relation to degrading treatment and respect for private life. Where abusive acts or practices are also criminal offences, the right to legal redress is fun- damental. In their review of a development project entitled 'Making Safeguarding Personal', Klee and Williams (2013) note the frustration people felt at a lack of retri- bution for known perpetrators of abuse. Viewing disabled people as victims of crime rather than as 'vulnerable adults' in such situations focuses attention on upholding their rights of access to protection and justice.

Supporting people to protect themselves can also be part of a social worker's role. In addition to shared risk assessment, this involves ensuring people have access both to information on sources of help and support and to legal advice and advocacy services. While becoming an employer undoubtedly develops confidence, some disabled adults directly employing PAs via direct payments or personal budgets may also need support and advice in relation to challenging poor practice. Hague et al. (2011) report that some disabled women had significant difficulties taking action against PAs, and they suggest greater use could be made of peer support and buddy systems among disabled people using direct payments.

Conclusion

Safeguarding is a key role for those working with disabled children and adults; the role is broad in scope and includes working in the context of domestic violence and hate crime, as well as investigating abusive practices in the home and in residential settings. Social workers may also be involved in preventative work, such as raising public awareness of abuse in communities, reducing social isolation, and maximizing the choice, control and power disabled people have over their own support. They may become engaged in direct therapeutic work with those who have experienced abuse; this could be in the form of one-to-one support, family group conferences, longer-term risk management work, or referral to professional counselling services. However, safeguarding does not involve work only with those experiencing abuse and neglect but also with perpetrators of abuse, some of whom may themselves be considered children or adults 'at risk'.

While safeguarding policy has defined disabled adults as inherently vulnerable, and research has identified disabled children as being at increased risk, safeguarding situations are complex, and social workers need to pay careful attention to the range of situational and structural factors that may increase the risk of abuse or neglect. Policy and practice guidance offer some direction, but professional judgement and shared decision-making are essential; a focus on human rights is also fundamental. Adopting such a rights-based approach, which seeks to uphold disabled people's right to live a life free from abuse, requires social workers to challenge negative perceptions of disabled people and to intervene in ways that do not focus on immediate physical safety alone.

Key messages

- Social workers have an essential role in safeguarding work.
- Assessments should not concentrate solely on people's impairments and the needs arising from them. Such limited focus may result in indicators of abuse and neglect being misinterpreted or overlooked.
- While it is an important concept in safeguarding, 'vulnerability' is a value-laden term. Adopting a critical understanding of both vulnerability and risk which considers the range of contributory factors ensures that practice remains anti-oppressive.
- There is a range of law and policy guidance relevant to safeguarding practice with disabled people. However, professional judgement informed by a commitment to human rights is fundamental. Without this, practice can become overprotective and, at worst, abusive.

Activities

- How can social workers ensure that disabled children are able to disclose abuse? What strategies could be put in place for Chloe?
- Duffy and Gillespie (2009) suggest that there is no conflict between safeguarding and personalization but, rather, misunderstanding of the two ideas. What are your thoughts about this?
- What strategies would you explore with Michael to maximize his choice and control while ensuring the risks of abuse and neglect are managed?

Suggested further reading

Hague, G., Thiara, R., Magowan, P., and Mullender, A. (2007) *Making the Links: Disabled Women and Domestic Violence: Final Report*. Bristol: Women's Aid.

Laws, L. (2009) Personalization and safeguarding, in Newman, S. (ed.), *Personalization: Practical Thoughts and Ideas from People Making it Happen*. Brighton: Pavilion.

Stalker, K. and McArthur, K. (2012) 'Child abuse, child protection and disabled children: a review of recent research', *Child Abuse Review*, 21(1), 24-40.

11 Collaborative Practice

Issues considered in this chapter:

- Collaboration in the context of social work with disabled people
- Collaborative practice with disabled people's organizations
- Working with key partners in health, education and housing
- Working with carers

Introduction

While social workers practise as autonomous professionals, Rees (2014: 130) highlights that such autonomy 'does not equate with working independently from other health and social care professionals'. This chapter explores collaborative practice in the context of social work with disabled people. Described as a dominant characteristic of *contemporary* social work across all social care settings (Morris 2008), emphasis on collaboration in both policy and practice actually has a long history (Pollard et al. 2014). However, while attention focused initially on collaboration at a strategic level, there is now increased emphasis on joint working at the front-line level (Morris 2008; Laming 2009) and, 'in the present era, social workers cannot avoid multi-professional practice' (Smith 2009: 136).

Collaborative working has been seen both as a solution to the challenges of meeting people's often interrelated health and social care needs (Morrison and Glenny 2012) and as a means of providing services in an efficient and cost-effective way (Crawford 2012). It is therefore unsurprising that it has received increasing political support and is a key feature of health and social care law and policy (Whittington 2003; Rose 2011). Examples include the Children Act 1989, in which inter-agency collaboration is a key principle, New Labour's *Modernising Social Services* (DoH 1998b), with its clear focus on partnerships across statutory and non-statutory agencies, and *Putting People First* (DoH 2007b), which highlights collaboration across all public services as key to the realization of the personalization agenda. More recently, the Children Act 2004, the Care Act 2014, the Social Services and Well-Being (Wales) Act 2014, and the Children and Families Act 2014 all place duties of cooperation, integration and partnership working on local authorities in relation to their social care functions.

Despite the plethora of policy and legislation and a common sense supposition that working collaboratively is advantageous (Payne 2002; Rose 2011), numerous commentators note the contested nature of the relationship between collaborative practice and actual benefits for service users owing to an inconclusive evidence base (Leiba and Weinstein 2003; Rose 2011; Quinney and Hafford-Letchfield 2012) and a dearth of relevant research, particularly that relating to social care outcomes rather than social care processes (Rummery 2003; Goodman et al. 2011; Rose 2011; Crawford 2012; Morrison and Glenny 2012; Glasby and Miller 2015). However, the body of empirical research is growing (Gridley et al. 2014; Pollard et al. 2014), and this supports the perception that collaborative working can improve service-user satisfaction. Service users, including those with long-term conditions and physical impairments, have also repeatedly expressed a desire for professionals to work more closely together (Barton 2003; Sixsmith et al. 2014) and often experience a lack of collaboration as a disabling barrier:

> ... within three months I had probably had visits from four different professions ... I never had so many people in my life. (Parent of a disabled child, cited in Goddard et al. 2000 and Dowling 2011: 76)

> ... it is almost as if the disabled person is put in the role of detective. You have to go out and track things down. (Disabled adult, cited in Atkins 2001 and Barton 2003:103)

Failure to collaborate successfully can have serious and harmful consequences, as highlighted in a range of high-profile Serious Case Reviews into the deaths of both children and adults (Crawford 2012). Therefore social workers, and, indeed, other health and social care professionals (Douglas and Martin 2014; Sellman et al. 2014), are expected to be skilled in collaborative practice; this is particularly so in the context of an increasingly diverse and complex network of health and social care provision (Colyer 2008; Goodman et al. 2011), including self-directed and self-funded care arrangements. For social workers, this expectation is stated clearly in the Professional Capabilities Framework (Domain 8) and in professional codes and standards (HCPC SoP 9; Care Council for Wales *Code of Professional Practice for Social Care*, 3.6 and 6.6; SSSC *Code of Practice for Social Service Workers and Employers*, 4.4, 6.5 and 6.7). Furthermore, there is an expectation that collaborative and interprofessional working is covered in qualifying social work programmes (Laming 2003; Crawford 2012), and a particular emphasis on interdisciplinary and interprofessional learning is advocated (Gridley et al. 2014).

For social workers in disability settings, collaborative activity may include the coordination of multidisciplinary meetings, interprofessional assessments, and the implementation of multi-provider care and support packages. Considering such work, whom do you consider to be the key collaborative partners? You may have identified health professionals, teachers, the police, housing officers and support staff from the voluntary sector. While these are all important, Marks (2008: 46) highlights that effective social work practice demands first and foremost 'effective and genuine collaboration between [social workers] *and service users*'. Morris (2008) and Crawford (2012) both emphasize the risk of service users becoming marginalized when social workers focus predominantly on their collaborative relationships with other professionals. As such, best practice demands that service users are 'not only ... at the centre of collaborative practice, but ... also the focus of it' (ibid.: 89).

What is collaborative practice?

Attempts to describe collaborative practice are met with 'definitional complexity' (Morrison and Glenny 2012: 367). Numerous researchers refer to the array of terms used to describe the activity of joint working, and a number have already been used in this chapter: partnership working, cooperation, interprofessional work, integration and multidisciplinary working. Among other terms are interdisciplinary coordination and multi-agency working. Jan Horwath (2009) observes a tendency in practitioners to use these terms interchangeably (cited in Rose 2011). Do you consider them to be referring to the same thing? Fuller definitions of these terms can be found in *Collaboration in Social Work Practice* (Weinstein et al. 2003) or on the website of the UK Centre for the Advancement of Interprofessional Education (www. caipe.org.uk). A useful summary is provided by Pollard et al. (2014: 12): 'the prefix *multi* tends to indicate the *involvement* of personnel from different professions, disciplines or agencies ... The prefix *inter* tends to imply collaboration, particularly in areas such as decision making.' Whittington (2003) suggests that the phrase 'collaborative practice' is a useful way of uniting the various terms, hence its adoption in this chapter's title. However, what the array of terms highlights is that collaborative practice involves social workers operating closely within their *own* organizations and profession, with *other* organizations and agencies, with *other* professionals from different disciplines, and most importantly, with service users and carers.

The complexity in definition echoes the challenges in achieving effective collaboration in practice. As a result of these challenges, disabled people, particularly those with complex needs, report experiencing uncoordinated and fragmented care and support services (Gridley et al. 2014). Consider your own experiences on placement or in the workplace. What challenges and barriers to effective collaboration have you experienced or encountered? Research studies identify a range of barriers to success (Rose 2011):

- *structural*   differing organization boundaries (for example, differing geographical areas of responsibility); boundary disputes; lack of clarity in relation to overall accountability or an absence of overall accountability;
- *procedural and financial*   differing computer systems and databases that do not share information; individual agency record-keeping; complex funding arrangements and lack of flexibility in access to available budgets;
- *professional*   differing perspectives, practice models and values (for example, medical and social models of disability); status differences and interprofessional rivalry; different professional language and jargon; blurred boundaries between professions in terms of function and role; differing evidence base;
- *personal*   personality clashes and poor professional relationships.

Engaging in effective collaborative practice involves working together to dismantle these barriers and is therefore highly skilled work. While structural and organizational changes such as co-location, pooled budgets and joint commissioning have sought to address some of these, Payne (2002) and Rummery (2003) observe that such changes are no guarantee of effective collaboration; this is because positive collaborative relationships 'are largely built upon *human* relationships' (Bob Hudson 2000; cited in Rose 2011: 8; emphasis added). As members of a profession that focuses on the importance of relationships and interpersonal skills such as communication, networking and coordination, social workers can therefore make a very positive contribution to collaborative endeavour. This chapter now turns to consider collaborative practice with key partners encountered by social workers in disability settings.

Working with disabled people's organizations and the third sector ▨

Context

There are a growing number of organizations working *for* disabled people which are controlled and managed *by* disabled people. This includes not only local agencies but also national bodies, such as the UK Disabled People's Council, and international umbrella organizations. The emergence and growth of these organizations, and the development of the disabled people's movement, has seen the social model of disability, which they adopt, have increasing influence on disability policy and practice (Mackie 2012). In Britain, one of the early user-led disability rights organizations was the Union of Physically Impaired Against Segregation (UPIAS), established in 1974. The UK Disabled People's Council now represents over 300 member organizations, among them disabled people's coalitions and Centres for Independent Living (UK Disabled People's Council 2015). In addition to supporting these member organizations, the council operates worldwide as a member of Disabled People's International, which works to promote disabled people's human rights globally.

Taking inspiration from the independent living movement in the USA, Centres for Independent Living (CILs), or Centres for Integrated Living (French and Swain 2008), are now established in the UK and are supported by the National Centre for Independent Living, founded in 1997. Working in partnership with health agencies and local authorities, CILs employ disabled people and provide a range of services –information and advice, support with personal budget and direct payment management, support to recruit appropriate personal assistants, peer support and peer counselling, equipment repair and maintenance services, and advocacy. They may also offer disability awareness training and support users to develop a range of daily living and employment-related skills (Higham and Torkington 2009).

Case profile: Jatinder

Jatinder is a 22-year-old man who lives in an adapted property with his parents and sister. He has a range of physical impairments and receives support with his personal care. His mother originally provided this but, owing to her health problems, Jatinder now receives assistance from local agency care workers. Jatinder wishes to have greater control over his support as he feels a lack of flexibility is impacting on his independence and social life. He has heard about direct payments and has received literature from the local authority adult social care department about them, but he remains unsure and unclear. Jatinder meets with staff at the local Centre for Independent Living to talk through direct payments and meets other young disabled adults using them, who share their experiences. Jatinder transfers to direct payments and, together with other users, the CIL, and colleagues from the local authority adult social care team, co-produces a short video and leaflet about the service to replace the literature sent by the local authority. Jatinder is now researching the centre's database of accessible holiday venues, as he and his friends plan a summer break.

While disabled people's organizations and CILs provide a range of support services to individuals, Evans (2008) highlights their wider role in influencing statutory social care services, promoting the concept of independent living, and supporting disabled people to access the services to which they are legally entitled. She observes that, in order to achieve this, organizations have adopted two strategies: facilitating disabled people's empowerment and acquiring power from statutory professionals. While Jatinder's contact with the CIL resulted in a positive outcome for him, collaboration between the users, the organization and statutory professionals has resulted in improved adult social care services per se.

Community and social care services for disabled people are also provided by a range of third-sector agencies, including local and national charitable organizations such as the Stroke Association, Age UK, Sense and Scope. These organizations may offer advice and information services, carer support, group and social activities, training, and personal assistance which are 'complementary and supplementary to public welfare provision' (Jenkins et al. 2013: 252). There is evidence that service users value this support, particularly that which is provided over a longer period. However, it is important to note that the disabled people's movement has been highly critical of some of the national charitable organizations, notably the Leonard Cheshire Foundation, owing to their continued provision of segregated services such as residential care, their poor representation of disabled people, their low levels of disabled staff, and their high salaries for senior staff (Clark 2003) (see chapter 4).

Good practice in collaboration with disabled people's organizations

Referring to a number of successful local initiatives, Dowling (2011) argues that independent living, personal assistance and outreach support can all be developed by local non-statutory organizations in collaboration with social workers. Indeed, Higham and Torkington (2009: 45) suggest that establishing alliances with users and user-led organizations provides real 'potential for change'; as such, Vic Finkelstein argued that social workers should concentrate on such alliances, rather than pursuing increased alliance with the medical professions (Sapey 2009). While user-controlled, disabled people's organizations have welcomed the involvement of professional allies: 'We need professionals to be our allies and advocates, not our enemies' (disabled adult in NISW 2001; cited in Barton 2003:104).

If collaborative practice with disabled people's organizations means becoming allies, what does this mean in practice? Evans (2008) notes that it involves the sharing of professional power and suggests that social workers do this in two ways: by recognizing and valuing the expertise of disabled people; and by establishing links between social care senior management staff and leaders of disabled people's organizations. Bob Holman (1993) argued that such collective work with user-led organizations is challenging, as the social work profession has concentrated increasingly on the needs of individuals (cited in Sapey 2009). Placing social work students in disabled people's organizations during their training may be one way to develop an understanding of the importance and value of this work (Evans 2008).

Social workers should also actively refer disabled people to user-led organizations so that they can benefit from the advice, information and advocacy support available (Higham and Torkington 2009). In England, such referrals are increasingly important in view of the new duties relating to prevention, information and advice, and independent advocacy under the Care Act 2014. Indeed, failure to implement advocacy provisions can have serious consequences, as highlighted in social care enquiries and Serious Case Reviews (Simcock and Manthorpe 2013).

Working with health

Context

While it is important not to equate impairment with ill health, people with physical and sensory impairments may also have medical needs; for those with multiple and complex needs, the boundaries between health and social care may be blurred. Therefore, social workers in disability settings will undoubtedly have to work with health professionals. Leiba and Weinstein (2003) suggest that, in the UK, nursing professionals are the closest colleagues of social workers. However, social workers may also need to collaborate with occupational therapists, doctors, physiotherapists, rehabilitation assistants, speech and language therapists, and dieticians.

Over more than two decades, a plethora of policy and legislation has sought to improve joint working between health and social care (Coad 2008; Vatcher and Jones 2014) in both children's and adults' services, resulting in the reorganization and increased integration of services (Northern Ireland has had integrated health and social services structures since 1973 and now has Integrated Care Partnerships). This policy and legislation has taken different approaches: some can be seen as facilitative, such as the Health Act 1999, which enabled the pooling of health body and local authority budgets; others can be considered coercive, such as the Community Care (Delayed Discharges, etc.) Act 2003, which imposed reimbursement charges on local authorities failing to facilitate timely discharge (Whittington 2003). In 2004, national standards for children's health and social care services were set out in the *National Service Framework for Children, Young People and Maternity Services* (DoH 2004). Standards 6 to 10 applied to specific groups of children, including disabled children, and the framework highlighted that these standards were to be met by collaborating with local authorities (Coad 2008). A year later, the *National Service Framework for Long-Term Conditions* (DoH 2005b) was launched. This too stressed the importance of inter-agency working and collaboration between health and social care services for those with conditions such as Parkinson's disease, multiple sclerosis and epilepsy (Sixsmith et al. 2014).

More recently, the Health and Social Care Act 2012 has led to reform of the NHS in England, including the formation of GP-led clinical commissioning groups to replace primary care trusts. This Act also established health and well-being boards, which have responsibility for overseeing the integration of health and social care at the local level. In 2015, the Care Act 2014 placed a clear statutory duty on local authorities to promote the integration of health services with care and support, and the same year saw the launch of the Better Care Fund – a single pooled budget aimed at motivating the NHS and local authorities to work together more closely. These developments pose new opportunities and challenges for collaborative practice, particularly between GPs and social workers (Glasby and Miller 2015).

Social workers may collaborate with health professionals in a range of settings, including hospitals, GP practices and primary care services, integrated health and social care teams, or specialist joint-funded services such as those supporting people with HIV/AIDS or cancer. They may be involved in hospital discharge work, multidisciplinary meetings, and screening and assessments for NHS Continuing Healthcare, a care package arranged and funded solely by the NHS in England. They may also take a lead in coordinating 'joint care packages', where the care and support is funded and provided by both the NHS and the local authority. In addition to these tasks, McLaughlin (2015), in his study of two hospitals in Northern Ireland, found that service users particularly valued the emotional support offered by social workers, as well as their attention to practical challenges, such as the financial difficulties faced by parents of disabled children.

Difficulties that may arise

Despite the policy and legislative provision for collaboration, 'there is a long and inglorious history of the NHS and social services departments failing to work effectively together' (Rummery 2003: 202), which has impacted adversely on the experiences of disabled people:

> There is still little, or really no contact between the different agencies that care for me, especially between health and social services. I feel that, for people with complex problems, an annual review with all the professionals involved, and needless to say with the client and their family ... preferably at the clients'/patients' home, would be far more useful than the random meetings with all the different people over the year.
> (Disabled adult, cited in Barton 2003: 114)

Various barriers to effective collaboration between health and social care have been identified. Glasby and Miller (2015) refer to 'long-standing' differences in professional and organizational culture. For example, differing perspectives on risk have been observed between nurses and social workers (Leiba and Weinstein 2003), and there are also differences in language use and overall priorities (Hudson and Glasby 2015). These can lead to tension and conflict between members of a multidisciplinary team. In disability settings, differing models and understandings of disability (notably medical and social models), and the impact these have on approach to care and support, may create problems in collaborative practice (Morris 2008; Smith 2009).

With the increased organizational integration of health and social care services, fears have been expressed that health and medical models will dominate practice at the expense of social work and social models (Whittington 2003). Issues of status and hierarchy may undoubtedly impact on both collaborative practice and the experience of service users; Colyer (2008: 183) observes that the medical profession holds a 'superior position in the ... professional hierarchy' and may therefore seek to adopt an automatic position of leadership and priority. This is reflected in the words of a physiotherapist who worked in a residential hospital for young people with multiple impairments: 'It was the physiotherapists and the medical staff who were in charge and the teachers had to ask very kindly if they could possibly have access to the patients because the medical work was viewed as being so much more important' (Anna-Stina et al. 2008: 151).

A further barrier to collaborative practice is a lack of understanding between professionals about their respective roles and responsibilities (Arnott and Koubel 2012). Smith (2009) suggests that policy developments have exacerbated this by encouraging health professionals to focus solely on one aspect of social work activity, namely, safe and timely hospital discharge. The wider role of social work, such as the provision of psycho-emotional support, may therefore be misunderstood.

Good practice in collaboration with health

Hudson and Glasby (2015) argue that, owing to its emphasis on relationship-building and skills in managing change, the social work profession is well positioned to take a lead in improving collaborative practice across health and social care. However, Rummery (2003) reminds professionals that relationship-building among themselves must not be to the detriment of their relationships with service users and carers. Collaborative practice must therefore remain service user-centred. This may include ensuring that the perspectives, concerns and wishes of service users are valued and known by all members of the multidisciplinary team (Dow and Evans 2014), as well as working in cooperation with health colleagues to offer services that maximize their choice and control, such as the use of personal health budgets. Since October 2014, people in receipt of NHS Continuing Healthcare have had the right to a personal health budget, unless there are clear clinical or financial reasons that would make this inappropriate.

While social workers should maintain a distinct sense of their own professional identity (Crawford 2012), having a clear understanding of the roles and responsibilities of other professionals, and respecting their autonomy, can also enhance collaborative practice (Colyer 2008; Arnott and Koubel 2012). To what extent do you understand the roles of health colleagues with whom you have worked on placement or in your practice? Is this an area for future development? Social workers should be careful not to make stereotypical assumptions about the approaches of other professionals (Crawford 2012; Smith 2009); this is particularly true in relation to the model of disability that may inform their practice. Indeed, there is evidence that both occupational therapists and physiotherapists are more aware of and informed by social and affirmative models of disability (Anna-Stina et al. 2008; Ballantyne and Muir 2008). Furthermore, Spain (2008: 165), a disabled nurse, observes that 'doctors and nurses are beginning to admit that they are definitely not experts on disability and disability issues.'

In view of recent structural changes in the NHS, social workers will need to pay particular attention to their collaborative relationships with GPs and primary healthcare services. Relatively little is known about these relationships, and there have been calls for further research in this area (Glasby and Miller 2015). Social workers should consider being involved in such research, exploring the potential for improved collaboration in this context.

Working with education

Context

Education is a key determinant of life chances, and disabled people with qualifications fare better in employment, income and social participation than other disabled people (PMSU 2005; Riddell et al. 2010). Working relationships between social workers and education professionals are therefore crucial. Education and social care were brought together in directorates of children's services following the 2004 Children Act, and the recent Children and Families Act 2014 has introduced further requirements for collaboration (see chapter 8).

The role of teachers has expanded as a result of the policy drive towards early intervention; teachers are expected to have a commitment to collaboration (Training and Development Agency 2007) and sometimes act as lead professionals. They make an important contribution to achieving the five outcomes in *Every Child Matters* (Reese 2013). Children's centres and extended schools have resulted in the co-location of education professionals and other professionals.

Social workers may need to collaborate with teachers, classroom assistants, educational psychologists, early years practitioners, specialist advisers and practitioners (for example, in connection with sensory impairment and autistic spectrum conditions), and education social workers. The 2008 Children and Young Persons Act requires each school to appoint a 'designated teacher' to promote the educational achievement of looked after children, and this person will be a key contact when working with disabled children who are also looked after.

Collaboration is a matter for both children's and adults' social care; the responsibilities of social workers in adult services under the Care Act 2014 in connection with transition are discussed in chapter 8. This includes collaboration with institutions of further and higher education. It is important that social care support is effectively integrated with the support that colleges and universities provide. This can be either through 'reasonable adjustments' made in compliance with the Equality Act or through the disabled students' allowance for students in higher education. Planned changes from 2016 will shift the balance from individual funding towards universities making anticipatory adjustments to the way courses are delivered and reasonable adjustments for disabled individuals.

One of the policy drivers for increased collaboration has been poor educational outcomes for looked after children, among whom disabled children are over-represented. Statutory guidance (DfE 2014a) states that the *majority* of looked after children have special educational needs. Looked after children should have a Personal Education Plan (PEP) initiated by a social worker in collaboration with a 'designated teacher' and the child. Every child with SEN should also have an Individual Education Plan. Each local authority must appoint a 'virtual school head' (VSH) to oversee and promote the educational attainment of all looked after children and to monitor the quality of Personal Education Plans. For looked after children with special educational needs, the VSH should ensure that the Special Educational Needs and Disability Code of Practice is followed, that Education, Health and Care Plans work well with children's overall care plans, and that PEPs are effective in identifying undiagnosed special educational needs.

Teachers and social workers must now collaborate in holistic planning and the negotiation of shared outcomes in the education, health and care planning process under the Children and Families Act 2014 (see chapter 8). As the threshold for eligibility for an EHC Plan is the same as for the previous Statement of Special Educational Needs, education professionals will have a key role in identifying children who should undergo this interprofessional assessment.

Social workers also need to collaborate with education staff regarding children in need and safeguarding. Disabled children are disproportionately at risk of abuse and neglect (Stalker et al. 2010), and teachers, as the professionals who spend the most time face to face with such children, may be first to recognize potential problems.

Difficulties that may arise

In the push to break down barriers, differences between professional cultures are sometimes minimized. Bronstein and Abramson (2003), writing in an American context, maintain that, as a result of professional socialization, social workers show a greater tendency towards radicalism and teachers towards conservatism. They argue that diversity and other social issues are more central to the education of social workers than of teachers, and that teachers are more likely to locate problems within individual students, while social workers take a more ecological approach.

There may be challenges in negotiating a shared approach if there are similar differences in UK professional cultures. In addition, some social workers lack confidence in working with schools, as evidenced by recent British research into Personal Education Plans for looked after children (Haydn 2005).

Rushmer and Pallis (2002) point to the danger of blurred boundaries and of professionals working beyond their area of expertise. Policies of early intervention have led to education professionals and others using the common assessment framework and providing support without an early referral to social care. While this has been a positive development in many ways, a recent synthesis of the findings of Serious Case Reviews suggested that thresholds for referral to social care may be too high (Brandon et al. 2012). In the case of disabled children, for whom behaviours indicative of abuse may be misinterpreted as features of impairment (DCSF 2009), the lack of social work input at an early stage could in some cases increase the risk of safeguarding concerns being overlooked: 'Particularly in neglect cases it appeared that thresholds for referral to children's social care were not being met, and referrals were less likely to be accepted or did not progress' (Brandon et al. 2012: 119). This suggests that communication between social workers and other professionals, including educational professionals, has sometimes been inadequate to the task of identifying children who are most at risk.

Good practice in collaboration with education

There is clearly a need for effective dialogue between schools and social care about individual children at an early stage to ensure that risks are identified. Joint training about indicators of abuse and neglect, as well as thresholds for referral to social care, can improve interprofessional understanding and communication. Hothersall (2013) states that an explicit sense of professional identity, acknowledging differences in knowledge bases, theoretical orientations, values and skills, should be seen positively, while Sloper (2004) also stresses the importance of clarity about roles and responsibilities in interprofessional practice. This is particularly the case when disabled children are at risk of abuse or neglect.

Recent research has identified benefits of social care professionals working within extended schools. Wilkin et al. (2008) found that there was earlier identification of needs and quicker access to services, better understanding and knowledge of roles and responsibilities of other professionals, and a more coherent, holistic package of support for children. The placement of qualified social workers in schools may also lead to more effective interprofessional safeguarding practice.

Among examples of effective collaboration are co-located teams, including SEN and social care staff, and joint working arrangements for particular groups of children and young people, such as transition teams (Spivack et al. 2014). Craston et al. (2013) found that, before the piloting of the 2014 Children and Families Act, many local authorities already had multi-agency or joint working arrangements, including multi-agency panels to support children and young people with complex needs, often covering assessment planning and budget allocation. In most areas, early years services had led to the development of key workers to support families and the 'team around the child' approach. During the preparatory stage of the Pathfinder programme for the recent SEN and disability reforms, social workers' experience of delivering personalized support was particularly useful to education colleagues (Spivack et al. 2014).

The introduction of EHC Plans has offered teachers, social workers and others a way of working better together through the negotiation of outcomes towards which all can work (see chapter 8). The extension of personal budgets and direct payments is likely to lead to more personalized approaches in education, and Craston et al. (2013) found that this motivated professionals to identify desired outcomes with families. In fact, some respondents regarded personal budgets as crucial in leading to these conversations with families. However, a personal budget was not always necessary in order to achieve a personalized plan, as in some cases '[d]iscussions between the family, school and local authority took place to tailor the young person's education outcomes around their life targets and abilities' (Craston et al. 2013: 94). This indicates that a focus on outcomes has the potential to bring about a more personalized approach. Although the above example does not refer to social work, it is apparent that the involvement of social care in the Pathfinder programme was crucial in sharing experience and expertise in the delivery of personalized services with colleagues in education.

Working with housing

Context

It is well established that poor or unsuitable housing can have an adverse impact on people's physical and mental health (Quinney and Hafford-Letchfield 2012; Ritchie and Victory 2014). Studies suggest that this is particularly true for disabled people (Ritchie and Victory 2014). It is therefore essential that both health and social care services collaborate with housing providers and housing services in order to meet people's needs holistically. Such collaboration was recommended by, *inter alia*, the independent think tank the Smith Institute (Feinstein et al. 2008), and the requirement for partnership working in this field is evident in public policy and legislation. For example, in 2003, the government introduced the 'Supporting People' strategy, under which grants were provided to local authorities and used to coordinate and fund 'housing-related' support from a range of agencies in their area. With the aim of maintaining independent living and preventing or delaying admission into institutional care, Supporting People services provided a range of help to various service-user groups, including those with physical and sensory impairments. Since 2010, however, funding has been significantly reduced, resulting in many services closing and gaps in provision for those with needs that do not meet the thresholds of the local authority social care department.

Social workers may need to collaborate with a range of housing professionals and housing agencies – local authority housing departments, social landlords and housing associations, providers of specialist accommodation, housing officers and support workers, home improvement agencies, and care homes. Housing support workers in particular may undertake more direct work with disabled people than social workers (Quinney and Hafford-Letchfield 2012) and therefore be a key source of support and information; their potential importance in safeguarding situations is increasingly recognized (Parry 2013).

Housing issues for disabled people

For social workers working in disability settings, there are a range of situations in which housing issues arise and where collaboration with housing professionals is essential. In his study with thirty-one disabled young people living in Wales, Mackie (2012) observed that a number of participants would have welcomed greater contact with a social worker to discuss their housing options. Interconnected factors, such as inadequate information, limited availability of suitable accommodation, poor transitional arrangements and low priority, have all been identified as barriers for younger disabled people wishing to move out of the parental home (Hendey and Pascall 2002; Mackie 2012) (see chapter 3). Social workers can collaborate with housing agencies to dismantle these barriers by sharing information to identify the extent of need, coordinating the provision of information on housing options, and advocating on behalf of service users.

For some adults with physical impairments, particularly those with acquired impairments, new parents, and older adults, the existing home itself becomes disabling (Harris and Roulstone 2011; Ritchie and Victory 2014). This reflects Mackie's (2012) observation that mainstream housing design often fails to consider those with embodied difference. In such circumstances, social workers may need to collaborate with a range of housing providers, and also occupational therapy services, in order to facilitate the provision of appropriate adaptations. However, social workers should also consider collaboration with housing professionals at a strategic and planning level in order to support the design and development of accommodation that enables people to 'age in place', irrespective of any future acquired impairment (Taira and Carlson 2014).

In addition to issues of availability and accessibility, disabled people are at risk of experiencing poor quality housing (Department for Communities and Local Government 2009), fuel poverty and the subsequent exacerbation of pre-existing health conditions (Quinney and Hafford-Letchfield 2012; Handy 2014), homelessness (Ritchie and Victory 2014), and delays in receiving social care support as a result of 'ordinary residence' disputes between local authorities (Strong and Hall 2011; cited in Quinney and Hafford-Letchfield 2012). In England, the Care Act

2014 and its accompanying regulations have sought to offer clarity in relation to 'ordinary residence' rules, and they include the requirement that care and support provision should not be delayed during a period of dispute (Care and Support (Disputes Between Local Authorities) Regulations 2014, §2(1)). However, the Supreme Court case concerning the 'ordinary residence' of a disabled man known as PH, and involving three local authorities, highlights the complexity of this issue (*R (on the application of Cornwall Council)* v. *Secretary of State for Health [2015] UKSC 46*).

Good practice in collaboration with housing

The need to work collaboratively with housing professionals is clear, particularly when one considers the findings of Gillian Stewart and John Stewart (1993; cited in Quinney and Hafford-Letchfield 2012: 114), who report that 'social workers found assisting service users with housing problems [to be] one of the most difficult parts of their work ... and felt ill-prepared to undertake this work.' However, in collaborating closely with housing colleagues, social workers must be mindful not to do so in a way that excludes the service user, as illustrated in the words of a disabled young person in the study by Mackie: '[Name of Council] decided that I'd be moving. Well actually it was my parents, carer, social worker, and the council ... I went and saw the house and I'm happy with it but I do want to know who I'll be living with' (Mackie 2012: 814).

Social workers need to develop their legal literacy in relation to 'ordinary residence' rules and housing duties and have a good understanding of differences in tenure and how these impact on referral routes for rehousing and the provision of aids and adaptions. For example, those living in housing association accommodation may have access to a minor aids and adaptations budget held by the landlord, while those in privately rented or owner-occupied homes may need referral to a home improvement agency. Disabled owner-occupiers, disabled tenants, and landlords with disabled tenants may all be able to apply for a Disabled Facilities Grant to fund major adaptations. Ritchie and Victory (2014) highlight that, while knowledge of these referral processes is vital, the development of good working relationships between those employed in housing and those making referrals is key to positive outcomes for service users.

Quinney and Hafford-Letchfield (2012: 117) suggest that increased personalization in public services offers the chance to develop 'more innovative housing solutions' for disabled people. Social workers should work closely with service users, housing providers and other third-sector organizations to personalize support across health, social care and housing boundaries. One example of such innovation is the Housing Associations' Charitable Trust's up2us project. As part of this project, collaborative working between tenants of a supported living scheme, the housing association, the local authority and an independent living organization facilitated the collective use of personal budget funds to purchase night-time care and support services (SCIE and NHF 2012).

Working with carers

Context

According to the 2001 census, there are 6.5 million carers in the UK (cited in Carers UK 2014), and their role in and contribution to both social care and support for disabled people generally, and the successful implementation of the personalization agenda specifically, is increasingly acknowledged in policy as well as legislation (Greenwood et al. 2015; Seddon and Robinson 2015). For example, the Carers (Recognition and Services) Act 1995, *A National Strategy for Carers* (DoH 1999), the Carers and Disabled Children's Act 2000, the Carers (Equal Opportunities) Act 2004 and the *Carers at the Heart of 21st-Century Families and Communities* policy (HM Government 2008a), among others, all acknowledged carers' needs, increased their rights to assessment, and enabled local authorities to offer support.

While previous statutory rights were held by carers providing 'substantial amounts of care on a regular basis', the legal definition of a 'carer' has since been broadened in England and Wales by the Care Act 2014 and the Social Services and Well-Being (Wales) Act 2014 and is now rendered as 'An adult who provides or intends to provide care for another adult' (Section 10(3) Care Act 2014) or 'A person who provides or intends to provide care for an adult or disabled child' (Section 3(4) Social Services and Well-Being (Wales) Act 2014).

While such legal definitions and statutory rights exist, the way carers have been conceptualized by social care professionals and providers has varied. Twigg (1989; cited in Glendinning et al. 2015) devised a typology of carer–provider relationships in which carers are perceived to fulfil one of three roles: as a resource for the person cared for; as a co-worker; or as a co-client. Earlier legislation reflected a focus on the carer as either a resource (the support provided by the carer was considered merely as part of the service user's 'resources' and therefore reduced the amount of support needed from the local authority) or a co-worker (support required by the service user was central, but the carer's role was acknowledged; they were asked if they were willing and able to continue to provide care and what help they needed in order to continue). Referring to reduced amounts in personal budgets as a result of the existence of carer input, Glendinning et al. (2015) argue that contemporary practice continues to perceive carers predominantly as a resource. They suggest that less attention has been placed on the carer as co-client, when their own needs, interests and well-being are considered, despite statutory duties to do so. As you read the following case profile, consider the legal definition of 'carers' and Twigg's (1989) typology. Who is the carer in this scenario? How do you think they have been perceived by social care professionals?

Case profile: Elsie and Patrick

Elsie and Patrick are in their late seventies and have been married for fifty-three years. They are both profoundly Deaf, use British Sign Language, and maintain some contacts with the Deaf community. Recently, Patrick had hip replacement surgery, following which he underwent a period of rehabilitation at a local resource centre. During the social work assessment for his discharge, Elsie advised the social worker that she wished to provide support for him but could do so only in the evening owing to her own health problems: she has angina, arthritis and mild cognitive impairment. Since his return home, Patrick has been supported by care workers from a local agency for his morning routine; this is the only support funded by the local authority. Elsie prepares all the meals for them both and helps Patrick get ready for bed. Patrick continues to manage the finances and correspondence and organizes Elsie's medication. He also liaises with a local taxi service to transport them to the supermarket once a week, but they find this increasingly expensive.

Disabled people are often perceived as receivers rather than providers of care. However, the fact that over 40,000 people in receipt of a carer's allowance in 2013 were also receiving disability living allowance is an indication of the number of disabled people who are looking after someone else (Carers UK 2014). This includes people with complex impairments. Indeed, Hersh (2013) identified a number of deafblind people who were providing care for their older or disabled relatives. In the scenario above, both Elsie and Patrick could be considered to be carers. The nature of their caring relationship is reciprocal. This is common to many such relationships (Seddon and Robinson 2015), but it is not always recognized in social work assessments, which often suggest binary roles of carer and cared-for and assume what Seddon and Robinson (ibid.:14) refer to as a 'one way direction of care'. Such assessments fail to reflect the interdependence in such relationships, impacting on the appropriateness of the support provided.

Although some disabled people are carers, much of the early feminist writing drawing attention to the pressures on carers was based on the assumption that most informal work of this nature was carried out by non-disabled women. Feminist researchers from the 1970s onwards identified the extensive nature of the unpaid contribution of informal carers and the impact this had on their lives. Community care policies have stressed care *by* the community (DHSS 1981; HM Government 2012), and the carers' lobby has emphasized the savings this represents to the state (Buckner and Yeandle 2011). While recent statistics drawn from the 2011 census show that 58 per cent of carers are women, this percentage rises considerably for those who are in receipt of a carer's allowance and provide over thirty-five hours of care per week (Carers UK 2014). There was a focus on the sexual division of labour in the early feminist literature on carers (Finch and Groves 1983). However, disabled people, including disabled *women*, were represented in terms of dependency and burden. This led to an 'us and them' situation (Morris 1991) in which the interests of carers and disabled people were considered to be in opposition to each other. The arguments of non-disabled feminists against the familism and individualism of community care policies developed into calls for a more 'collective' approach involving the greater use of residential care (Finch and Groves 1983; Dalley 1988).

At the same time, disabled people were developing critiques of the controlling nature of the 'care' envisaged by community care policies and the carers' lobby: 'The concept of care seems to many disabled people a tool through which others are able to dominate and manage our lives' (Wood 1991: 199). Priestley (1998b) argues that 'care' involves a relationship of power and discipline in which the collective needs of disabled people are ignored. Care, irrespective of whether it was provided by the state or by informal carers, was rejected by disability activists, who argued for *personal assistance* under the control of disabled people. This would facilitate independent living (Morris 1993b), in which *independence* involves disabled people's control over their own lives rather than the ability to manage without any support (see chapter 9).

Attempts to reconcile these two opposing views have drawn on the work of feminists in the USA, who have identified an 'ethic of care' (Gilligan 1982) based on relationships and responsibilities rather than on rights and rules (Shakespeare 2000), though later feminist work has acknowledged that justice and equality are also important in caring relationships (Tronto 1993). Watson et al. (2004) have drawn on the ethic of care to suggest that the opposing views of the carers' lobby and the independent living movement can be reconciled by adopting a discourse of *interdependency*, which acknowledges that everyone is in need at some point in their lives (Kittay 2011). Shakespeare (2000) also asserts that the way forward is through dialogue between the philosophies of independent living and ethic of care. He supports barrier removal and personal assistance, as these are essential if interdependency is to be based on equality, but challenges untrammelled independence and individualism: 'We might then recognise that we are all dependent on each other, and that disabled people's limitations are not qualitatively different from those of other human beings' (Shakespeare 2000: 15).

Morris (1991) also challenged the way non-disabled feminists failed to acknowledge the contribution of disabled people as carers; this contribution is highlighted in the case profile above. Interdependency, the contribution of disabled people in caring, and the fact that both providers and recipients of care may be marginalized and impoverished by the experience (Ungerson 1997), have led to calls for the disability movement and the carers' lobby to make common cause for increased support (Thomas 2007).

Reflecting this common cause and the mutuality that is often present in caring relationships such as that of Patrick and Elsie, the Care Act 2014 and the Social Services and Well-Being (Wales) Act 2014 give carers and adults with support needs the same rights to assessment solely on the appearance of need. There is also a new duty on local authorities to meet the eligible needs of carers on an equal basis with those of the adults they are supporting. This represents a considerable strengthening of the rights of carers, including their right to be considered as a co-client and not just as a resource or co-worker (Glendinning et al. 2015); it also strengthens the access of both carers and adults with support needs to choice and control through personal budgets and direct payments.

Despite these increasing statutory rights, research highlights that the uptake of formal services among carers, particularly those from black and minority ethnic communities, remains low (Greenwood et al. 2015). This may impact on the well-being of both service users and carers; social workers should therefore be skilled at identifying carers, including those within reciprocal care relationships, and assist them in accessing assessment and support (Donskoy and Pollard 2014).

Good practice in collaboration with carers

Donskoy and Pollard (2014: 40) note that, owing to their 'intimate knowledge of service users as people living with a condition on an ongoing basis', carers can make a significant contribution to the work of interprofessional teams supporting disabled people. It is therefore essential that social workers collaborate closely with carers rather than focusing solely on other professionals (Douek 2003). In their study of spousal carers for adults who have had a stroke, Quinn et al. (2014) found that carers particularly valued healthcare staff who took the time to explain a range of issues related to their partners' condition. Elsie may benefit from clear information from healthcare professionals about Patrick's surgery, safe transfers, and ongoing rehabilitation potential, while Patrick could benefit from information about Elsie's medication. However, drawing on data from a twenty-year-long research programme, Seddon and Robinson (2015) note the often limited interaction between healthcare staff and carers. Social workers therefore have a role in ensuring all members of the interprofessional team engage with carers; this may include inviting them to multidisciplinary team meetings and facilitating dialogue between them and other professionals.

As highlighted by Elsie and Patrick's situation, care relationships are often reciprocal, and the needs of carers and service users are therefore interrelated (Donskoy and Pollard 2014). Social workers should consider how care and support services can meet these interrelated needs jointly rather than addressing them separately (Glendinning et al. 2015). Because of the complexity of people's relationships, this can be challenging work. Douek (2003) suggests that social workers should be creative in their approach, drawing on support that may be available from the voluntary sector, local groups and community organizations. The social worker working with Elsie and Patrick could make contact with the local Deaf club and also explore community transport options to reduce the cost of the weekly supermarket trip. Creative use of personal budgets should also be considered, as there is evidence to suggest that these can lead to improvements in carers' quality of life, experience of social care and overall well-being (Jones et al. 2014; Glendinning et al. 2015). Personal budget funds could be used for communication support and interpreter costs, enabling Elsie and Patrick to attend local carer support groups, or to fund accessible transport to Deaf club activities.

Consideration of interrelated needs should not negate carers' rights to a separate individual assessment, and social workers have legal and professional duties to offer these. Glendinning et al. (2015) observe that such assessments provide carers with an opportunity to express emotional needs and feelings in relation to their role. This is something which carers say they both need and value (Glendinning et al. 2015), but it often receives little attention in assessments: 'It's very much about the physical side of things, the lifting and handling, the taking to the toilet and the getting in and out of bed' (care manager, cited in Seddon and Robinson 2015). When completing carers' assessments, social workers should ensure they explore the emotional aspects of the role and offer individuals the opportunity to express their feelings in a safe and confidential space. This includes exploration of changes in the nature of relationships – for example, from romantic to caring – stress and coping, and any impact caring has on sexual relationships.

Conclusion

Collaborative working is a core and unavoidable feature of contemporary social work practice across social care settings, and social workers are expected to have the ability to work effectively with others. In an increasingly diverse landscape of health and social care provision, there are a growing number of organizations, agencies and professionals with whom social workers will need to cooperate. Numerous barriers to effective collaboration have been identified and, as such, successful joint working is highly skilled. Social workers are well positioned to facilitate and engage in collaborative practice on account of their relationship-building and communication skills. However, they also need a clear sense of their own professional identity and a good understanding of the role and responsibilities of other professionals. Student social work placements in multidisciplinary teams or non-traditional settings such as schools and disabled people's organizations are one way to develop this.

Social workers with disabled people may need to collaborate with professionals from health, education and housing; in safeguarding situations, they may also work closely with colleagues from the police and the criminal justice system. However, priority should be given to forming effective collaborative relationships with service users and carers; this includes relationships not only with individual disabled children, disabled adults, families and carers but also with user-led organizations. Sharing professional power with such organizations can enhance and inform social care provision so that it increasingly reflects the expressed priorities of disabled people.

Key messages

- There are clear professional expectations of social workers in relation to their ability to work effectively with other professionals, recognizing that collaborative working is an essential element of contemporary practice.
- There is evidence that a failure to collaborate effectively has an adverse impact on the experiences of disabled people using health and social care services.
- Social workers in disability settings may need to collaborate with colleagues in health, education and housing, as well as with carers and practitioners in the third sector.
- The focus of collaborative practice should be the service user, and social workers should invest in positive relationships with service users on an individual level and also by forming alliances with user-led disabled people's organizations.

Activities

- Revisit chapter 1 and identify the key partners involved in Helen's care and support. How well did professionals collaborate with Helen and with each other and how could collaborative practice have been enhanced?
- How could a social worker undertaking a carer's assessment reflect the reciprocal and interdependent nature of the relationship between Elsie and Patrick? Would you recommend a joint assessment or separate assessments?
- Reflect on your own social work education and/or continuous professional development activity. To what extent is this interprofessional and multidisciplinary? How could you develop this?

Suggested further reading

Crawford, K. (2012) *Interprofessional Collaboration in Social Work Practice.* London: Sage.

Seddon, D., and Robinson, C. (2015) Carer assessment: continuing tensions and dilemmas for social care practice, *Health & Social Care in the Community*, 23(1): 14–22.

Spivack, R., Craston, M., and Redman, R. (2014) *Evaluation of the Special Educational Needs and Disability Pathfinder Programme: Thematic Report: Collaborative Working with Social Care.* London: Department for Education.

Conclusion

This book has set out to promote the knowledge and understanding that social workers need to work with disabled people. It has been informed by a commitment to human rights; the need to address the social, cultural and environmental barriers that limit the opportunities of disabled people; and by our belief that these issues can be addressed only through equal partnership between social workers, disabled people and their organizations. This approach owes almost everything to the critique of social work, and social policy more generally, developed by the disability movement. However, despite the view expressed by some within the movement that social work no longer has a role with disabled people, it remains our view that it does have a contribution to make. Significantly, despite the many limitations of Helen's early encounters with social work several decades ago, described in chapter 1, the social worker 'made things happen' in a way that improved her quality of life and opportunities. With the developments in knowledge and understanding of disability and in policy that have occurred in recent years, there are opportunities for social workers.

In seeking to understand disability, we have explored theories and models, life course issues, and policy and legislation. We have also considered inequality, diversity and oppression. What has bound these issues together is the lived experience of disabled people. Many of the points that are made in the book are ably illustrated in Helen's first-person account. For example, she writes about the way agencies have sought to define her so as to fit her into their own systems; the focus on her impairment at the expense of her right to a good education; barriers to accessing and remaining in employment; and the need for social workers to see the 'whole person' rather than a medical condition and a list of limitations. Helen also describes her introduction to the social model as a 'Eureka moment': her realization that her difficulties were not an inevitable result of her impairment was a crucial turning point. Many of her experiences entirely validate the social model, with its emphasis on social and environmental barriers, and, although there is still a long way to go before all aspects of life are fully accessible, anti-discrimination legislation has at least ensured that disabled people no longer have to travel in the guard's van on our trains!

The distinction between disability and impairment drawn by the social model has been a thread running through this book, though we have also explored social relational approaches. These acknowledge the restrictions arising from impairment and identify the psycho-emotional effects of disabling barriers as well as the restrictions to activity that result. Helen refers to restrictions and pain resulting from her impairment as well as the social, physical and attitudinal barriers she experiences. As a profession that operates at the intersection of the individual and his or her environment, social work could utilize this approach to address structural oppression, the effects of impairment, and the impact of both on individuals, which may include internalized oppression.

We have also explored approaches which emphasize the universality of impairment. While this can be an effective challenge to the 'othering' of disabled people, we have concluded that it must not lead to the neglect of structural oppression. There is a need for social workers, in collaboration with disabled people and their organizations, to address the barriers that threaten participation and human rights.

Clearly disabled people are not homogeneous, and some have multiple identities or minority statuses. Disability can be experienced differently on the basis of these diverse identities, and social workers should ensure that this is recognized and that needs are appropriately met. Helen stresses the importance of her status as a woman, the impact this had on her dissatisfaction with the equipment provided for her, and the way it was ignored when medical decisions were made.

For disabled people, both impairment and disabling barriers can impede communication. Social workers need effective core communication skills as well as specialist skills and familiarity with diverse modes of communication when working with disabled people. Although they cannot be experts in every method or language, showing flexibility and a willingness to allow time to facilitate communication are important. Social workers may need to collaborate with family, friends, support workers and other professionals who are familiar with a disabled person's means of communication, fluent in British Sign Language, or familiar with a particular assistive technology. However, this is not a matter simply of technical proficiency. Social workers need to understand the psycho-social impact of communication impairment. They also need to be mindful of the importance of language, which should reflect social work values and the preferences of disabled people.

Communication is linked to other imperatives, such as choice, control, and participation in assessment and decision-making. This is equally important for children and adults. There should be respect for the knowledge that parents have about their child and for the expertise of disabled adults about their own lives. As Helen writes: 'Social workers must recognize that I have knowledge, skills and expertise in my own situation and work in partnership with me on equal terms.'

Personalization and interprofessional collaboration are key features of policy in both adults' and children's social care. Support should therefore be focused on the outcomes that service users desire and on the transfer of control to them from professionals. Self-assessment, personal budgets and direct payments are ways in which this can be facilitated. Service users will vary as to their need and preference for support in the planning process, and it is important that social workers are sensitive to this. In the midst of the various assessment, planning and resource-allocation mechanisms associated with personalization, it is as well to remember that person-centred practice and flexibility are not entirely dependent on these systems. The attitudes, commitment, skills and creativity of both social workers and service users also have an important part to play. However, effective collaboration with other professionals can be instrumental in delivering flexibility and better coordination of services. This may be promoted by the formal integration and co-location of staff and also by formal processes such as interprofessional panels and key worker systems. However, it is important for social workers to be clear about their role and statutory responsibilities within interprofessional teams, particularly in safeguarding situations.

Overall, it is commitment to human rights and service-user control that should guard against oppressive practice. Helen sums this up very effectively, as she concludes: 'I value social workers who recognize that my need for their involvement is not always related to my physical impairment. And I value social workers who protect and promote my rights – not just my rights as a user of social work services but my fundamental human rights.'

The social work profession has seen significant changes over the last fifteen years; these include a change of professional regulator (for social workers in England), a change in professional qualification and the emergence of new routes to qualification, the appointment of two chief social workers, and the arrival and, at the time of writing, forthcoming closure of the College of Social Work. Those working with disabled people will face a number of additional future changes and challenges. The closure of the Independent Living Fund and increased austerity and resource pressures are occurring concurrently with new statutory duties to engage in preventative work and the new statutory rights for self-funders and carers. In addition to developing their legal literacy in relation to the new legislation, social workers also need to adapt to new ways of working in a world of greater personalization and self-directed support; this requires close attention to risk enablement in an increasingly risk-averse society. In facing these challenges, social workers must act as close and equal allies with disabled people and their organizations; and despite – or perhaps because of – these challenges, social work with disabled people will remain a highly rewarding and interesting area of practice.

References

Abberley, P. (1987) The concept of oppression and the development of a social theory of disability, *Disability, Handicap & Society*, 2(1): 5–19.

Abberley, P. (1993) Disabled people and normality, in Swain, J., French, S., Barnes, C., and Thomas, C., eds, *Disabling Barriers – Enabling Environments*. London: Sage (in association with the Open University).

Abberley, P. (1996) Work, Utopia and impairment, in Barton, L., ed., *Disability and Society: Emerging Issues and Insights*. London: Longman.

Abbott, D., Jepson, M., Hastie, J., Carpenter, J., Gibson, B., and Smith, B. (2014) *Men Living with Long-Term Conditions: Exploring Gender and Improving Social Care*. London: NIHR School for Social Care Research.

Abbott, D., Morris, J., and Ward, L. (2001) *The Best Place to Be? Policy, Practice and the Experiences of Residential School Placements for Disabled Children*. York: Joseph Rowntree Foundation/York Publishing Services.

Abendstern, M., Hughes, J., Clarkson, P., Tucker, S., and Challis, D. (2014) Exploring the contribution of self-assessment to preventative services in social care, *British Journal of Social Work*, 44: 729–46.

About Families Partnership (2012) *Parenting and Support: Topic Report*. Centre for Research on Families and Relationships (CRFR), http://aboutfamilies.files.wordpress.com/2012/10/about-families-report-4-parenting-and-support.pdf.

Alderson, P. (1993) *Children's Consent to Surgery*. Buckingham: Open University Press.

Allred, K., and Hancock, C. (2012) On death and disability: reframing educators' perceptions of parental response to disability, *Disability Studies Quarterly*, 32(4), http://dsq-sds.org/article/view/1737.

Andrew, P. (2012) *The Social Construction of Age*. Bristol: Multilingual Matters.

Anna-Stina, French, S., and Swain, J. (2008) In practice from the viewpoint of a physiotherapist, in Swain, J., and French, S., eds, *Disability on Equal Terms*. London: Sage.

Anon (2012) Tactile glove lets hearing and vision impaired send text messages, http://b3.zcubes.com/v.aspx?mid=81793&title=tactile-glove-lets-hearing-and-vision-impaired-send-text-messages-.

Arnott, J., and Koubel, G. (2012) Interprofessional working and the community care conundrum, in Koubel, G., and Bungay, H., eds, *Rights, Risks, and Responsibilities: Interprofessional Working in Health and Social Care*. Basingstoke: Palgrave Macmillan.

Association of Directors of Adult Social Services (2009) *Common Resource Allocation Framework*. London: Association of Directors of Adult Social Services.

Association of Directors of Adult Social Services (2011) *ADASS Budget Survey 2011*, www.adass.org.uk/Content/Article.aspx?id=1407.

Association of Directors of Adult Services and Department of Health (2010) *The Future of Social Work in Adult Services*, www.skillsforcare.org.uk/Document-library/Social-work/Effective-deployment/The future of social work in adult social services - Advice note 2.pdf.

Association of Directors of Social Services (2005) *Safeguarding Adults: A National Framework of Standards for Good Practice and Outcomes in Adult Protection Work*. London: Association of Directors of Social Services.

Atkinson, D., Jackson, M., and Walmsley, J. (1998) *Forgotten Lives: Exploring the History of Learning Disability*. Bristol: British Institute of Learning Disability.

Audit Commission (2002) *Special Education Needs: A Mainstream Issue*. London: Audit Commission.

Audit Commission (2003) *Services for Disabled Children*. London: Audit Commission.

Avery, D. (1999) Talking 'tragedy': identity issues in the parental story of disability, in Corker, M., and French, S., eds, *Disability Discourse*. Buckingham: Open University Press.

Baker, C. (2007) Disabled children's experience of permanency in the looked after system', *British Journal of Social Work*, 37(7): 1173–88.

Balderston, S. (2013) After disablist hate crime: which interventions work to resist victimhood and build resilience with survivors?, in Roulstone, A., and Mason-Bish, H., eds, *Disability, Hate Crime and Violence*. London: Routledge.

Ballantyne, E., and Muir, A. (2008) In practice from the viewpoint of an occupational therapist', in Swain, J., and French, S., eds, *Disability on Equal Terms*. London: Sage.

Balmer, N., Pleasance, P., Buck, A., and Walker, H. C. (2006) Worried sick: the experience of debt problems and their relationship with health, illness and disability, *Social Policy and Society*, 5: 39–51.

Baltes, P., and Baltes, M. M. (1990) Psychological perspectives on successful aging: the model of selective optimization with compensation, in Baltes, P., and Baltes, M. M., eds, *Successful Aging: Perspectives from the Behavioral Sciences*. Cambridge: Cambridge University Press, pp. 1–34.

Barnartt, S. N., and Mandell, B. (2013) *Disability and Intersecting Statuses*. Bingley: Emerald.

Barnes, C. (1991) *Disabled People in Britain and Discrimination*. London: Hurst.

Barnes, C. (1992) *Disabling Imagery and the Media*, http://disability-studies.leeds.ac.uk/files/library/Barnes-disabling-imagery.pdf.

Barnes, C., and Mercer, G. (2006) *Independent Futures: Creating User-Led Disability Services in a Disabling Society*. Bristol: Policy Press.

Barnes, C., and Mercer, G. (2010) *Exploring Disability*. 2nd edn, Cambridge: Polity.

Barnett, D., Clements, M., Kaplan-Estrin, M., and Fialka, J. (2003) Building new dreams: supporting parents' adaptation to their child with special needs, *Infants & Young Children*, 16(3): 184–200.

Baron-Cohen, S. (2002) Is Asperger syndrome necessarily viewed as a disability?, *Focus on Autism and Other Developmental Disabilities*, 17(3): 186–92.

Baron-Cohen, S., Scott, F. J., Allison, C., Williams, J., Bolton, P., Matthews, F. E., and Brayne, C. (2009) Prevalence of autism-spectrum conditions: UK school-based population study, *British Journal of Psychiatry*, 194(6): 500–9.

Barton, C. (2003) Allies and enemies: the service user as care co-ordinator, in Weinstein, J., Whittington, C., and Leiba, T., eds, *Collaboration in Social Work Practice*. London: Jessica Kingsley.

Baxter, K., and Glendinning, C. (2011) Making choices about support services: disabled adults' and older people's use of information, *Health and Social Care in the Community*, 19(3): 272–9.

Bayat, M. (2007) Evidence of resilience in families of children with autism, *Journal of Intellectual Disability Research*, 51(9): 702–14.

Bazalgette, L., Bradley, W., and Ousbey, J. (2011) *The Truth about Suicide*. London: Demos.

Bennett, E. (2009) *What Makes my Family Stronger: A Report into What Makes Families with Disabled Children Stronger – Socially, Emotionally and Practically*, www.cafamily.org.uk/media/392373/research_and_reportswhat_makesmyfamilystrongerwhatmakes_families_with_disabled_children_stronger_socially__emotionally_and_practically2009.pdf.

Benson, D. (2014) Education (school), in Cameron, C., ed., *Disability Studies: A Student's Guide*. London: Sage.

Beresford, B. (1995) *Expert Opinions: A National Survey of Parents Caring for a Severely Disabled Child*. Bristol: Policy Press.

Beresford, B. (2004) On the road to nowhere? Young disabled people and transition, *Child: Care, Health and Development*, 30(6): 581–7.

Beresford, B., Rabiee, P., and Sloper, P. (2007a) Outcomes for parents of disabled children, https://www.york.ac.uk/inst/spru/pubs/rworks/aug2007-03.pdf.

Beresford, B., Rabiee, P. and Sloper, P. (2007b) *Priorities and Perceptions of Disabled Children and Young People and Their Parents Regarding Outcomes from Support Services*, http://php.york.ac.uk/inst/spru/research/summs/priorpercep.php.

Beresford, P. (2009) *Whose Personalization?*. London: Compass.

Beresford, P. (2014) *Personalization: Critical and Radical Debates in Social Work*. Bristol: Policy Press.

Beresford, P., and Clark, S. (2009) *Improving the Wellbeing of Disabled Children and Young People through Improving Access to Positive and Inclusive Activities*. London: Centre for Excellence and Outcomes in Children's and Young People's Services.

Beresford, P., Fleming, J., Glynn, M., Bewley, C., Croft, S., Branfield, F., and Postle, K. (2011) *Supporting People: Towards a Person-Centred Approach*. Bristol: Policy Press.

Blacher, J. (1984) Sequential stages of parental adjustment to the birth of a child with handicaps: fact or artefact?, *Mental Retardation,* 22(2): 55–68.

Blackburn, C., Spencer, N., and Read, J. (2010) Prevalence of childhood disability and the characteristics and circumstances of disabled children in the UK: secondary analysis of the Family Resources Survey', *BMC Pediatrics,* 10(21), www.biomedcentral.com/content/pdf/1471-2431-10-21.pdf.

Blackburn, C., Spencer, N., and Read, J. (2012) Children with neurodevelopmental disabilities, in Davies, P. S. C., ed., *Annual Report of the Chief Medical Officer 2012: Our Children Deserve Better: Prevention Pays*. London: Department of Health.

Blatterer, H. (2007) Adulthood: the contemporary redefinition of a social category, *Sociological Research Online,* 12(4), www.socresonline.org.uk/12/4/3.html.

Bodsworth, S. M., Clare, I., Simblett, S. K., and Deafblind UK (2011) Deafblindness and mental health: psychological distress and unmet need among adults with dual sensory impairment, *British Journal of Visual Impairment,* 29(1): 6–26.

Bondi, L. (2008) On the relational dynamics of caring: a psychotherapeutic approach to emotional and power dimensions of women's care work, *Gender, Place and Culture,* 15(3): 249–65.

Bonell, S., McInerny, T., and O'Hara, J. (2011) *Neurodevelopmental Psychiatry: An Introduction for Medical Students*. South London and Maudsley NHS Foundation Trust, www.rcpsych.ac.uk/pdf/ Neurodevelopmental psychiatry - an introduction for medical students.pdf.

Borsay, A. (2005) *Disability and Social Policy in Britain since 1750: A History of Exclusion*. Basingstoke: Palgrave Macmillan.

Boushel, M., Whiting, R., and Taylor, I. (2010) *How We Become Who We Are: The Teaching and Learning of Human Growth and Development, Mental Health and Disability on Qualifying Social Work Programmes*. London: Social Care Institute for Excellence.

Braddock, D. L., and Parish, S. L. (2001) An institutional history of disability, in Albrecht, G. L., Seelman, K. D., and Bury, M., eds, *Handbook of Disability Studies*. London: Sage.

Brandon, M., Sidebotham, P., Bailey, S., Belderson, P., Hawley, C., Ellis, C., and Megson, M. (2012) *New Learning from Serious Case Reviews: A Two Year Report for 2009–2011*. London: Department for Education.

brap (2011) *'Who Moved my Samosa?' Managing Conflicts about Equality and Diversity: A Practical Guide*. Birmingham: brap.

Brawn, E. (2014) *Priced Out: Ending the Financial Penalty of Disability by 2020*. London: Scope.

Brawn, E., Bush, M., Hawkings, C., and Trotter, R. (2013) *The Other Care Crisis: Making Social Care Funding Work for Disabled Adults in England*. London: Scope, Mencap, National Autistic Society, Sense, and Leonard Cheshire Disability.

Brennan, M., Horowitz, A., and Su, Y. P. (2005) Dual sensory loss and its impact on everyday competence, *Gerontologist,* 45(3): 337–46.

British Association of Social Workers (2012) *Code of Ethics for Social Work,* http://cdn.basw.co.uk/ upload/basw_112315-7.pdf.

Broach, S., Clements, L., and Read, J. (2010) *Disabled Children: A Legal Handbook*. London: Legal Action Group/Council for Disabled Children.

Bronstein, L. R., and Abramson, J. S. (2003) Understanding socialization of teachers and social workers: groundwork for collaboration in the schools, *Families in Society,* 84(3): 1–8.

Brother, M. (2003) It's not just about ramps and braille: disability and sexual orientation, in Zappone, K., ed., *Re-Thinking Identity: The Challenge of Diversity*. Dublin: Joint Equality and Human Rights Forum.

Buckner, L., and Yeandle, S. (2011) *Valuing Carers 2011: Calculating the Value of Carers' Support*, http://circle.leeds.ac.uk/files/2012/08/110512-circle-carers-uk-valuing-carers.pdf.

Burchardt, T. (2000) *The Dynamics of Being Disabled*, Case Paper 036. London: LSE.

Burton, J. (2012) Physical disability, in Greenfields, M., Dalrymple, R., and Fanning, A., eds, *Working with Adults at Risk of Harm*. Maidenhead: Open University Press.

Butler, S. (2009) Personal–professional relationships, *Talking Sense*, Winter 2009 www.sense.org.uk/content/talking-sense-personal-professional-relationships.

Bywater, J., and Jones, R. (2007) *Sexuality and Social Work: Transforming Social Work Practice*. Exeter: Learning Matters.

Calderbank, R. (2000) Abuse and disabled people: vulnerability or social indifference?, *Disability & Society*, 15(3): 521–34.

Cameron, C. (2014) Harassment and hate crime, in Cameron, C., ed., *Disability Studies: A Student's Guide*. London: Sage.

Campbell, J., and Oliver, M. (1996) *Disability Politics: Understanding our Past, Changing our Future*. London: Routledge.

Care Quality Commission (2012) *Health Care for Disabled Children and Young People*. London: Care Quality Commission.

Carers UK (2014) *Facts about Carers: Policy Briefing*. London: Carers UK.

Carpenter, B., and Egerton, J. (2007) *Family Structures: Working in Partnership through Early Support: Distance Learning Text*. London: Department for Education and Skills/Department of Health.

Castle, R. (2007) Disabled social workers: contribution and difficulties. Unpublished thesis, Staffordshire University.

Cemlyn, S. (2008) Human rights practice: possibilities and pitfalls for developing emancipatory social work, *Ethics and Social Welfare*, 2(3): 222–42.

Children's Society (2011) *4 in every 10: Disabled Children Living in Poverty*. London: Children's Society.

Clark, A., Hayes, R., Jones, K., and Lievesley, N. (2009) *Ageism and Age Discrimination in Social Care in the United Kingdom: A Review from the Literature*. Centre for Policy on Ageing, www.cpa.org.uk/information/reviews/CPA- ageism_and_age_discrimination_in_social_care-report.pdf.

Clark, J. L. (2014) *Where I Stand: On the Signing Community and my Deafblind Experience*. Minneapolis: Handtype Press.

Clark, L. (2003) Leonard Cheshire vs. the Disabled People's Movement: A Review, http://disability-studies.leeds.ac.uk/files/library/Clark-Laurence-leonard-cheshire.pdf.

Clarke, H. (2006) *Preventing Social Exclusion for Disabled Children and their Families*. London: Department for Education and Skills.

Clarke, H., and McKay, S. (2008) *Exploring Disability, Family Formation and Break-Up: Reviewing the Evidence*, DWP Research Report no. 514. Norwich: The Stationery Office.

Clarke, M., Donlan, C., Lister, C., Wright, J., Newton, C., and Cherguit, J. (2006) The provision of communication aids to children in England: an analysis of applications to the Communication Aids Project, *Child: Care, Health and Development*, 33(5): 569–75.

Clarke, S., Sloper, P., Moran, N., Cusworth, L., Franklin, A., and Beecham, J. (2011) Multi-agency transition services: greater collaboration needed to meet the priorities of young people with complex needs as they move into adulthood, *Journal of Integrated Care*, 19(5): 30–40.

Clements, L. (2011) Social care law developments: a sideways look at personalization and tightening eligibility criteria, *Elder Law Journal*, 1: 47–52.

Clements, L. (2015) The Care Act 2014 Overview, updated briefing (July 2015), www.lukeclements.co.uk/wp-content/uploads/2015/07/0-Care-Act-notes-updated-2015-09.pdf.

Clibbens, J., and Sheppard, M. (2007) Are children with learning disabilities really 'children first'? A needs and outcome evaluation of policy, *Social and Public Policy Review*, 1(2).

Coad, J. (2008) Bringing together child health and social care provision: challenges and opportunities for multi-agency working, in Morris, K., ed., *Social Work and Multi-Agency Working: Making a Difference*. Bristol: Policy Press.

Cockerill, H., Elbourne, D., Allen, E., Scrutton, D., Will, E., McNee, A., Fairhurst, C., and Baird,

G. (2014) Speech, communication and use of augmentative communication in young people with cerebral palsy: the SH&PE population study, *Child: Care, Health and Development*, 40(2): 149–57.

Coleman, N., Sykes., W., and Groom, C. (2013a) *Barriers to Employment and Unfair Treatment at Work: A Quantitative Analysis of Disabled People's Experiences*, Research Report 88. Manchester: Equality and Human Rights Commission.

Coleman, N., Sykes., W., and Walker, A. (2013b) *Crime and Disabled People: Baseline Statistical Analysis of Measures from the Formal Legal Inquiry into Disability-Related Harassment*. Manchester: Equality and Human Rights Commission.

Collingbourne, T. (2014) The Care Act 2014: a missed opportunity?, *Web Journal of Current Legal Issues*, 20(3).

Collins, M., Langer, S., Welch, V., Wells, E., Hatton, C., Robertson, J., and Emerson, E. (2014) A break from caring for a disabled child: parent perceptions of the uses and benefits of short break provision in England, *British Journal of Social Work*, 44(5): 1180–96.

Colyer, H. (2008) Responsibilities and accountabilities in interprofessional working, in Koubel, G., and Bungay, H., eds, *Rights, Risks and Responsibilities: Interprofessional Working in Health and Social Care*. Basingstoke: Palgrave Macmillan.

Communication Trust (2011) *Don't Get Me Wrong*. London: Communication Trust.

Connors, A., and Stalker, K. (2003) *The Views and Experiences of Disabled Children and their Siblings: A Positive Outlook*. London: Jessica Kingsley.

Connors, A., and Stalker, K. (2007) Children's experiences of disability: pointers to a social model of childhood disability, *Disability & Society*, 22(1): 19–33.

Contact a Family (2011) *Forgotten Families: The Impact of Isolation on Families with Disabled Children across the UK*, www.cafamily.org.uk/media/381636/forgotten_isolation_report.pdf.

Cooke, P., and Standen, P. J. (2002) Abuse and disabled children: hidden needs ...?, *Child Abuse Review*, 11: 1–18.

Cooper, H. (2013) The oppressive power of normalcy in the lives of disabled children: deploying history to denaturalize the notion of the 'normal child', in Curran, T., and Runswick-Cole, K., eds, *Disabled Children's Childhood Studies: Critical Approaches in a Global Context*. Basingstoke: Palgrave Macmillan.

Corbett, J. (1997) A proud label, in Pointon, A., and Davies, C., eds, *Framed: Interrogating Disability in the Media*. London: British Film Institute.

Corker, M. (1999) Differences, conflations and foundations: the limits to 'accurate' theoretical representation of disabled people's experiences, *Disability & Society*, 14(5): 627–42.

Coulshed, V., and Orme, J. (2012) *Social Work Practice: An Introduction*. 5th edn, Basingstoke: Palgrave Macmillan.

Council for Disabled Children (2014) EHC outcomes pyramid, www.councilfordisabledchildren.org.uk/resources/ehc-outcomes-pyramid.

Cousins, J. (2006) *Every Child is Special: Placing Disabled Children for Permanence*. London: British Association for Adoption and Fostering.

Craston, M., Thom, G., Purdon, S., Bryson, C., Lambert, C., and James, N. (2014) *Special Educational Needs and Disability Pathfinder Programme Evaluation: Summary of Interim Impact Findings*. London: Department for Education.

Craston, M., Thom, G., and Spivack, R. (2013) Evaluation of the SEND pathfinder programme: process and implementation, DfE Research Report 295, https://www.gov.uk/government/uploads/system/uploads/attachment_data/file/206486/DFE-RR295.pdf.

Crawford, K. (2012) *Interprofessional Collaboration in Social Work Practice*. London: Sage.

Criminal Justice Joint Inspection (2013) *Living in a Different World: Joint Review of Disability Hate Crime*. London: HMCPSI, HMIC, HMI Probation.

Crow, L. (1996) Including all of our lives: renewing the social model of disability, in Barnes, C., and Mercer, G., eds, *Exploring the Divide: Illness and Disability*. Leeds: Disability Press, pp. 55–72.

Crown Office and Procurator Fiscal Service (2014) *Hate Crime in Scotland 2013–14*, www.copfs.gov.uk/images/Documents/Equality_Diversity/Hate Crime in Scotland 2013-14.pdf.

CPS (Crown Prosecution Service) (2007) *Policy for Prosecuting Cases of Disability Hate Crime.* London: Crown Prosecution Service.

CPS (Crown Prosecution Service) (2014) *Hate Crimes and Crimes against Older People Report 2013–2014.* London: Crown Prosecution Service.

CSCI (Commission for Social Care Inspection) (2008) *Cutting the Cake Fairly: CSCI Review of Eligibility Criteria for Social Care.* London: Commission for Social Care Inspection.

CSCI (Commission for Social Care Inspection) (2009) *Supporting Disabled Parents: A Family or Fragmented Approach?* London: Commission for Social Care Inspection.

Dalley, G. (1988) *Ideologies of Caring: Rethinking Community and Collectivism.* Basingstoke: Palgrave Macmillan.

Darling, R. B., and Heckert, D. A. (2010) Orientations toward disability: differences over the life-course, *International Journal of Disability, Development and Education,* 57(2): 131–43.

Davidson-Pain, C., and Corbett, J. (1995) A double coming out: gay men with learning disabilities, *British Journal of Learning Disabilities,* 23: 147–51.

Davis, J. (2004) Disability and childhood: deconstructing the stereotypes, in Swain, J., French, S., Barnes, C., and Thomas, C., eds, *Disabling Barriers – Enabling Environments.* 2nd edn, London: Sage.

Davis, J. M., and Watson, N. (2001) Where are the children's experiences? Analysing social and cultural exclusion in 'special' and 'mainstream' schools, *Disability & Society,* 16(5): 671–87.

Davis, K. (1993) Power, oppression and disability, http://disability-studies.leeds.ac.uk/files/library/DavisK-resourcenotes.pdf.

Davis, K. (2004) The crafting of good clients, in Swain, J., French, S., Barnes, C., and Thomas, C., eds, *Disabling Barriers – Enabling Environments.* 2nd edn, London: Sage.

Davis, L. J. (1997) Constructing normalcy, in Davis, L. J., ed., *The Disability Studies Reader.* London: Routledge.

DCSF (Department for Children, Schools and Families) (2009) *Safeguarding Disabled Children: Practice Guidance.,* London: DCSF.

DCSF (Department for Children, Schools and Families) (2010a) *Short Breaks: Statutory Guidance on How to Safeguard and Promote the Welfare of Disabled Children Using Short Breaks.* London: DCSF.

DCSF (Department for Children, Schools and Families (2010b) *Children Act 1989 Guidance and Regulations,* Vol. 2: *Care Planning, Placement and Case Review.* London: DCSF.

DCSF (Department for Children, Schools and Families) and DoH (Department of Health) (2008) *Transition: Moving on Well: A Good Practice Guide for Health Professionals and their Partners on Transition Planning for Young People with Complex Health Needs or a Disability.* London: DoH.

DCSF (Department for Children, Schools and Families), DoH (Department of Health), Council for Disabled Children and National Children's Bureau (2007) *A Transition Guide for All Services: Key Information for Professionals about the Transition Process for Disabled Young People.* Nottingham: DCSF.

Dean, J. (2003) *Unaddressed: The Housing Aspirations of Young Disabled People in Scotland.* York: Joseph Rowntree Foundation.

Debenham, C. (2012) *An Assessment of the Needs of Lesbian, Gay, Bisexual and Transgender (LGB and T) People in the East Sussex Area Using or Needing to Use Adult Social Care's Services.* Lewes: East Sussex County Council.

Dendy, M. (1903) The feeble minded, *Economic Review,* 1(3): 257–79.

Department for Communities and Local Government (2009) *English House Condition Survey 2007: Annual Report,* www.esds.ac.uk/doc/6449/mrdoc/pdf/6449ehcs_annual_report_2007.pdf.

Department for Communities and Local Government (2010) *Citizenship Survey.* London: Department for Communities and Local Government.

Department of Education and Science (1978) *Special Education Needs: Report of the Committee of Enquiry into the Education of Handicapped Children and Young People (the Warnock Report).* London: HMSO.

Depoy, E., and Gilson, S. (2008) Social work practice with disability: moving from the perpetuation of a client category to human rights and social justice, *Journal of Social Work Values and Ethics*, 5(3).

Derbyshire, L. (2013) A mug or a teacup and saucer, in Curran, T., and Runswick-Cole, K., eds, *Disabled Children's Childhood Studies: Critical Approaches in a Global Context*. Basingstoke: Palgrave Macmillan.

Deutsch, M. (2005) Forms of oppression, www.beyondintractability.org/essay/forms-of-oppression.

DfE (Department for Education) (2011) *Support and Aspiration: A New Approach to Special Educational Needs and Disability*. London: Department for Education.

DfE (Department for Education) (2014a) *Promoting the Education of Looked After Children: Statutory Guidance for Local Authorities*. London: Department for Education.

DfE (Department for Education) (2014b) *Special Educational Needs in England: January 2014*, https://www.gov.uk/government/statistics/special-educational-needs-in-england-january-2014.

DfE (Department for Education) and DoH (Department of Health) (2014) *Special Educational Needs and Disability Code of Practice: 0 to 25 Years: Statutory Guidance for Organizations which Work with and Support Children and Young People who Have Special Educational Needs or Disabilities*. London: Department for Education and Department of Health.

DfES (Department for Education and Skills) (1997) *Green Paper: Excellence for All Children: Meeting Special Educational Needs*. London: Department for Education and Skills.

DfES (Department for Education and Skills) (2003) *Every Child Matters*. London: The Stationery Office.

DfES (Department for Education and Skills) (2004) *Removing Barriers to Achievement: The Government's Strategy for SEN*. London: Department for Education and Skills.

DoH (Department of Health) (1998a) *Disabled Children: Directions for their Future Care*. London: The Stationery Office.

DoH (Department of Health) (1998b) *Modernising Social Services*. London: Department of Health.

DoH (Department of Health) (1999) *Caring about Carers: A National Strategy for Carers*. London: Department of Health.

DoH (Department of Health) (2000a) *Assessing Children in Need and their Families: Practice Guidance*. London: The Stationery Office.

DoH (Department of Health) (2000b) *No Secrets: Guidance on Developing and Implementing Multi-Agency Policies and Procedures to Protect Vulnerable Adults from Abuse*. London: Department of Health.

DoH (Department of Health) (2003) *Direct Payments Guidance: Community Care, Services for Carers and Children's Services (Direct Payments) Guidance, England 2003*. London: Department of Health.

DoH (Department of Health) (2004) *National Service Framework for Children, Young People and Maternity Services*. London: Department of Health.

DoH (Department of Health) (2005a) *Independence, Well-Being and Choice: Our Vision for the Future of Social Care for Adults in England*. London: Department of Health.

DoH (Department of Health) (2005b) *National Service Framework for Long-Term Conditions*. London: Department of Health.

DoH (Department of Health) (2006) *Our Health, Our Care, Our Say: A New Direction for Community Services*. London: Department of Health.

DoH (Department of Health) (2007a) *Briefing 13: Disabled Lesbian, Gay and Bisexual (LGB) People*. London: Department of Health.

DoH (Department of Health) (2007b) *Putting People First: A Shared Vision and Commitment to the Transformation of Adult Social Care*. London: Department of Health.

DoH (Department of Health) (2008) *LAC (DH)(2008)1: Transforming Adult Social Care*. London: Department of Health.

DoH (Department of Health) (2009) *Report on the Consultation: The Review of No Secrets Guidance*. London: Department of Health.

DoH (Department of Health) (2010a) *Practical Approaches to Safeguarding and Personalization*. London: Department of Health.

DoH (Department of Health) (2010b) *Prioritising Need in the Context of Putting People First: A Whole*

System Approach to Eligibility for Social Care – Guidance on Eligibility Criteria for Adult Social Care. London: Department of Health.

DoH (Department of Health) (2010c) *Prioritising Need in the Context of Putting People First: A Whole Systems Approach to Eligibility Criteria.* London: Department of Health.

DoH (Department of Health) (2010d) *A Vision for Adult Social Care: Capable Communities and Active Citizens.* London: Department of Health.

DoH (Department of Health) (2012a) *Reforming the Law for Adult Care and Support: The Government's Response to Law Commission Report 326 on Adult Social Care.* London: The Stationery Office.

DoH (Department of Health) (2012b) *Transforming Care: A National Response to Winterbourne View Hospital: Final Report.* London: Department of Health.

DoH (Department of Health) (2014) *Care and Support Statutory Guidance: Issued under the Care Act 2014.* London: Department of Health.

DoH (Department of Health) and DfES (Department for Education and Skills) (2004) *National Service Framework for Children, Young People and Maternity Services: Disabled Children and Young People and Those with Complex Health Needs.* London: Department of Health.

DoH (Department of Health), Home Office and DfEE (Department for Education and Employment) (1999) *Working Together to Safeguard Children.* London: The Stationery Office.

DHSS (Department of Health and Social Security) (1981) *Growing Older.* London: The Stationery Office.

Diversity Trust, Somerset LINk and NHS Somerset (2012) *Lesbian, Gay, Bisexual & Transgender Experiences in Somerset: Somerset Social Care Services: Our Recommendations.* Yeovil: Diversity Trust, Somerset LINk and NHS Somerset.

Dobson, B., and Middleton, S. (1998) *Paying to Care: The Cost of Childhood Disability.* York: YPS.

Dominelli, L. (2002) *Anti-Oppressive Social Work Theory and Practice.* Basingstoke: Palgrave Macmillan.

Donskoy, A.-L., and Pollard, K. (2014) Interprofessional working with service users and carers, in Thomas, J., Pollard, K., and Sellman, D., eds, *Interprofessional Working in Health and Social Care: Professional Perspectives.* 2nd edn, Basingstoke: Palgrave Macmillan.

Douek, S. (2003) Collaboration or confusion? The carers' perspective, in Weinstein, J., Whittington, C., and Leiba, T., eds, *Collaboration in Social Work Practice.* London: Jessica Kingsley.

Douglas, F., and Martin, H. (2014) Occupational therapy, in Thomas, J., Pollard, K., and Sellman, D., eds, *Interprofessional Working in Health and Social Care: Professional Perspectives.* 2nd edn, Basingstoke: Palgrave Macmillan.

Dow, L., and Evans, N. (2014) Medicine, in Thomas, J., Pollard, K., and Sellman, D., eds, *Interprofessional Working in Health and Social Care: Professional Perspectives.* 2nd edn, Basingstoke: Palgrave Macmillan.

Dowling, M. (2011) Children with disabilities: international perspectives for developing practice, in Seden, J., Matthews, S., McCormick, M., and Morgan, A., eds, *Professional Development in Social Work: Complex issues in Practice.* Abingdon: Routledge.

Doyle, L. (1979) *The Political Economy of Health.* London: Pluto Press.

Drake, R. (1999) *Understanding Disability Policies.* Basingstoke: Macmillan.

Drewett, A. Y. (2010) Social rights and disability: the language of 'rights' in community care policies, *Disability & Society,* 14(1): 115–28.

Duffy, S. (2011) *A Fair Society and the Limits of Personalization.* Sheffield: Centre for Welfare Reform.

Duffy, S. (2012) *An Apology.* Sheffield: Centre for Welfare Reform.

Duffy, S., and Gillespie, J. (2009) *Personalization & Safeguarding,* www.in-control.org.uk/media/52833/personalisation%20safeguarding%20discussion%20paper%20version%201.0.pdf.

Dunn, M., Clare, I., and Holland, A. (2008) To empower or to protect? Constructing the 'vulnerable adult' in English law and public policy, *Legal Studies,* 28(2): 234–53.

Dupré, M. (2012) Disability culture and cultural competency in social work, *Social Work Education: The International Journal,* 31(2): 168–83.

DWP (Department for Work and Pensions) (2006) *A New Deal for Welfare: Empowering People to Work.* London: DWP.

DWP (Department for Work and Pensions) (2008) *No One Written Off: Reforming Welfare to Reward Responsibility*. London: DWP.

DWP (Department for Work and Pensions) (2010) *Public Consultation: Disability Living Allowance Reform*. London: DWP.

Edwards, H., and Richardson, K. (2003) The child protection system and disabled children, in NWGCPD, ed., *'It Doesn't Happen to Disabled Children': Child Protection and Disabled Children*. London: National Society for the Prevention of Cruelty to Children.

Edwards, M. L. (1997) Deaf and dumb in ancient Greece, in Davis, L. J., ed., *The Disability Studies Reader*. London: Routledge.

Egan, G. (2010) *The Skilled Helper: A Problem-Management and Opportunity-Development Approach to Helping*. 9th edn, Belmont, CA: Brooks/Cole.

EHRC (Equality and Human Rights Commission) (2011) *Hidden in Plain Sight: Inquiry into Disability-Related Harassment*. London: EHRC.

Elias, N. (1978) *The Civilizing Process*, Vol. 1: *The History of Manners*. Oxford: Blackwell.

Ellis, J. B. (1989) Grieving for the loss of the perfect child: parents of children with handicaps, *Child and Adolescent Social Work*, 6(4): 259–70.

Ellis, K. (2005) Disability rights in practice: the relationship between human rights and social rights in contemporary social care, *Disability & Society*, 20(7): 691–704.

Ellis, K. (2011) 'Street-level bureaucracy' revisited: the changing face of frontline discretion in adult social care in England, *Social Policy & Administration*, 45(3): 221–44.

Emerson, E., and Hatton, C. (2005) *The Socio-Economic Circumstances of Families Supporting a Child at Risk of Disability in Britain in 2002*. Institute for Health Research, Lancaster University.

Emerson, E., and Roulstone, A. (2014) Developing an evidence base for violent and disablist hate crime in Britain: findings from the Life Opportunities Survey, *Journal of Interpersonal Violence*, 29(17): 3086–104.

Emerson, J., and Bishop, J. (2012) Videophone technology and students with deaf-blindness: a method for increasing access and communication, *Journal of Visual Impairment & Blindness*, 106(10): 622–33.

Erikson, E. H. (1968) *Identity, Youth and Crisis*. New York: W. W. Norton.

Esmail, S., Munro, B., and Gibson, N. (2007) Couple's experience with multiple sclerosis in the context of their sexual relationship, *Sexuality and Disability*, 25(4): 163–77.

Evans, C. (2008) In practice from the viewpoint of disabled people, in Swain, J., and French, S., eds, *Disability on Equal Terms*. London: Sage.

Evans, C. (2012) Increasing opportunities for co-production and personalization through social work student placements in disabled people's organizations, *Social Work Education: The International Journal*, 31(2): 235–40.

Every Disabled Child Matters (2015) *Right from the Start: What We Want from the Next Government*, www.edcm.org.uk/media/159113/edcm-right-from-the-start_web.pdf.

Family Fund (2014) *Tired All the Time: The Impact of Sleep Difficulties on Families with Disabled Children*. York: Family Fund.

Faulkner, A. (2012) *The Right to Take Risks: Service Users' Views of Risk in Adult Social Care*. York: Joseph Rowntree Foundation.

Feinstein, L., Lupton, R., Hammond, C., Mujtaba, T., Salter, E., and Sorhaindo, A. (2008) *The Public Value of Social Housing: A Longitudinal Analysis of the Relationship between Housing and Life Chances*. London: Smith Institute.

Ferguson, I. (2007) Increasing user choice or privatizing risk? The antinomies of personalization, *British Journal of Social Work*, 37(3): 387–403.

Ferguson, I. (2012) Personalization, social justice and social work: a reply to Simon Duffy, *Journal of Social Work Practice*, 26(1): 55–73.

Finch, J., and Groves, D. (1983) *A Labour of Love*. London: Routledge & Kegan Paul.

Finkelstein, V. (1980) *Attitudes and Disabled People: Issues for Discussion*, http://disability-studies.leeds.ac.uk/files/library/finkelstein-attitudes.pdf.

Finkelstein, V. (2001) The social model repossessed, http://disability-studies.leeds.ac.uk/files/library/finkelstein-soc-mod-repossessed.pdf.

Finkelstein, V. (2004) Modernising services?, in Swain, J., French, S., Barnes, C., and Thomas, C., eds, *Disabling Barriers – Enabling Environments*. 2nd edn, London: Sage.

Fitzgerald, G. (2008) No secrets, safeguarding adults and adult protection, in Pritchard, J., ed., *Good Practice in Safeguarding Adults: Working Effectively in Adult Protection*. London: Jessica Kingsley.

Formby, E. (2012) *Solidarity but Not Similarity? LGBT Communities in the Twenty-First Century*. Centre for Education and Inclusion Research, Sheffield Hallam University.

Fortier, L. M., and Wanless, R. L. (1984) Family crisis following the diagnosis of a handicapped child, *Family Relations*, 33(1): 13–24.

Foster, M., Harris, J., Jackson, K., Morgan, H., and Glendinning, C. (2006) Personalised social care for adults with disabilities: a problematic concept for frontline practice, *Health and Social Care in the Community*, 14(2): 125–35.

Foucault, M. (1979) My body, this paper, this fire, *Oxford Literary Review*, 4(1): 9–28.

Franklin, A., and Sloper, P. (2009) Supporting the participation of disabled children and young people in decision-making, *Children & Society*, 23(1): 3–15.

Fraser, G. (2013) When we deny our own vulnerability, we cope by being cruel to others, *The Guardian*, 25 October.

Fraser, N. (1997) From redistribution to recognition? Dilemmas of justice in a 'postsocialist' age, in Fraser, N., ed., *Justice Interruptus: Critical Reflections on the 'Postsocialist' Condition*. New York: Routledge.

French, S. (2004a) 'Can you see the rainbow?': The roots of denial, in Swain, J., French, S., Barnes, C., and Thomas, C., eds, *Disabling Barriers – Enabling Environments*. 2nd edn, London: Sage.

French, S. (2004b) Enabling relationships in therapy practice, in Swain, J., Clark, J., French, S., Reynolds, F., and Parry, K., eds, *Enabling Relationships in Health and Social Care*. Oxford: Butterworth–Heinemann.

French, S., and Swain, J. (2008) The perspective of the disabled people's movement, in Davies, M., ed., *The Blackwell Companion to Social Work*. 3rd edn, Oxford: Blackwell.

French, S., and Swain, J. (2012) *Working with Disabled People in Policy and Practice: A Social Model*. Basingstoke: Palgrave Macmillan.

Freund, P. (1982) *The Civilized Body: Social Domination, Control and Health*. Philadelphia: Temple University Press.

Freund, P. (1990) The expressive body: a common ground for the sociology of emotions and health and illness, *Sociology of Health & Illness*, 12(4): 452–77.

Gaylard, D. (2009) Assessing adults, in Mantell, A., ed., *Social Work Skills with Adults*. Exeter: Learning Matters.

Gill, C. (2006) Disability, constructed vulnerability and socially conscious palliative care, *Journal of Palliative Care*, 22(3): 183–90.

Gilligan, C. (1982) *In a Different Voice: Psychological Theory and Women's Development*. Cambridge, MA: Harvard University Press.

Gillman, M. (2008) In practice from the viewpoint of a social worker, in Swain, J., and French, S., eds, *Disability on Equal Terms*. London: Sage, pp. 171–6.

Glasby, J. (2011) *Whose Risk is it Anyway? Risk and Regulation in an Era of Personalization*. York: Joseph Rowntree Foundation.

Glasby, J. (2014) The controversies of choice and control: why some people might be hostile to English social care reforms, *British Journal of Social Work*, 44: 252–66.

Glasby, J., and Miller, R. (2015) New conversations between old players? The relationship between general practice and social care, *Journal of Integrated Care*, 23(2): 42–52.

Gleeson, B. J. (1997) Disability studies: a historical materialist view, *Disability & Society*, 12(2): 179–202.

Glendinning, C., Challis, D., Fernandez, J., Jacobs, S., Jones, K., Knapp, M., Manthorpe, J., Moran, N., Netten, A., Stevens, M., and Wilberforce, M. (2008) *The National Evaluation of the Individual Budgets Pilot Programme (Research Findings)*. York: Social Policy Research Unit.

Glendinning, C., Mitchell, W., and Brooks, J. (2015) Ambiguity in practice? Carers' roles in personalised social care in England, *Health & Social Care in the Community*, 23(1): 23–32.

Glenn, F. (2007) *Growing Together, or Drifting Apart? Children with Disabilities and their Parents' Relationships.* London: One Plus One.

Goffman, I. (1964) *Stigma: Notes on the Management of Identity.* Harmondsworth: Penguin.

Goldbart, J., and Caton, S. (2010) *Communication and People with the Most Complex Needs: What Works and Why This is Essential.* London: Mencap.

Goodinge, S. (2000) *A Jigsaw of Services: Inspection of Services to Support Disabled Adults in their Parenting Role.* London: Department of Health.

Goodman, C., Drennan, V., Manthorpe, J., Gage, H., Trivedi, D., Shah, D., Scheibl, F., Poltawski, L., Handley, M., Nash, A., and Iliffe, S. (2011) *A Study of the Effectiveness of Interprofessional Working for Community-Dwelling Older People: Final Report.* London: National Institute for Health Rsearch.

Göransson, L. (2008) *Dövblindhet i ett livsperspektiv: Strategier och metoder för stöd.* Finspång: Mo Gårds Förlag.

Gordon, D., Parker, R., Loughtran, F., and Heslop, P. (2000) *Disabled Children in Britain: A Re-analysis of the OPCS Disability Surveys.* London: The Stationery Office.

Gore, E., and Parchar, G. (2010) *Rights and Reality: Disabled People's Experience of Accessing Goods and Services.* London: Leonard Cheshire Disability.

Gravell, C. (2012) *Cruelty: People with Learning Disabilities and their Experience of Harassment, Abuse and Related Crime in the Community.* London: Lemos & Crane.

Greenwood, N., Habibi, R., Smith, R., and Manthorpe, J. (2015) Barriers to access and minority ethnic carers' satisfaction with social care services in the community: a systematic review of qualitative and quantitative literature, *Health & Social Care in the Community*, 23(1): 64–78.

Gridley, K., Brooks, J., and Glendinning, C. (2014) Good practice in social care for disabled adults and older people with severe and complex needs: evidence from a scoping review, *Health & Social Care in the Community*, 22(3): 234–48.

Guasp, A. (2012) *Gay in Britain: Lesbian, Gay and Bisexual People's Experiences and Expectations of Discrimination.* London: Stonewall.

Guasp, A., Gammon, A., and Ellison, G. (2013) *Homophobic Hate Crime: The Gay British Crime Survey 2013.* London: Stonewall.

Hague, G., Thiara, R., Magowan, P., and Mullender, A. (2007) *Making the Links: Disabled Women and Domestic Violence: Final Report.* Bristol: Women's Aid.

Hague, G., Thiara, R., and Mullender, A. (2011) Disabled women, domestic violence and social care: the risk of isolation, vulnerability and neglect, *British Journal of Social Work*, 41(1): 148–65.

Handy, C. (2014) Housing, health and social care – an introduction, *Journal of Integrated Care*, 22(1): 4–9.

Hanisch, H. (2011) Disabled adolescence – spaces, places and plans for the future: a case study, *European Journal of Disability Research*, 5(2): 93–103.

Hanks, J. R., and Hanks, L. M. (1980) The physically handicapped in certain non-occidental societies, in Phillips, W., and Rosenberg, J., eds, *Social Scientists and the Physically Handicapped.* London: Arno Press.

Hansbro, J., Shah, P., Uren, Z., Lone, J., Cuciureanu, F., Gifford, G., and Sotiropoulou, N. (2013) *Fulfilling Potential: Building a Deeper Understanding of Disability in the UK Today.* London: Department for Work and Pensions.

Haraldsdóttir, F. (2013) Simply children, in Curran, T., and Runswick-Cole, K., eds, *Disabled Children's Childhood Studies: Critical Approaches in a Global Context.* Basingstoke: Palgrave Macmillan.

Harpur, P. (2011) Embracing the new disability rights paradigm: the importance of the Convention on the Rights of Persons with Disabilities, *Disability & Society*, 21(1): 1–14.

Harris, J. (2010) The use, role and application of advanced technology in the lives of disabled people in the UK, *Disability & Society*, 25(4): 427–39.

Harris, J., and Roulstone, A. (2011) *Disability, Policy and Professional Practice.* London: Sage.

Harris, J., Foster, M., Jackson, K., and Morgan, H. (2005) *Outcomes for Disabled Service Users*. Social Policy Research Unit, University of York.

Harris, M., and Mohay, H. (1997) Learning to look in the right place: a comparison of attentional behaviour in deaf children with deaf and hearing mothers, *Journal of Deaf Studies and Deaf Education*, 2: 96–102.

Harrison, J., Spafford, R., and Wiseman, R. (2011) *Impact of the Short Break Programme on the Prevention of Disabled Children Entering the Looked After System*, Together for Disabled Children, www.cafamily.org.uk/media/399551/research_and_reports_impact_of_the_short_break_programme_on_the_prevention_of_disabled_children_entering_the_looked_after_system.pdf.

Hart, P. (2008) Sharing communicative landscapes with congenitally deafblind people: it's a walk in the park!, in Zeedyk, M. S., ed., *Promoting Social Interaction for Individuals with Communicative Impairments: Making contact*. London: Jessica Kingsley.

Hassenfeld, Y. (1987) Power in social work practice, *Social Service Review*, 61(3): 469–83.

Hatton, C., and Waters, J. (2011) *The National Personal Budget Survey*. Lancaster: In Control and Lancaster University.

Hatton, C., and Waters, J. (2013) *The Second POET Survey of Personal Budget Holders and Carers*. London: Think Local, Act Personal.

Hawkins, L., Fook, J., and Ryan, M. (2001) Social workers' use of the language of social justice, *British Journal of Social Work*, 31: 1–13.

Hawkins, P. (2014) Disability is diverse, www.sbs.com.au/news/article/2014/08/19/comment-disability-diverse.

Haydn, C. (2005) More than a piece of paper? Personal education plans and 'looked after' children in England, *Child and Family Social Work*, 10(4): 343–52.

Hayes, M., and Black, R. S. (2003) Troubling signs: disability, Hollywood movies and the construction of a discourse of pity, *Disability Studies Quarterly*, 23(2): 114–32.

Health and Social Care Information Centre (2013) *Community Care Statistics Social Services Activity: England 2012–13: Provisional Release*. London: Health and Social Care Information Centre.

Helen Sanderson Associates (2012) Support planning and review: physical impairment, http://old.helensandersonassociates.co.uk/Our_Work/How/Support_Planning.html.

Hendey, N., and Pascall, G. (2002) *Disability and Transition to Adulthood: Achieving Independent Living*. Hove: Pavillion, for Joseph Rowntree Foundation.

Hendry, M., Pasterfield, D., Lewis, R., Carter, B., Hodgson, D., and Wilkinson, C. (2013) Why do we want the right to die? A systematic review of the international literature on the views of patients, carers and the public on assisted dying, *Palliative Medicine*, 27(1): 13–26.

Hersh, M. (2013) Deafblind people, communication, independence, and isolation, *Journal of Deaf Studies and Deaf Education*, doi:10.1093/deafed/ent022.

Higgins, A., Sharek, D., Nolan, M., Sheerin, B., Flanagan, P., Slaicuinaite, S., McDonnell, S., and Walsh, H. (2012) Mixed methods evaluation of an interdisciplinary sexuality education programme for staff working with people who have an acquired physical disability, *Journal of Advanced Nursing*, 68(11): 2559–69.

Higham, P., and Torkington, C. (2009) Partnerships with people who use services and carers, in Higham, P., ed., *Post-Qualifying Social Work Practice*. London: Sage.

Hines, S. (2007) Transgendering care: practices of care within transgender communities, *Critical Social Policy*, 27(4): 462–86.

Hirst, M., and Baldwin, S. (1994) *Unequal Opportunities: Growing up Disabled*. London: The Stationery Office.

HM Government (2008a) *Carers at the Heart of 21st-Century Families and Communities*. London: Department of Health.

HM Government (2008b) *Staying Safe: Action Plan*. London: Department for Children, Schools and Families, http://webarchive.nationalarchives.gov.uk/20130401151715/http://www.education.gov.uk/publications/eOrderingDownload/DCSF-00151-2008.pdf.

HM Government (2012) *Caring for our Future: Reforming Care and Support*, Cm 8378. London: Department of Health.

HM Government (2013) *Working Together to Safeguard Children. A Guide to Inter-Agency Working to Safeguard and Promote the Welfare of Children*. London: The Stationery Office.

HM Government (2015) *Working Together to Safeguard Children: A Guide to Inter-Agency Working to Safeguard and Promote the Welfare of Children*. London: The Stationery Office.

HM Treasury and DfES (Department for Education and Skills) (2007) *Aiming High for Disabled Children: Better Support for Families*. London: HM Treasury.

Hochschild, A. (1983) *The Managed Heart: Commercialization of Human Feeling*. Berkeley: University of California Press.

Hodge, S. (2007) Why is the potential of augmentative and alternative communication not being realized? Exploring the experiences of people who use communication aids, *Disability & Society*, 22(5): 457–71.

Hoffmaster, B. (2006) What does vulnerability mean?, *Hastings Center Report*, 36(2): 38–45.

Home Office (2007) *Achieving Best Evidence in Criminal Proceedings: Guidance on Interviewing Victims and Witnesses, and Using Special Measures*. London: Home Office Communication Directorate.

Home Office (2012) Statistical news release: hate crimes, England and Wales 2011/12, https://www. gov.uk/government/uploads/system/uploads/attachment_data/file/191722/hate-crimes-1112-snr.pdf.

Hothersall, S. (2013) Social workers, in Littlechild, B., and Smith, R., eds, *A Handbook for Interprofessional Practice in the Human Services: Learning to Work Together*. Harlow: Pearson Education.

House of Commons Education and Skills Committee (2006) *Special Educational Needs*, Vol. 1. London: The Stationery Office.

House of Commons Public Accounts Committee (2013) *Department for Work and Pensions: Management of Medical Services*. London: The Stationery Office.

Howe, D. (2006) Disabled children, parent–child interaction and attachment, *Child and Family Social Work*, 11: 95–106.

Hudson, A., and Glasby, J. (2015) Social work: a 'forgotten' piece of the integration jigsaw?, *Journal of Integrated Care*, 23(2): 96–103.

Hughes, B., and Paterson, K. (1997) The social model of disability and the disappearing body: towards a sociology of impairment, *Disability & Society*, 12(3): 325–40.

Hughes, K., Bellis, M. A., Jones, L., Wood, I., Wood, S., Bates, G., Ecklet, L., McCoy, E., Mikton, C., Shakespeare, T., and Officer, A. (2012) Prevalence and risk of violence against adults with disabilities: a systematic review and meta-analysis of observational studies, *The Lancet*, 380(9845): 899–907.

Hunt, P. (1966a) A critical condition, in Hunt, P., ed., *Stigma: The Experience of Disability*. London: Geoffrey Chapman.

Hunt, P. (1966b) *Stigma: The Experience of Disability*, http://disability-studies.leeds.ac.uk/files/library/Hunt-CONTENTS.pdf.

Hunt, P. (1981) Settling accounts with the parasite people: a critique of 'A Life Apart' by E. J. Miller and G. V. Gwynne, *Disability Challenge*, 1(May), 37–50, http://disability-studies.leeds.ac.uk/files/library/UPIAS-Disability-Challenge1.pdf.

Ife, J. (2012) *Human Rights and Social Work: Towards Rights Based Practice*. Cambridge: Cambridge University Press.

IFF Research (2008) *Employment Aspects and Workforce Implications of Direct Payments*. London: IFF Research.

Illich, I., Zola, I. K., McKnight, J., Caplan, J., and Shaiken, H. (1977) *Disabling Professions*. London: Marion Boyars.

Ingstad, B., and Whyte, S. R. (1995) *Disability and Culture*. London: University of California Press.

Ivaldi, G. (2000) *Surveying Adoption*. London: British Association for Adoption and Fostering.

IVR (Institute for Volunteering Research) (2004) *Volunteering for All: Exploring the Link between Volunteering and Social Exclusion*. London: IVR.

Jenkins, L., Brigden, C., and King, A. (2013) Evaluating a third sector community service following stroke, *Journal of Integrated Care*, 21(5): 248–62.

Jeppsson Grassman, E., Holme, L., Taghizadeh Larsson, A., and Whitaker, A. (2012) A long life with a particular signature: life course and aging for people with disabilities, *Journal of Gerontological Social Work*, 55(2): 95–111.

Johnson, F. (2011) Problems with the term and concept of 'abuse': critical reflections on the Scottish adult support and protection study, *British Journal of Social Work*, 42(5): 833–50.

Johnson, R., Thom, G., and Prabhakar, M. (2011) *Individual Budgets for Families with Disabled Children Final Evaluation Report: The Family Journey*, Research Report DFE-RR145b. London: Department for Education.

Jones, K., Netten, A., Rabiee, P., Glendinning, C., Arksey, H., and Moran, N. (2014) Can individual budgets have an impact on carers and the caring role?, *Ageing and Society*, 34(1): 157–75.

Jones, L., Bellis, M. A., Wood, S., Hughes, K., McCoy, E., Eckley, L., Bates, G., Mikton, C., Shakespeare, T., and Officer, A. (2012) Prevalence and Risk of violence against children with disabilities: a systematic review and meta-analysis of observational studies, *The Lancet*, 380(9845): 899–907, http://dx.doi.org/10.1016/S0140-6736(12)60692-8.

Joyner, S. (2012) Co-production in social care, in Loeffler, E., Taylor-Gooby, D., Bovaird, T., Hine-Hughes, F., and Wilkes, L., eds, *Making Health and Social Care Personal and Local: Moving from Mass Production to Co-Production*. Birmingham: Governance International.

Just Fair (2014) *Dignity and Opportunity for All: Securing the Rights of Disabled People in the Austerity Era*. London: Just Fair.

Kandel, I., and Merrick, J. (2003) The birth of a child with disability: coping by parents and siblings, *Scientific World Journal*, 3(2003): 741–50.

Katbamna, S., Ahmad, W., Bhakta, P., Baker, R., and Parker, G. (2004) Do they look after their own? Informal support for South Asian carers, *Health & Social Care in the Community*, 12(5): 398–406.

Katz, I., La Placa, V., and Hunter, S. (2007) *Barriers to Inclusion and Successful Engagement of Parents in Mainstream Services*. York: Joseph Rowntree Foundation.

Kearney, P., and Griffin, T. (2001) Between joy and sorrow: being a parent of a child with developmental disability, *Journal of Advanced Nursing*, 34(5): 582–92.

Kelly, C. (2011) Making 'care' accessible: personal assistance for disabled people and the politics of language, *Critical Social Policy*, 31(4): 562–82.

Kemshall, H. (2002) *Risk, Social Policy and Welfare*. Buckingham: Open University Press.

Kendall-Tackett, K., Lyon, T., Taliaferro, G., and Little, L. (2005) Why child maltreatment researchers should include children's disability status in their maltreatment studies, *Child Abuse and Neglect*, 29: 147–51.

Kingsley, E. P. ([1987] 2001) Welcome to Holland, in Klein, S. D., and Schive, K., eds, *You Will Dream New Dreams: Inspiring Personal Stories by Parents of Children with Disabilities*. New York: Kensington Books.

Kittay, E. F. (2011) The ethics of care, dependence, and disability, *Ratio Juris: An International Journal of Jurisprudence and Philosophy of Law*, 24(1): 49–58.

Klee, D., and Williams, C. (2013) *Making Safeguarding Personal*. London: Local Government Association.

Knott, C., and Scragg, T. (2007) *Reflective Practice in Social Work*. Exeter: Learning Matters.

Koprowska, J. (2014) *Communication and Interpersonal Skills in Social Work: Transforming Social Work Practice*. 4th edn, London: Sage.

Kottow, M. H. (2003) The vulnerable and the susceptible, *Bioethics*, 17(5/6): 460–71.

Kübler-Ross, E. (1969) *On Death and Dying*. New York: Routledge.

Labour Shadow Department for Work and Pensions (2013) *Making Rights a Reality for Disabled People*. London: Labour Party.

Ladd, P. (2003) *Understanding Deaf Culture: In Search of Deafhood*. Clevedon: Multilingual Matters.

Lamb, B. (2005) *Time to Get Equal in Volunteering: Tackling Disablism*. London: Scope.

Laming, W. H. (2003) *The Victoria Climbié Inquiry*. London: The Stationery Office.

Laming, W. H. (2009) *The Protection of Children in England: A Progress Report*. London: The Stationery Office.

Lapper, A. (2005) *My Life in my Hands*. London: Simon & Schuster.

Leadbetter, C. (2004) *Personalization through Participation: A New Script for Public Services*. London: Demos.

Leece, J. (2003) *Direct Payments: A Practitioner's Guide*. Birmingham: Venture Press.

Leece, J. (2012) The emergence and development of the personalization agenda, in Davies, M., ed., *Social Work with Adults*. Basingstoke: Palgrave Macmillan.

Leece, J., and Leece, D. (2010) Personalization: perceptions of the role of social work in a world of brokers and budgets, *British Journal of Social Work*, 41(2): 204–23.

Leiba, T., and Weinstein, J. (2003) Who are the participants in the collaborative process and what makes collaboration succeed or fail?, in Weinstein, J., Whittington, C., and Leiba, T., eds, *Collaboration in Social Work Practice*. London: Jessica Kingsley.

Levitas, R. (1996) The concept of social exclusion and the new Durkheimian hegemony, *Critical Social Policy*, 16(1): 5–20.

Levitas, R. (2005) *The Inclusive Society: Social Exclusion and New Labour*. 2nd edn, Basingstoke: Palgrave Macmillan.

Linton, S. (1998) *Claiming Disability: Knowledge and Identity*. New York: New York University Press.

Livingstone, S., and Palmer, T. (2012) *Identifying Vulnerable Children Online and What Strategies Can Help Them*, UK Council for Child Internet Safety, www.saferinternet.org.uk/downloads/Research_Highlights/Vulnerable_children_report_final.pdf.

Lopez, A., Rodriguez, I., Ferrero, F. J., Valledor, M., and Campo, J. C. (2014) Low-cost system based on electro-oculography for communication of disabled people, in *Multi-Conference on Systems, Signals & Devices (SSD)*, Barcelona, 11–14 February 2014, pp. 1–6.

Love, A., Cooke, P., and Taylor, P. (2003) The criminal justice system and disabled children, in NWGCPD, ed., *'It Doesn't Happen to Disabled Children': Child Protection and Disabled Children*. London: National Society for the Prevention of Cruelty to Children.

Luna, P. S., Osorio, E., Cardiel, E., and Hedz, P. (2002) Communication aid for speech disabled people using Morse codification, in *Second Joint EMBSBMES Conference*, Houston, Texas, 23–26 October, pp, 2434–5.

Lund, E., and Vaughn-Jensen, J. (2012) Victimisation of children with disabilities, *The Lancet*, 380(9845): 867–9, http://dx.doi.org/10.1016/S0140-6736(12)61071-X.

Lymbery, M., and Morley, K. (2012) Self-directed support and social work, *Practice: Social Work in Action*, 24(5): 315–27.

Lyon, N., Barnes, M., and Sweiry, D. (2006) *Families with Children in Britain: Findings from the 2004 Families and Children Study (FACS)*, DWP Research Report. London: Department for Work and Pensions.

Maas-Lowit, M., and Hothersall, S. (2010) Protection, in Maas-Lowit, M., and Hothersall, S., eds, *Need, Risk and Protection in Social Work Practice*. Exeter: Learning Matters.

McCabe, M., and Taleporos, G. (2003) Sexual esteem, sexual satisfaction, and sexual behaviour among people with physical disability, *Archives of Sexual Behavior*, 32(4): 359–69.

McConnell, D., Savage, A., Sobsey, D., and Uditsky, B. (2015) Benefit-finding or finding benefits? The positive impact of having a disabled child, *Disability & Society*, 30(1): 29–45.

MacInnes, T., Tinson, A., Gaffney, D., Horgan, G., and Baumberg, B. (2014) *Disability, Long Term Conditions and Poverty*. York: Joseph Rowntree Foundation.

Mackenzie, C., Bennett, A., and Cairney, M. (2011) Active citizenship and acquired neurological communication difficulty, *Disability and Rehabilitation*, 33(3): 187–94.

Mackie, P. K. (2012) Housing pathways of disabled young people: evidence for policy and practice, *Housing Studies*, 27(6): 805–21.

McLaughlin, J. (2015) Social work in acute hospital settings in Northern Ireland: the views of service users, carers and multi-disciplinary professionals, *Journal of Social Work*, doi: 10.1177/1468017314568843.

McLaughlin, J., Goodley, D., Clavering, E., and Fisher, P. (2008) *Families Raising Disabled Children: Enabling Care and Social Justice*. Basingstoke: Palgrave Macmillan.

McRuer, R. (2006) *Crip Theory: Cultural Signs of Queerness and Disability*. New York: New York University Press.

Mallett, R., and Runswick-Cole, K. (2014) *Approaching Disability: Critical Issues and Perspectives*. London: Routledge.

Mandelstam, M. (2010) *Quick Guide to Community Care Practice and the Law*. London: Jessica Kingsley.

Mandelstam, M. (2013) *Safeguarding Adults and the Law*. 2nd edn, London: Jessica Kingsley.

Manthorpe, J. (2013) How to be a 'culturally competent' social worker – what the research says, www.communitycare.co.uk/articles/18/02/2013/118928/how-to-be-a-culturally-competent-social-worker-what-the-research-says.htm.

Manthorpe, J., Hussein, S., and Stevens, M. (2012) Communication with migrant workers: the perspectives of people using care services in England, *Practice: Social Work in Action*, 24(5): 299–314.

Manthorpe, J., Stevens, M., Rapaport, J., Challis, D., Jacobs, S., Netten, A., Jones, K., Knapp, M., Wilberforce, M., and Glendinning, C. (2010) Individual budgets and adult safeguarding: parallel or converging tracks? Further findings from the evaluation of the individual budget pilots, *Journal of Social Work*, 11(4): 422–38.

Manthorpe, J., Stevens, M., Rapaport, J., Harris, J., Jacobs, S., Challis, D., Netten, A., Knapp, M., Wilberforce, M., and Glendinning, C. (2008) Safeguarding and system change: early perceptions of the implications for adult protection services of the English individual budgets pilots – a qualitative study, *British Journal of Social Work*, 39(8): 1465–80.

Marchant, R. (2001) Working with disabled children, in Foley, P., Roche, J., and Tucker, S., eds, *Children in Society: Contemporary Theory, Policy and Practice*. Basingstoke: Palgrave Macmillan.

Marchant, R., and Jones, M. (2000) Assessing the needs of disabled children and their families, in Department of Health, ed., *Assessing Children in Need and their Families: Practice Guidance*. London: The Stationery Office.

Marchant, R., and Jones, M. (n.d.) Disabled children and young people: 21 years of policy, https://actionforchildren.org.uk/media/63676/disabled_children.pdf.

Marchant, R., and Page, M. (2003) Child protection practice with disabled children, in NWGCPD, ed., *'It Doesn't Happen to Disabled Children': Child Protection and Disabled Children*. London: National Society for the Prevention of Cruelty to Children.

Marini, I., Glover-Graf, N., and Millington, M. (2012) *Psychosocial Aspects of Disability: Insider Perspectives and Strategies for Counselors*. New York: Springer.

Marks, D. (2008) Physical disability, in Davies, M., ed., *The Blackwell Companion to Social Work*. 3rd edn, Oxford: Blackwell.

Marmot, M., and Wilkinson, R. (1999) *Social Determinants of Health*. Oxford: Oxford University Press.

Martin, J. (2007) *Safeguarding Adults*. Lyme Regis: Russell House.

Martin, J. (2013) *Report on an Investigation into Complaint Numbers 12 012 268 and 12 005 756 against Thurrock Council*. Coventry: Local Government Ombudsman.

Martin, N. (2011) Disability identity – disability pride, *Perspectives: Policy and Practice in Higher Education*, 16(1): 14–18.

Martinez, F. (2014) Edinburgh International Book Festival 2014 [Live Interview with Mark Thomas], http://writerpictures.net/2014/08/eibf-2014-francesca-martinez/.

Mason, M. (1992) Internalised oppression, in Rieser, R., and Mason, M., eds, *Disability Equality in the Classroom: A Human Rights Issue*. London: Disability Equality in Education.

Mayall, B. (1993) Children and childhood, in Hood, S., Mayall, B., and Oliver, S., eds, *Critical Issues in Social Research*. Buckingham: Open University Press.

Mencap (2003) *Breaking Point: A Report on Caring without a Break for Children and Adults with Severe or Profound Learning Disabilities*, https://www.mencap.org.uk/sites/default/files/documents/2008-04/campaigns_breaking_point_0408.pdf.

Mencap (2013) *Short Breaks Support is Failing Family Carers: Reviewing Progress 10 Years on from Mencap's First Breaking Point Report*, https://www.mencap.org.uk/sites/default/files/documents/Short_Breaks_report.pdf.

Menzies Lyth, I. E. P. (1960) Social systems as a defense against anxiety: an empirical study of the nursing services of a general hospital, *Human Relations*, 13: 95–121.

Middleton, L. (1996) *Making a Difference: Social Work with Disabled Children*. Birmingham: Venture Press.

Middleton, L. (1999) *Disabled Children: Challenging Social Exclusion*. Oxford: Blackwell.

Miller, D. (2003) Disabled children and abuse, in NWGCPD, ed., *'It Doesn't Happen to Disabled Children': Child Protection and Disabled Children*. London: National Society for the Prevention of Cruelty to Children.

Miller, E., and Gwynne, G. (1972) *A Life Apart*. London: Tavistock.

Miller, N., Kirk, A., Kaiser, M., and Glos, L. (2014) Disparities in access to health care among middle-aged and older adults with disabilities, *Journal of Aging and Social Policy*, 26(4): 324–46.

Milne, A., Sullivan, M. P., Tanner, D., Richards, S., Ray, M., Lloyd, L., Beech, C., and Phillips, J. (2014) *Social Work with Older People: A Vision for the Future*. London: The College of Social Work, www.cpa.org.uk/cpa-lga-evidence/College_of_Social_Work/Milneetal%282014%29-Social workwitholderpeople-avisionforthefuture.pdf.

Milner, J., and O'Byrne, P. (2009) *Assessment in Social Work*. Basingstoke: Palgrave Macmillan.

Minkler, M., and Fadern, P. (2002) 'Successful aging': a disability perspective, *Journal of Disability Policy Studies*, 12(4): 229–35.

Mitchell, M., and Howarth, C. (2009) *Trans Research Review*. Manchester: Equality and Human Rights Commission.

Mitchell, M., Beninger, K., Rahim, N., and Arthur, S. (2013) *Implications of Austerity for LGBT People and Services*. London: NatCen Social Research.

Mitchell, W., Baxter, K., and Glendinning, C. (2012) *Updated Review of Research on Risk and Adult Social Care in England*. York: Joseph Rowntree Foundation.

MNDA (Motor Neurone Disease Association) (2013) *Speech and Communication*. Northampton: MNDA.

Molloy, H., and Vasil, L. (2002) The social construction of Asperger syndrome: the pathologising of difference?, *Disability & Society*, 17(6): 659–69.

Monbiot, G. (2014) Cleansing the stock, *The Guardian*, 21 October.

Mooney, A., Owen, C., and Statham, J. (2008) *Disabled Children: Numbers, Characteristics and Local Service Provision*, Research Report No DCSF-RR042. London: Department for Children, Schools and Families.

Moore, M., and Slee, R. (2013) Disability studies, inclusive education and exclusion, in Watson, N., Roulstone, A., and Thomas, C., eds, *Routledge Handbook of Disability Studies*. London: Routledge.

Moriarty, J. (2014) Personalization for people from black and minority ethnic groups, Race Equality Foundation, http://cdn.basw.co.uk/upload/basw_111150-6.pdf.

Morris, J. (1991) *Pride against Prejudice: Transforming Attitudes to Disability*. London: Women's Press.

Morris, J. (1993a) Feminism and disability, *Feminist Review*, 43: 57–70.

Morris, J. (1993b) *Independent Lives?: Community Care and Disabled People*. Basingstoke: Palgrave Macmillan.

Morris, J. (1996) *Feminism and Disability*. London: Women's Press.

Morris, J. (1998a) *Accessing Human Rights: Disabled Children and the Children Act*. Barkingside: Barnardo's.

Morris, J. (1998b) *Don't Leave Us Out: Involving Disabled Children and Young People with Communication Impairments*. York: Joseph Rowntree Foundation.

Morris, J. (1999) *Hurtling into the Void: Transition to Adulthood for Young Disabled People with Complex Health and Support Needs*. Brighton: Pavilion.

Morris, J. (2003) *Barriers to Independent Living: A Scoping Paper Prepared for the Disability Rights Commission*. London: Disability Rights Commission.

Morris, J. (2004) Independent living and community care: a disempowering framework, *Disability & Society*, 19(5): 427–42.

Morris, J. (2005) *Children on the Edge of Care: Human Rights and the Children Act*. York: Joseph Rowntree Foundation.

Morris, J. (2011a) Impairment and disability: constructing an ethics of care which promotes human rights, *Hypatia*, 16(4): 1–16.

Morris, J. (2011b) *Rethinking Disability Policy*. York: Joseph Rowntree Foundation, www.jrf.org.uk/publications/rethinking-disability-policy.

Morris, J. (2013) Why we need to build on the Independent Living Fund, jennymorrisnet.blogspot.co.uk/2013/11/why-we-need-to-build-on-the-independent-living-fund.

Morris, J. (2014a) Communication is at the heart of being human, jennymorrisnet.blogspot.co.uk/2014/06/communication-is-at-heart-of-being-human.html?m=1.

Morris, J. (2014b) *Independent Living Strategy: A Review of Progress*. London: In Control and Disability Rights UK.

Morris, J. (2014c) Personal budgets and self-determination, jennymorrisnet.blogspot.co.uk/2014/04/personal-budgets-and-self-determination.html.

Morris, J., and Wates, M. (2006) *Supporting Disabled Parents and Parents with Additional Needs*. London: Social Care Institute for Excellence.

Morris, J., and Wates, M. (2007) *Working Together to Support Disabled Parents*. London: Social Care Institute for Excellence.

Morris, K. (2008) Setting the Scene, in Morris, K., ed., *Social Work and Multi-Agency Working: Making A Difference*. Bristol: Policy Press.

Morrison, M., and Glenny, G. (2012) Collaborative inter-professional policy and practice: in search of evidence, *Journal of Education Policy*, 27(3): 367–86.

Mullaly, B. (2007) *The New Structural Social Work*. 3rd edn, Oxford: Oxford University Press.

Munro, E. (2011) *The Munro Review of Child Protection: Final Report: A Child Centred System*. London: The Stationery Office.

Murray, P. (2006) Being in school? Exclusion and the denial of psychological reality, in Goodley, D., and Lawthom, R., eds, *Disability and Psychology: Critical Introductions and Reflections*. Basingstoke: Palgrave Macmillan.

National Assembly for Wales (2000) *In Safe Hands: Implementing Adult Protection Procedures in Wales*. Cardiff: National Assembly for Wales.

National Children's Bureau (2014) 1 in 10 adults have used abusive language towards a disabled person, www.ncb.org.uk/news/1-in-10-adults-have-used-abusive-language-towards-a-disabled-person.

Needham, C., and Carr, S. (2012) *Co-Production: An Emerging Evidence Base for Adult Social Care Transformation*. London: Social Care Institute for Excellence.

Newbronner, L., Chamberlain, R., Bosanquet, K., Bartlett, C., Sass, B., and Glendinning, C. (2011) *Keeping Personal Budgets Personal: Learning from the Experiences of Older People, People with Mental Health Problems and their Carers*. London: Social Care Institute for Excellence.

NISW (National Institute for Social Work) (2001) *Putting the Person First*. NISW Briefing No. 31. London: NISW.

NWGCPD (National Working Group on Child Protection and Disability) (2003) *'It Doesn't Happen to Disabled Children': Child Protection and Disabled Children*. London: National Society for the Prevention of Cruelty to Children.

Office for Disability Issues (2014) Disability facts and figures, http://odi.dwp.gov.uk/disability-statistics-and-research/disability-facts-and-figures.php.

OFSTED (2012) *Protecting Disabled Children: Thematic Inspection*, www.ofsted.gov.uk/resources/120122.

Oldman, C. (2002) Later life and the social model of disability: a comfortable partnership?, *Ageing and Society*, 22(6): 791–806.

Oliver, M. (1990) *The Politics of Disablement*. Basingstoke: Palgrave Macmillan.

Oliver, M. (1996a) A sociology of disability or a disablist sociology, in Barton, L., ed., *Disability and Society: Emerging Issues and Insights*. London: Longman.

Oliver, M. (1996b) *Understanding Disability: From Theory to Practice*. Basingstoke: Palgrave Macmillan.

Oliver, M. (2004) If I had a hammer: the social model in action, in Swain, J., French, S., Barnes, C., and Thomas, C., eds, *Disabling Barriers – Enabling Environments*. 2nd edn, London: Sage.

Oliver, M. (2009) *Understanding Disability: From Theory to Practice*. 2nd edn, Basingstoke: Palgrave Macmillan.

Oliver, M., Sapey, B., and Thomas, P. (2012) *Social Work with Disabled People*. 4th edn, Basingstoke: Palgrave Macmillan.

Olkin, R. (2002) Could you hold the door for me? Including disability in diversity, *Cultural Diversity & Ethnic Minority Psychology*, 8(2): 130–7.

O'Loughlin, M., and O'Loughlin, S. (2012) *Social Work with Children and Families*. Exeter: Sage/Learning Matters.

Olsen, R., and Tyers, H. (2004) *Think Parent: Supporting Disabled Adults as Parents*. London: National Family and Parenting Institute.

Olshansky, S. (1962) Chronic sorrow: a response to having a mentally defective child, *Social Casework*, 43(4): 190–3.

Oosterhoorn, R., and Kendrick, A. (2001) No sign of harm: issues for disabled children communicating about abuse, *Child Abuse Review*, 10(4): 243–53.

Orme, J. (2002) Social work: gender, care and justice, *British Journal of Social Work*, 32: 799–814.

Osborne, C. (2013) How the latest research on safeguarding disabled children should inform social work, www.communitycare.co.uk/articles/22/02/2013/118947/how-the-latest-research-on-safeguarding-disabled-children-should-inform-social-work.htm.

Parekh, A., MacInnes, T., and Kenway, P. (2010) *Monitoring Poverty and Social Exclusion 2010*. York: Joseph Rowntree Foundation.

Parrott, L., and Madoc-Jones, I. (2008) Reclaiming information and communication technologies for empowering social work practice, *Journal of Social Work*, 8(2): 181–97.

Parry, I. (2013) Adult safeguarding and the role of housing, *Journal of Adult Protection*, 15(1): 15–25.

Parsons, T. (1951) *The Social System*. London: Routledge & Kegan Paul.

Parton, N. (2011) Child protection and safeguarding in England: changing and competing conceptions of risk and their implications for social work, *British Journal of Social Work*, 41: 854–75.

Partridge, M. (2013) Including people with learning difficulties from Chinese backgrounds: an ethnography of three services. Unpublished thesis, University of Bristol.

Pascall, G., and Hendy, N. (2004) Disability and transition to adulthood: the politics of parenting, *Critical Social Policy*, 24(2): 165–86.

Patmore, C., Qureshi, H., Nicholas, E., and Bamford, C. (1998) *Outcomes Project: Department of Health Report 1357 2.98*. York: University of York.

Paul, A., and Cawson, P. (2002) Safeguarding disabled children in residential settings: what we know and what we don't know, *Child Abuse Review*, 11(5): 262–81.

Pavey, S., Douglas, G., and Hodges, L. (2009) *The Needs of Older People with Acquired Hearing and Sight Loss*. London: Thomas Pocklington Trust.

Payne, M. (2002) Coordination and teamwork, in Adams, R., Dominelli, L., and Payne, M., eds, *Critical Practice in Social Work*. Basingstoke: Palgrave Macmillan.

Penhale, B., and Parker, J. (2008) *Working with Vulnerable Adults*. Abingdon: Routledge.

Perry, B. (2003) Where do we go from here? Research hate crime, *Internet Journal of Criminology*, www.internetjournalofcriminology.com/Where Do We Go From Here. Researching Hate Crime. pdf.

Peters, S. (2000) Is there a disability culture? A syncretisation of three possible world views, *Disability & Society*, 15(4): 583–601.

Phillips, J., Ajrouch, K., and Hillcoat-Nalletamby, S. (2010) *Key Concepts in Social Gerontology*. London: Sage.

Picardie, R. (1998) *Before I Say Goodbye*. London: Penguin.

Pilling, D., and Barrett, P. (2008) Text communication preferences of deaf people in the United Kingdom, *Journal of Deaf Studies and Deaf Education*, 13(1): 92–103.

Pinney, A. (2005) *Disabled Children in Residential Placements*. London: Department for Education and Skills.

Platts, M., Hughes, J., Lenehan, C., and Morris, J. (1996) *We Miss Her When She Goes Away: Respite Services for Children with Learning Disabilities and Complex Health Needs*. Manchester: NDT.

PMSU (Prime Minister's Strategy Unit) (2005) *Improving the Life Chances of Disabled People*. London: PMSU.

Pollard, K., Sellman, D., and Thomas, J. (2014) The need for interprofessional working, in Thomas, J., Pollard, K., and Sellman, D., eds, *Interprofessional Working in Health and Social Care: Professional Perspectives*. 2nd edn, Basingstoke: Palgrave Macmillan.

Powell, M. (2007) *Understanding the Mixed Economy of Welfare*. Bristol: Policy Press.

Power, D., Power, M. R., and Rehling, B. (2007) German deaf people using text communication: short message service, TTY, relay services, fax and e-mail, *American Annals of the Deaf*, 152(3): 291–301.

Prideaux, S. (2005) *Not So New Labour: A Sociological Critique of New Labour's Policy and Practice*. Bristol: Policy Press.

Prideaux, S., Roulstone, A., Harris, J., and Barnes, C. (2009) Disabled people and self-directed support schemes: reconceptualising work and welfare in the 21st century, *Disability & Society*, 24(5): 557–69.

Priestley, M. (1998a) Constructions and creations: idealism, materialism and disability theory, *Disability & Society*, 13(1): 75–94.

Priestley, M. (1998b) *Disability Politics and Community Care*. London: Jessica Kingsley.

Priestley, M. (2000) Adults only: disability, social policy and the life course, *Journal of Social Policy*, 29(3): 421–39.

Priestley, M. (2003a) *Disability: A Life Course Approach*. Cambridge: Polity.

Priestley, M. (2003b) A life course approach, *Disability Studies Quarterly*, 23(2): 1–5.

Priestley, M. (2014) Generating debates: why we need a life-course approach to disability issues, in Swain, J., French, S., Barnes, C., and Thomas, C., eds, *Disabling Barriers – Enabling Environments*. 3rd edn, London: Sage.

Pritchard, J. (2008) Introduction, in Pritchard, J., ed., *Good Practice in Safeguarding Adults: Working Effectively in Adult Protection*. London: Jessica Kingsley.

Purdam, K., Afkhami, R., Olsen, W., and Thornton, P. (2008) Disability in the UK: measuring equality, *Disability & Society*, 23(1): 53–65.

Putnam, M. (2002) Linking aging theory and disability models: increasing the potential to explore aging with physical impairment, *The Gerontologist*, 42(6): 799–806.

Putnam, M. (2012) Can aging with disability find a home in gerontological social work?, *Journal of Gerontological Social Work*, 55(2): 91–4.

Quarmby, K. (2011) *Scapegoat: Why We Are Failing Disabled People*. London: Portobello Books.

Quinn, K., Murray, C., and Malone, C. (2014) Spousal experiences of coping with and adapting to caregiving for a partner who has a stroke: a meta-synthesis of qualitative research, *Disability and Rehabilitation*, 36(3): 185–98.

Quinney, A., and Hafford-Letchfield, T. (2012) *Interprofessional Social Work: Effective Collaborative Approaches*. Exeter: Learning Matters.

Rabiee, P., Priestley, M., and Knowles, J. (2001) *Whatever Next? Young Disabled People Leaving Care*, http://disability-studies.leeds.ac.uk/files/2011/10/finalreport1.pdf.

Read, J., and Clements, L. (2001) *Disabled Children and the Law: Research and Good Practice*. London: Jessica Kingsley.

Rees, D. (2014) Physiotherapy, in Thomas, J., Pollard, K., and Sellman, D., eds, *Interprofessional Working in Health and Social Care: Professional Perspectives*. Basingstoke: Palgrave Macmillan.

Reese, M. (2013) Teachers and education, in Littlechild, B., and Smith, R., eds, *A Handbook for Interprofessional Practice in the Human Services: Learning to Work Together*. Harlow: Pearson Education.

Reeve, D. (2002) Negotiating psycho-emotional dimensions of disability and their influence on iden-tity constructions, *Disability & Society*, 7(5): 493–508.

Reeve, D. (2004a) Counselling and disabled people: help or hindrance?, in Swain, J., French, S., Barnes, C., and Thomas, C., eds, *Disabling Barriers – Enabling Environments*. 2nd edn, London: Sage.

Reeve, D. (2004b) Psycho-emotional dimensions of disability and the social model, in Barnes, C., and Mercer, G., eds, *Implementing the Social Model of Disability*. Leeds: Disability Press.

Reeve, D. (2008) *Negotiating* Disability in Everyday Life: The Experience of Psycho-Emotional Disablism. Unpublished thesis, Lancaster University.

Reeve, D. (2012) Preparation for practice: can philosophy have a place in helping students incorpo-rate the social model of disability within their praxis?, *Social Work Education: The International Journal*, 31(2): 227–34.

Reeve, D. (2014) Psycho-emotional disablism and internalised oppression, in Swain, J., French, S., Barnes, C., and Thomas, C., eds, *Disabling Barriers – Enabling Environments*. 3rd edn, London: Sage.

Rembis, M. A. (2010) Beyond the binary: rethinking the social model of disabled sexuality, *Sexuality & Disability*, 28: 51–60.

Renshaw, C. (2008) Do self-assessment and self-directed support undermine traditional social work with disabled people?, *Disability & Society*, 23(3): 283–6.

Riddell, S., Edward, S., Weedon, E., and Ahlgren, L. (2010) *Disability, Skills and Employment: A Review of Recent Statistics and Literature on Policy and Initiatives*. Manchester: Equality and Human Rights Commission.

Riddick, B. (2001) Dyslexia and inclusion: time for a social model of disability perspective?, *International Studies in Sociology of Education*, 11(3): 223–36.

Ridgeway, S. M. (1993) Abuse and deaf children: some factors to consider, *Child Abuse Review*, 2: 166–73.

Ritchie, J., and Victory, C. (2014) Housing, in Thomas, J., Pollard, K., and Sellman, D., eds, *Interprofessional Working in Health and Social Care: Professional Perspectives*. 2nd edn, Basingstoke: Palgrave Macmillan.

Roberts, K., and Lawton, D. (2001) Acknowledging the extra care parents give their disabled children, *Child: Care, Health and Development*, 27(4): 307–19.

Robertson, J., Hatton, C., Emerson, E., Wells, E., Collins, M., Langer, S., and Welch, V. (2009) *The Impacts of Short Break Provision on Disabled Children and Families: An International Literature Review*, Research Report DCSF-RR222. London: Department for Children, Schools and Families.

Roebroeck, M., Jahnsen, R., Carona, C., Kent, R., and Chamberlain, M. (2009) Adult outcomes and lifespan issues for people with childhood-onset physical disability, *Developmental Medicine and Child Neurology*, 51: 670–8.

Rose, W. (2011) Effective multi-agency work in children's services, in Seden, J., Matthews, S., McCormick, M., and Morgan, A., eds, *Professional Development in Social Work*. Abingdon: Routledge.

Roulstone, A. (2012) 'Stuck in the middle with you': towards enabling social work with disabled people, *Social Work Education: The International Journal*, 31(2): 142–54.

Roulstone, A., and Barnes, C. (2005) *Working Futures? Disabled People, Policy and Social Inclusion*. Bristol: Policy Press.

Roulstone, A., and Mason-Bish, H. (2013) *Disability, Hate Crime and Violence*. Abingdon: Routledge.

Roulstone, A., and Prideaux, S. (2012) *Understanding Disability Policy*. Bristol: Policy Press.

Rummery, K. (2003) Social work and multi-disciplinary collaboration in primary health care, in Weinstein, J., Whittington, C., and Leiba, T., eds, *Collaboration in Social Work Practice*. London: Jessica Kingsley.

Runswick-Cole, K. (2011) Time to end the bias towards inclusive education?, *British Journal of Special Education*, 38(3): 112–19.

Rushmer, R., and Pallis, G. (2002) Inter-professional working: the wisdom of integrated working and the disaster of blurred boundaries, *Public Money and Management*, 23(1): 59–66.

Ryan, J., and Thomas, F. (1987) *The Politics of Mental Handicap*. London: Penguin.

Safilios-Rothschild, C. (1970) *The Sociology and Social Psychology of Disability and Rehabilitation*. New York: Random House.

Sapey, B. (2002) Disability, in Thompson, N., ed., *Loss and Grief: A Guide for Human Services Practitioners*. Basingstoke: Palgrave Macmillan.

Sapey, B. (2009) Engaging with the social model of disability, in Higham, P., ed., *Post-Qualifying Social Work Practice*. London: Sage.

Sapey, B., Turner, R., and Orton, S. (2004) *Access to Practice: Overcoming the Barriers to Practice Learning for Disabled Social Work Students*. Southampton: SWAPltsn, http://eprints.lancs.ac.uk/id/eprint/603.

Satz, A. (2008) Disability, vulnerability and the limits of antidiscrimination, *Washington Law Review*, 83: 513–68.

Savage, F. (2011) Hate crime: the only way is Essex, www.disabilitynow.org.uk/blog/hate-crime-only-way-essex.

SCIE (Social Care Institute for Excellence) (2010a) *Age Equality and Age Discrimination in Social Care: An Interim Practice Guide*, www.scie.org.uk/publications/guides/guide35/files/guide35.pdf.

SCIE (Social Care Institute for Excellence) (2010b) *Personalization Briefing: Implications for Social Workers in Adults' Services*. London: SCIE.

SCIE (Social Care Institute for Excellence) (2011) *Personalization for Someone with a Physical Disability*, www.scie.org.uk/socialcaretv/video-player.asp?guid=91834b9d-26ef-44ba-9055-c9720606edf9 [video].

SCIE (Social Care Institute for Excellence) (2012) *People Not Processes: The Future of Personalisation and Independent Living*. London: SCIE.

SCIE (Social Care Institute for Excellence) and NHF (National Housing Federation) (2012) *Personalization Briefing: Implications for Housing Providers*. London: SCIE.

SCIE (Social Care institute for Excellence) with Consortium of LGBT Voluntary and Community Organizations (2011) *Personalization Briefing: Implications for lesbian, Gay, Bisexual and Transgendered (LGBT) People*. London: SCIE.

Scope (2003) *Right from the Start: Good Practice in Sharing the News*. London: Scope.

Scope (2014a) New research: majority of disabled people fear change to assisted suicide law, 17 July, www.scope.org.uk/media/press-releases/july-2014/assisted-suicide-law#Opinium%20assisted%20suicide%20research%20reference.

Scope (2014b) New research: parents of disabled children 'frustrated', 'stressed' and 'exhausted' by battle for support, press release, 11 September, www.scope.org.uk/media/press-releases/sept-2014/parents-disabled-children-battle-support.

Scope (2014c) *What is the Social Model of Disability?*, www.youtube.com/watch?v=0e24rfTZ2CQ [video].

Scorgie, K., and Sobsey, D. (2000) Transformational outcomes associated with parenting children who have disabilities, *Mental Retardation*, 38(3): 323–38.

Scorgie, K., Wilgosh, D., and Sobsey, D. (2004) The experience of transformation in parents of children with disabilities: theoretical considerations, *Developmental Disabilties Bulletin*, 32(1): 84–110.

Scottish Government (2010a) *Getting it Right for Young Carers: The Young Carers Strategy for Scotland, 2010–2015*, www.gov.scot/Resource/Doc/319441/0102105.pdf.

Scottish Government (2010b) *Self-Directed Support: A National Strategy for Scotland*. Edinburgh: Scottish Government.

Scottish Government (2012) *Getting it Right for Every Child*. Edinburgh: Scottish Government.

Scull, A. (1979) *Museums of Madness: The Social Organizations of Insanity in Nineteenth-Century England*. London: Penguin.

Seddon, D., and Robinson, C. (2015) Carer assessment: continuing tensions and dilemmas for social care practice, *Health & Social Care in the Community*, 23(1): 14–22.

Sellman, D., Godsell, M., and Townley, M. (2014) Nursing, in Thomas, J., Pollard, K., and Sellman, D., eds, *Interprofessional Working in Health and Social Care: Professional Perspectives*. 2nd edn, Basingstoke: Palgrave Macmillan.

Sense (2006) *Fill in the Gaps: A Toolkit for Professionals Working with Older Deafblind People*. London: Sense.

Shakespeare, T. (2000) *Help*. Birmingham: Venture Press.

Shakespeare, T. (2006) *Disability Rights and Wrongs*. London: Routledge.

Shakespeare, T. (2008) Disability, genetics and eugenics, in Swain, J., and French, S., eds, *Disability on Equal Terms*. London: Sage.

Shakespeare, T. (2014) *Disability Rights and Wrongs Revisited*. 2nd edn, Abingdon: Routledge.

Shakespeare, T., and Watson, N. (1998) Theoretical perspectives on research with disabled children, in Stalker, K., and Ward, L., eds, *Growing Up with Disability*. London: Jessica Kingsley.

Shakespeare, T., and Watson, N. (2001) The social model of disability: an outdated ideology?, *Research in Social Science and Disability*, 2: 9–28.

Shildrick, M., and Price, J. (1996) Breaking the boundaries of the broken body: mastery, materiality and ME, *Body and Society*, 2(4): 93–113.

Shilling, C. (1993) *The Body and Social Theory*. London: Sage.

Sidebotham, P., and Appleton, J. (2012) Revolutions in safeguarding?, *Child Abuse Review*, 21: 1–6.

Siegler, M., and Osmond, H. (1974) *Models of Madness, Models of Medicine*. New York: Macmillan.

Simcock, P., and Manthorpe, J. (2013) Deafblind and neglected or deafblindness neglected? Revisiting the case of Beverley Lewis, *British Journal of Social Work*, http://bjsw.oxfordjournals.org/content/early/2013/05/14/bjsw.bct088.full.pdf.

Sin, C. H., and Fong, J. (2009) The impact of regulatory fitness requirements on disabled social work students, *British Journal of Social Work*, 39(8): 1518–39.

Sin, C. H., Hedges, A., Cook, C., Mguni, N., and Comber, N. (2009) *Disabled People's Experiences of Targeted Violence and Hostility*. Manchester: Equality and Human Rights Commission.

Sinclair, J. (2012) Don't mourn for us, *Autonomy: The Critical Journal of Interdisciplinary Autism Studies*, 1(1): 1–4.

Singer, J. (1999) 'Why can't you be normal for once in your life?' From a 'problem with no name' to the emergence of a new category of difference, in Corker, M., and French, S., eds, *Disability Discourse*. Buckingham: Open University Press.

Sixsmith, J., Callender, M., Hobbs, G., Corr, S., and Huber, J. W. (2014) Implementing the National Service Framework for Long-Term (Neurological) Conditions: service user and service provider experiences, *Disability and Rehabilitation*, 36(7): 563–72.

Skills for Care (2012) *The State of the Adult Social Care Sector and Workforce in England, 2012*. www.skillsforcare.org.uk/NMDS-SC-intelligence-research-and-innovation/NMDS-SC/Workforce-intelligence-publications/The-state-of-the-adult-social-care-sector-and-workforce-in-England-2012.aspx.

Skitteral, J. (2013) Transitions? An invitation to think outside y/our problem box, get fire in your belly and put pebbles in the pond, in Curran, T., and Runswick-Cole, K., eds, *Disabled Children's Childhood Studies: Critical Approaches in a Global Context*. Basingstoke: Palgrave Macmillan.

Slasberg, C. (2014) Social care sector leaders urged to change direction on personal budgets, www.theguardian.com/social-care-network/2014/apr/09/social-care-change-direction-personal-budgets.

Sloper, P. (2004) Facilitators and barriers for co-ordinated multi-agency services, *Child: Care, Health and Development*, 30(6): 571–80.

Sloper, P., Mukherjee, S., Beresford, B., Lightfoot, J., and Norris, P. (1999) *Real Change, Not Rhetoric: Putting Research into Practice in Multi-Agency Services*. Bristol: Policy Press.

Sloper, P., Rabiee, P., and Beresford, B. (2007) *Outcomes for Disabled Children*, Research Works, 2007–02, Social Policy Research Unit, University of York.

Smith, K., Lader, D., Hoare, J., and Lau, I. (2012) *Hate Crime, Cyber Security and the Experience of Crime among Children: Findings from the 2010/11 British Crime Survey: Supplementary Volume 3 to Crime in England and Wales 2010/11*. London: Home Office.

Smith, R. (2009) Inter-professional learning and multi-professional practice for PQ, in Higham, P., ed., *Post-Qualifying Social Work Practice*. London: Sage.

Social Services Inspectorate (1998) *Removing Barriers for Disabled Children: Inspection of Services to Disabled Children and their Families*. London: Department of Health.

Söderström, S., and Ytterhus, B. (2010) The use and non-use of assistive technologies from the world of information and communication technology by visually impaired young people: a walk on the tightrope of peer inclusion, *Disability & Society*, 25(3): 303–15.

Spain, R. (2008) In practice from the viewpoint of a disabled nurse, in Swain, J., and French, S., eds, *Disability on Equal Terms*. London: Sage.

Sparrow, R. (2005) Defending Deaf culture: the case of cochlear implants, *Journal of Political Philosophy*, 13(2): 135–52.

Spiers, J. (2000) New perspectives on vulnerability using emic and etic approaches, *Journal of Advanced Nursing*, 31(3): 715–21.

Spivack, R., Craston, M., and Redman, R. (2014) *Evaluation of the Special Educational Needs and Disability Pathfinder Programme: Thematic Report: Collaborative Working with Social Care*. London: Department for Education.

Stalker, K., and Connors, C. (2003) Communicating with disabled children, *Adoption and Fostering*, 27(1): 26–35.

Stalker, K., and Moscardini, L. (2012) *A Critical Review and Analysis of Current Research and Policy Relating to Disabled Children and Young People in Scotland: A Report to Scotland's Commissioner for Children and Young People*. Edinburgh: Scotland's Commissioner for Children and Young People.

Stalker, K., Green Lister, P., Lerpiniere, J., and McArthur, K. (2010) *Child Protection and the Needs and Rights of Disabled Children and Young People: A Scoping Study*. Glasgow: University of Strathclyde.

Stanley, N., Ridley, J., Manthorpe, J., Harris, J., and Hurst, A. (2007) *Disclosing Disability: Disabled Students and Practitioners in Social Work, Nursing and Teaching*. London: Social Care Workforce Research Unit.

Strong, S., and Hall, C. (2011) *Feeling Settled Project: Guide for Those Involved in Changing a Service from a Residential Care Home to Support Living where the People Stay in the Same Place*. Bath: NDTI.

Sullivan, P. M., and Knutson, J. F. (2000) Maltreatment and disabilities: a population-based epidemiological study, *Child Abuse and Neglect*, 24: 1257–73.

Sutton, J. (2012) Sutton v Norfolk County Council, http://jansutton.blogspot.co.uk/2012/08/sutton-v-norfolk-county-council.html.

Swain, J., and French, S. (2000) Towards an affirmation model of disability, *Disability & Society*, 15(4): 569–82.

Swinbourne, C. (2012) Communication barriers in sex education put deaf people at risk, *The Guardian*, 5 December, www.theguardian.com/society/2012/dec/05/sex-education-communication-deaf-people-risk.

Taira, E. D., and Carlson, J. (2014) *Aging in Place: Designing, Adapting, and Enhancing the Home Environment*. Abingdon: Routledge.

Thiara, R. K., Hague, G., and Mullender, A. (2011) Losing out on both counts: disabled women and domestic violence, *Disability & Society*, 26(6): 757–71.

Thomas, C. (1999) *Female Forms: Experiencing and Understanding Disability*. Buckingham: Open University Press.

Thomas, C. (2004) How is disability understood?, *Disability & Society*, 19(6): 563–8.

Thomas, C. (2007) *Sociologies of Disability and Illness: Contested Ideas in Disability Studies and Medical Sociology*. Basingstoke: Palgrave Macmillan.

Thomas, P. (2011) 'Mate crime': ridicule, hostility and targeted attacks against disabled people, *Disability & Society*, 26(1): 107–11.

Thompson, N. (2006) *Anti-Discriminatory Practice*. 4th edn, Basingstoke: Palgrave Macmillan.

Thompson, N. (2011a) *Effective Communication: A Guide for the People Professions*. 2nd edn, Basingstoke: Palgrave Macmillan.

Thompson, N. (2011b) *Promoting Equality: Working with Diversity and Difference*. 3rd edn, Basingstoke: Palgrave Macmillan.

Training and Development Agency (2007) *Professional Standards for Qualified Teacher Status and Regulations for Initial Teacher Training*. London: Training and Development Agency.

Tremain, S. (2001) On the government of disability, *Social Theory and Practice*, 27: 617–36.

Tronto, J. C. (1993) *Moral Boundaries: A Political Argument for an Ethic of Care*. London: Routledge.

Trotter, R. (2012) *Over-Looked Communities, Over-Due Change: How Services Can Better Support BME Disabled People*. London: Scope.

Tu, T., Lambert, C., Shah, J. N., Westwood, P., Bryson, C., Purdon, S., Mallender, J., Bertranou, E., Jhita, T., and Roberts, S. (2013) *Evaluation of the Right to Control Trailblazers: Synthesis Report*. London: Office for Disability Issues.

Tutton, P., Finnegan, C., MacDermott, A., Edwards, S., and Huzzey, R. (2011) *Double Disadvantage: The Barriers and Business Practices Making Debt a Problem for Disabled People*. London: Citizens Advice.

Twigg, J. (1989) Models of carers: how do social care agencies conceptualise their relationship with informal carers?, *Journal of Social Policy*, 18(1): 53–66.

UK Disabled People's Council (2015) About us, www.ukdpc.net/site/about-us.

UNESCO (1994) *The Salamanca Statement and Framework for Action on Special Needs Education*, Paris: UNESCO.

Ungerson, C. (1997) Give them money: is cash a route to empowerment?, *Social Policy and Administration*, 31(1): 45–53.

UPIAS (Union of Physically Impaired Against Segregation) and Disability Alliance (1976) *Fundamental Principles of Disability*, http://disability-studies.leeds.ac.uk/files/library/UPIAS-fundamental-principles.pdf.

Vatcher, A., and Jones, K. (2014) Social work, in Thomas, J., Pollard, K., and Sellman, D., eds, *Interprofessional Working in Health and Social Care: Professional Perspectives*. 2nd edn, Basingstoke: Palgrave Macmillan.

Verbrugge, L. M., and Yang, L.-S. (2002) Aging with disability and disability with aging, *Journal of Disability Policy Studies*, 12(4): 253–67.

Vernon, A. (1999) The dialectics of multiple identities and the disabled people's movement, *Disability & Society*, 14, 385-398.

Vernon, A. (2002) *User-Defined Outcomes of Community Care for Asian Disabled People*. Bristol: Policy Press.

VIPER Project Team (2012) *The VIPER Project: What We Found*, http://viper.councilfordisabledchildren.org.uk/media/7836/what-we-found.pdf.

Ward, C. (2012) *Perspectives on Ageing with a Learning Disability*. York: Joseph Rowntree Foundation.

Warnock, M. (2005) *Special Educational Needs: A New Look*. London: Philosophy of Education Society of Great Britain.

Waters, J., and Hatton, C. (2014) *Third National Personal Budget Survey: Experiences of Personal Budgets Holders and Carers across Adult Social Care and Health*. London: Think Local, Act Personal.

Watson, N. (2004) The dialectics of disability: a social model for the 21st century?, in Barnes, C., and Mercer, G., eds, *Implementing the Social Model of Disability*. Leeds: Disability Press.

Watson, N. (2014) Moral wrongs, disadvantages and disability: a critique of critical disability studies, *Disability & Society*, 29(4): 638–50.

Watson, N., McKie, K., Hughes, B., Hopkins, D., and Gregory, S. (2004) (Inter)dependence, needs and care. the potential for disability and feminist theorists to develop an emancipatory model, *Sociology*, 38(2): 331–50.

Watson, N., Shakespeare, T., Cunningham-Burley, S., Barnes, C., Corker, M., Davis, J., and Priestley, M. (1999) *Life as a Disabled Child: A Qualitative Study of Young People's Experiences and Perspectives*. University of Edinburgh, Department of Nursing Studies.

Weinstein, J., Whittington, C., and Leiba, T. (2003) *Collaboration in Social Work Practice*. London: Jessica Kingsley.

Welch, V., Hatton, C., Wells, E., Collins, M., Langer, S., Robertson, J., and Emerson, E. (2010) *The Impact of Short Breaks on Families with a Disabled Child: Report One of the Quantitative Phase*, Research Report DFE-RR063. London: Department for Education.

Welsh Assembly Government (2011) *Direct Payments Guidance: Community Care, Services for Carers and Children's Services (Direct Payments) (Wales) Guidance 2011*. Cardiff: Welsh Assembly Government.

Welsh Government (2014) *Policy Intent: Regulations and Other Subordinate Legislation under the Social Services and Well-Being Bill*. Cardiff: Welsh Government.

Whittington, C. (2003) Collaboration and partnership in context, in Weinstein, J., Whittington, C., and Leiba, T., eds, *Collaboration in Social Work Practice*. London: Jessica Kingsley.

Wilkin, A., Muirfield, J., Lamont, E., Kinder, K., and Dyson, P. (2008) *The Value of Social Care Professionals Working in Extended Schools*. Slough: National Foundation for Educational Research.

Wilson, A., and Beresford, P. (2000) 'Anti-oppressive practice': emancipation or appropriation?, *British Journal of Social Work*, 30(5): 553–73.

Winzer, M. A. (1997) Disability and society before the eighteenth century: dread and despair, in Davis, L. J., ed., *The Disability Studies Reader*. London: Routledge.

Wirral Borough Council (2012) *Adult Safeguarding Peer Challenge*. Wirral: Local Government Association.

Wolfensberger, W. (1995) Social role valorization is too conservative: no, it is too radical, *Disability & Society*, 10(3): 365–8.

Wolfensberger, W., and Thomas, S. (1983) *PASSING (Program Analysis of Service Systems' Implementation of Normalization Goals): Normalization Criteria and Ratings Manual*. 2nd edn, Toronto: National Institute on Mental Retardation.

Wood, C. (2011) *Tailor Made: 'Personalization Must Work for Those who Need it Most …'*. London: Demos.

Wood, R. (1991) Care of disabled people, in Dalley, G., ed., *Disability and Social Policy*. London: Policy Studies Institute.

Woodcock, J., and Tregaskis, C. (2008) Understanding structural and communication barriers to ordinary family life for families with disabled children: a combined social work and social model of disability analysis, *British Journal of Social Work*, 38(1): 55–71.

Young, A., and Hunt, R. (2011) *Research with d/Deaf people*. London: NIHR School for Social Care Research.

Young, I. M. (1990) *Justice and the Politics of Difference*. Princeton, NJ: Princeton University Press.

Zarb, G., and Oliver, M. (1993) *Ageing with a Disability: What Do They Expect after All These Years?* York: Joseph Rowntree Foundation.

Zola, I. K. (2005) Toward the necessary universalizing of a disability policy, *Milbank Quarterly*, 83(4): 1–27.

Index